THE Tragic
Black Buck

AFRICAN AMERICAN LITERATURE AND CULTURE

Expanding and Exploding the Boundaries

Carlyle V. Thompson
General Editor

Vol. 1

PETER LANG
New York • Washington, D.C./Baltimore • Bern
Frankfurt am Main • Berlin • Brussels • Vienna • Oxford

Carlyle Van Thompson

THE Tragic Black Buck

RACIAL MASQUERADING IN THE AMERICAN LITERARY IMAGINATION

PETER LANG
New York • Washington, D.C./Baltimore • Bern
Frankfurt am Main • Berlin • Brussels • Vienna • Oxford

Library of Congress Cataloging-in-Publication Data

Thompson, Carlyle Van.
The tragic black buck: racial masquerading in the American literary imagination /
Carlyle Van Thompson.
p. cm. — (African American literature and culture; v. 1
Includes bibliographical references and index.
1. American fiction—20th century—History and criticism. 2. African American men
in literature. 3. American fiction—African American authors—History and criticism.
4. Identity (Psychology) in literature. 5. Passing (Identity) in literature. 6. Group
identity in literature. 7. Tragic, The, in literature. 8. Deception in literature.
9. Racism in literature. 10. Race in literature. I. Title. II. Series.
PS374.N4T48   813'.52093552—dc22   2003025666
ISBN 0-8204-6206-3
ISSN 1528-3887

Bibliographic information published by **Die Deutsche Bibliothek**.
Die Deutsche Bibliothek lists this publication in the "Deutsche
Nationalbibliografie"; detailed bibliographic data is available
on the Internet at http://dnb.ddb.de/.

Cover design by Sophie Boorsch Appel

The paper in this book meets the guidelines for permanence and durability
of the Committee on Production Guidelines for Book Longevity
of the Council of Library Resources.

© 2004 Peter Lang Publishing, Inc., New York
275 Seventh Avenue, 28th Floor, New York, NY 10001
www.peterlangusa.com

Printed in the United States of America

*This book is proudly dedicated to
Cynthia D. Pullen-Thompson and Jabari James Joseph
Jawara Thompson along with my parents: Rogers
Grier Thompson and Edith Mayble Thompson*

CONTENTS

ACKNOWLEDGMENTS

This project of racial masquerade and misrepresentation comes out of my gradu-ate studies at Columbia University and my work with the distinguished literary scholar Robert G. O'Meally, who taught his first graduate course on racial passing at Columbia University. His enduring support has been critical.

While I was at Medgar Evers College, this project was strongly advanced in the CUNY Faculty Publications Program with the important feedback and sugges-tions of Nora Eisenburg, Linda Grasso, Katie Hogan, Frederick De Naples, and Cheryl Fish. I would also like to acknowledge the enduring support of my CUNY colleagues and friends George Cunningham and James L. de Jongh. Also, thanks go to James L. de Jongh and the IRADAC/CAAN Conference for their support on Charles Waddell Chesnutt's *The House Behind the Cedars*. Linda Susan Jackson, a superb teacher, poet, collaborator, and colleague at Medgar Evers College, has been especially helpful to this project and is a person who is always there for spiri-tual support, humor, and intellectual engagement. My talented students at Medgar Evers College patiently listened to my provocative ideas and unknowingly offered me the challenge to expand and explode the traditional boundaries of literary anal-ysis; I am grateful to have the opportunity to teach at a progressive institution whose namesake epitomizes an enduring challenge to the market-driven, narcissis-tic, hedonistic, and hegemonic dogma of worldwide white supremacist culture. One particular critically engaging black student, Lisa Allen, was especially helpful in my consideration and analysis of F. Scott Fitzgerald's *The Great Gatsby*. Rein-forcing the concept that teaching is an act of reciprocity, Allen by her challenges pushed me to look deeper into the novel. The tremendous academic success of other knowledgeable MEC students like James Worley, Kevin Brown, Oladapo Yeku, Andrea Sears, and Melissa Jackson speaks to the nontraditional intellectual possibilities that can happen only at Medgar Evers College. These students are reading, writing, and critically thinking themselves into subjectivity in a manner that does not reinforce and reinscribe the pathology of white supremacy, gender objectification, or class and color hegemony. I am extremely grateful to Patricia Lespiansse for her intellectual feedback and technical assistance. F. Leon Wilson, a long-time friend and comrade, has always been there for me with his superb technical assistance and his intellectual tenacity.

Special thanks and gratitude go to Haki R. Madhubuti, the Distinguished Professor of Chicago State University; Edison O. Jackson, president of Medgar Evers College; and Michael Eric Dyson, of the University of Pennsylvania—all truly revolutionary intellectuals who without reservation have supported my intellectual development. I am also extremely thankful to Bernado Pace, of Borough of Manhattan Community College (CUNY), and James West, of the University of Pennsylvania, for their support for my work on *The Great Gatsby*. With my life partner and friend Cynthia D. Pullen-Thompson by my side, this project was made more rich and abundant than I could have conceived; I am grateful for her enduring love and support. As intellectual friends from the City University of New York—Center for Worker Education, Carolyn Lewis, Sophronia Fuller, and Jannie Johnson inspire me to continue to grow and to share a vision of libratory intellectualism.

FOREWORD

This project examines the too often paradoxical phenomenon in American literature of light-skinned black male individuals who pass for white; these adventurous men can be viewed as black "bucks." Focusing on four novels of the first third of the twentieth century, I argue that black individuals who assume a white identity represent a paradox in that passing for white represents a challenge to the hedonistic and hegemonic ideology of biological white supremacy. Yet, some black individuals who pass for white also represent the denial of blackness in terms of their family, their history, and their culture. I examine the issues of race, gender, class, and law in the literature of passing involving the tropes of historical and theoretical miscegenation, mimicry, and masquerade. Dynamics of skin color, hair texture, physical features, and language are equally critical to my examination. These dynamics suggest how interracial conflict produces, perpetuates, and propagates *intraracial* conflict. The narratives of passing examined here are Charles Waddell Chesnutt's *The House Behind the Cedars* (1900), James Weldon Johnson's *The Autobiography of an Ex-Coloured Man* (1912), F. Scott Fitzgerald's *The Great Gatsby* (1925), and William Faulkner's *Light in August* (1932); these writers explore racial passing as a masquerade.

These four novels about black men who assume a white identity dramatically reveal that the too often tragic and comic performance of passing occurs not because of self-hatred but because of America's racist society and the need for socioeconomic survival and subjectivity. The literature of passing enduringly suggests the larger issues of national identity formation and class subjectivity in America.

To be a true American (too often meaning white) inherently means to pass, to attain the socioeconomic privileges associated with whiteness. Too often, light-skinned black individuals who pass for white and who challenge the laws and the extralegal sanctions against miscegenation and the philosophy of white supremacy become tragically and comically characterized as outsiders who have the illusion of inclusion.

1

INTRODUCTION:
BLACK BUCKS BEING AS WHITE
AS THEY WANNA BE

The Historical and Theoretical Roots of Black People Passing for White

All Black people pass. Passing is lying about who you are. Whenever a Black person is talking to a white person they're misrepresenting themselves.
—WALTER MOSLEY

There are white Americans so to speak and black Americans. But any fool can see that the white people are not really white, and that the black people are not black. They are all interrelated one way or another.
—ALBERT MURRAY, *The Omni-American*

Wendell B. Harris's film *Chameleon Street* (1989) relates the authentic story of William Douglas Street, an intelligent but unstable Michigan black man who, through a succession of impersonations, successfully infiltrates the white professional world. As his last name deftly implies, Street is a roaming and rootless individual. Driven by his wife's constant refrain, "Make some money, Make some money," Street as chameleon and con artist dexterously moves from scam to scam. Masquerading as a physician with a Harvard degree who performs surgery, as a Yale graduate student, as a corporate lawyer, and so on, Street "passes" to achieve socioeconomic agency in a white patriarchal and racist society. Yet his clandestine plans of deception are short lived because he is constantly being found out. While serving a prison sentence for fraud, he uses his prevaricating and performative adeptness to feign an epileptic seizure in order to escape a sexual assault by another manipulating black inmate. Grounded by Street's frustrated attempts to "make some money" and his sardonic humor, this escape from sexual violence augments the film's characterizations of Street's crafty performance as both tragic and comic.

In the film's most intriguing scene, Street attends a masquerade party dressed as the Beast from Jean Cocteau's *Beauty and the Beast* (1946). There he wins the grand prize for having the finest costume. Here the film reinforces the perception that white society accepts only those black people who engage in the masquerade of passing. Although William Douglas Street, a caramel-color-complexioned individual, cannot physically pass for white, his quest for socioeconomic subjectivity in the patriarchal white world reveals that crossing geographic boundaries, forsaking family, changing one's name, prevaricating, and performing are too often critical for black people's success in the white world. *Chameleon Street,* with a wide-eyed lens on the quest of an imaginative black man seeking economic agency by constantly transforming himself, becomes an appropriate metaphor for the literature in which light-skinned black individuals pass and masquerade as white. With heavy overtones of black male sexuality and economics, Street represents the dangerous black buck or dangerously free black man who threatens white society because of his unwillingness to conform to racist dictates.

Working from the premise that a significant amount of American literature represents a mixture of black and white cultures,[1] in *The Tragic Black Buck* I examine the paradoxical phenomenon of black males who pass for white and the social and political construction of race in the modernist literature of passing from 1900 to 1932. This period is critical because of black people's enduring challenge to the intense social and economic stratifications based on race. The literary texts examined here are Charles Waddell Chesnutt's *The House Behind the Cedars* (1900), James Weldon Johnson's *The Autobiography of an Ex-Coloured Man* (1912), F. Scott Fitzgerald's *The Great Gatsby* (1925), and William Faulkner's *Light in August* (1932). *The Tragic Black Buck* represents the first study, as far as I know, to analyze these four novels within the historical and literary framework of miscegenation, mimicry, and masquerade, along with the signifying trope of the black man as a buck. The concept of the black man as a buck resides in the historical breeding of black men and women in an effort to increase the number of slaves. Indeed, the Middle Passage and slavery in America reproduced its own product, black bodies for consumption and tremendous white wealth. Along with the threat of sexual violence by white male slave masters, black women were forced to have children by black men who were forced to have sexual intercourse with them. Many slave owners did use certain black males as studs; here the black man as a buck was born. Incest was a by-product of the sexual violence and sexual coercion. Linking black male slaves to animals, white society considered slaves literally subhuman, beasts. They were dangerous, breeding animals who were never more content than when toiling in the fields; idle, they were shiftless drunkards and potential rapists of white women.

Interracial sexual relations between white women and black men, and between black women and white men, flourished in colonial and antebellum America.[2] This racial amalgamation raises critical issues. America's conceptualization and construction of both black and white identities is determined by race. As Aldon Nielson argues, race is a "consummately empty signifier that is constituted out of a people's desire . . . to name themselves as not 'other.'" An "empty signifier," race inscribes meaning only when allocated particular political, social, and cultural constructions by groups or individuals.[3] Thus, in this project I argue that the phenomenon of passing for white is a kind of Faustian paradigm that represents a profound paradox that both challenges the doctrine of white supremacy (the essentialism of whiteness) and requires a denial of one's blackness at the same time that it reaffirms the existing racial hierarchy of white power and white privilege. Personhood is whiteness, and whiteness means possibility and privilege.[4] Paradoxically, within racist constructions, whiteness defines blackness and blackness defines whiteness.

In this work, passing is defined as a black individual's desire and attempt to transform his or her racial identity or racial classification by winning acceptance as white in the white world. Passing, in its most common usage, means "passing for white": masking one's African ancestry and cultural background in order to cross the color line in America from the black to the white side.[5] Extending and expanding the term "passing," I employ the term "masquerade" to denote the behavior of black people who pass for white because that term suggests the psychologically prevaricating act of performance that encompasses both aggression and repression. Individuals who pass for white encounter a psychological confusion that Marjorie Garber defines as "category crisis": "a failure of definitive distinction, a borderline that becomes permeable"; hence, the individual who passes becomes "a mechanism of displacement from one blurred boundary to another."[6] With black people too often being treated as pariahs, passing offers a plethora of possibilities. Passing for white may be defined as psychologically adaptive behavior and a performance that responds to America's systematic prowhite and antiblack ideology. In essence, passing is a strategy for survival and even socioeconomic advancement in the face of racial hegemony.

For the strategy of passing to be effective, it is generally critical that one's phenotype be light or white enough: that one's hair texture be straight, wavy, or curly enough; and that one possess thin lips and a high-bridged nose—all features that tend to resemble those of the majority of white people. Simply put, one must look white to pass; however, this ocular element reveals that too often racial appearance becomes paramount. Although the literature of passing places a significant emphasis on these corporeal features, we discover that class, gender, geography, education (literacy), and language play an important role in one's ability to pass. Passing embraces whiteness and denies blackness. Passing embraces possibilities of advancement and allows movement away from racial socioeconomic restrictions. Passing fulfills the desire for the power and possibility of blackness being cast in a predominant white role. Consequently, passing epitomizes the paradox between the reality of blackness and the appearance of whiteness; passing is the trick or the joke of illusion. Because of the inherent disadvantages and advantages in this mas-querade, this racial subterfuge has both tragic and comic dimensions for the black individual and especially for the dominant white society that targets black people with systemic racial intolerance.

The psychologically adaptive performance of passing, with its tragic and comic dimensions, is rooted in the history of black people enslaved by whites in America. Black people's journey from "behind the veil" to selfhood has always been pro-foundly ironic. People of African descent were subjected to legal and illegal op-pression in the "land of liberty," founded by white male slave owners who sought religious, economic, and political freedom for themselves. Resisting the dual op-pression, black people's sojourn was one from slavery to freedom. Yet, America, through the racist ideology of white men like Thomas Jefferson and his *Notes on the State of Virginia* (1782), has violently arranged itself around two races; it is through the violence (mainly the rape of black women) that mulattoes began to appear. These mulattoes as a disturbing presence represent the middle ground of racial discourse; they self-consciously manipulated the hegemonic boundaries of race. Because of their light skin and white features, mulattoes were generally more ac-cepted into the margins of white society. This quasi acceptance increased their possibilities for crossing geographic and class boundaries, moving from field slave to house slave and from slavery to freedom. Accordingly, many mulattoes had the opportunity to attain freedom by passing for white. Once free, many of these blacks challenged slavery and racism. Not surprisingly, many black abolitionists and activists such as Frederick Douglass, Booker T. Washington, W. E. B. Du Bois, Charles Waddell Chesnutt, and Walter White were light-skinned individuals. In contrast to these black individuals, whites such as Henry David Thoreau, Ralph Waldo Emerson, and Mark Twain challenged America's racist culture. Hence, it is of little wonder that many black and white writers contemplate issues of race and color.

Primarily because of the psychological, physical, and economic violence of white supremacy rooted in the fantasy of a black-free America, some black individ-uals have sought socioeconomic agency in the possibilities inherent in creating a "mask." As Houston A. Baker Jr. suggests, some black people responded to the vio-lent rituals by signifying on and using the "minstrel mask," thereby creating a dif-ferent face. Tracing the movement of the minstrel mask, Baker argues:

> That mask is a space of habitation not only for repressed spirits of sexuality, lucid play, id satisfaction, castration anxiety, and a mirror stage of development, but also for the deep-seated denial of the indisputable humanity of inhabitants of and de-scendants from the continent of Africa. And it is, first and foremost, the mastery of the minstrel mask by blacks that constitutes a primary move in Afro American discur-sive modernism.[7]

The amalgamation of blacks and whites during slavery and afterward functions concurrently with ongoing racial violence. After the founding of this country, there were three significant phases of black and white violence: (1) an initial phase of sporadic black revolts (and plots for revolts) during the period of enslavement; (2) a middle, long-term era of mainly white-initiated violence (riots and lynching, especially) carried out to maintain postslavery white supremacy in America; and (3) the cycle of massive urban rebellions in reaction to the economic, psychological, and physical violence suffered by blacks in the United States in the 1960s and beyond.[8]

It is the middle phase that demands our attention here; in this postslavery era, the United States government and many whites initiated illegal violent acts to maintain white supremacy. One of the main reasons for this violence was whites' anxiety that too many black people refused to accept a subordinate socioeconomic status. Lynching for such offenses as "speaking disrespectfully to whites," "failure to give way on a sidewalk," or "acting like a white man" suggests whites' desire to tyrannize black people. The last offense suggests a form of passing. Lynching and other forms of mob violence became an integral aspect of the post-Reconstruction system of white supremacy. From 1892 to 1903, some 1,985 blacks were killed by Southern lynch mobs.[9] While white men lynched black men, they were often imaging black men raping white women. For example, in Tulsa, Oklahoma (Wallstreet was the name of the black section of Tulsa), in 1921, and in Rosewood, Florida, in 1923, two white women separately made the false charge that black men assaulted them. Both of these black towns were burned and destroyed by mobs of white males seeking vengeance against black males who had failed to stay in their place.[10]

The lynch-burning of black men was a common thread in white racial violence. Additionally, the sexual mutilation of black men during these circus-like lynchings was a prominent feature that attracted numbers of white onlookers by the thousands; the grand prize in these rituals—the black man's genitals. This heinous act suggests a love-hate relationship. Sula, in Toni Morrison's novel of the same name, sarcastically highlights the paradox of the black male phallus: "White men love you [black men]. They spend so much time worrying about your penis they forget their own. *The only thing they want to do is cut off a nigger's privates. And if that ain't love and respect I don't know what is*[11] (emphasis added). Hence, an abnormal amount of castration anxiety hovered over acts of miscegenation between black men and white women; whether consensual or contrived, it was often punished by the riotous frenzy of lynch-burning. Frantz Fanon suggests that too often in racist societies the black man becomes stereotyped as a terrifying phallus. As Fanon argues, whereas the Jew symbolizes intellectual danger, the black symbolizes biological danger.[12] If we consider that sexual violence by white males was conquering the "sexual beast," the rape of black women during and after slavery was a form of castration. Hence, self-renunciation and denial of their blackness by those who pass symbolically suggests the phenomenon of self-castration and an acceptance and attachment of the symbolic representation of power: the white phallus.

Historically, American violence was also directed at white males who violated the customs of the day by engaging in intimate relationships with black women. Just as black men were stereotyped as rapists, black women were stereotyped as promiscuous. Within America's Eurocentric ethos, black people are often viewed as the antithesis of virtue, as evil incarnate. In addition to the violence of this period, membership in the Ku Klux Klan, the largest white supremacy group for most of the twentieth century, reached five million in the late 1920s. Masked in its members' whiteness, the Klan was a critical force in spreading racial discourse through its acts of economic, physical, and psychological terrorism. Not surprisingly, this period of racial brutality mirrors the period when the frequency of passing reached its zenith. According to some estimates, as many as 100,000 or as few as 10,000 to 25,000 black individuals crossed over yearly. Walter White believed that 12,000 black people passed annually.[13] While such significant numbers confirmed whites' anxiety, black people believed that high numbers represented revenge for their continuous oppression. Possibly more accurate studies of this phenomenon were done by the sociologists John H. Burma and Horace Mann Bond. During 1946, Burma estimated that some 2,500 to 2,750 blacks passed over to join some 110,000 who had already crossed over.[14] In 1931, Bond suggested that those who passed and those who desired to pass had done so and that those who remained had decided to focus their resources "upon the immediate task of racial survival."[15] It is likely that from 1880 to 1925, years of intense racial violence, blacks crossed the color line in significant numbers.

As the literature of passing reveals, many white people were concerned with miscegenation and with the number of black people who crossed socioeconomic boundaries, whereas for those light enough to pass, violence served as a catalyst to escape blackness. Accordingly, slave narratives are the literary foundation for my analysis of the literature of passing. Like the slave narratives, the literature of passing encompasses bondage, flight, and freedom. For example, Frederick Douglass's *Narrative of the Life of Frederick Douglass, an American Slave* (1845) is a "passing" narrative in that he disguised himself as a sailor and passed from slavery to freedom; once free, he changed his name. In the literature of passing, socioeconomic restrictions encompass bondage, whereas escape from blackness and passing for white encompass flight and freedom. Then, too, the social phenomenon places emphasis on socioeconomic agency, but the literature of passing encompasses this aspect and gives a melodramatic effect through the use of coincidences, revelations, and the usually tragic conclusions.

By tracing this phenomenon of passing as manifested in character development, plot structure, and rhetorical strategy, the literature of passing suggests a transition from the story of the desire to escape and one strategy for escaping from the overt racial oppression associated with slavery and its immediate legacy to the story of black people primarily seeking socioeconomic agency. Although enslaved and freed blacks had different motives for passing, those black individuals who passed for white represented the boldest challenge to the legal and extralegal systems of oppression. As Michel Foucault makes clear, "no matter how terrifying a given system may be, there always remain the possibilities of resistance, disobedience, and oppositional groupings."[16] Conversely, the literature of passing also denotes how passing represents the internalization of beliefs and values associated with the ingrained tenets of white supremacy. This duality of desire or Du Boisian "double consciousness" establishes the paradoxical phenomenon of passing.

Whereas the desire for freedom during slavery directly challenged oppression, the desire expressed in the literature for socioeconomic agency among free blacks who passed suggests a hegemonic classification of race in America. Race in America establishes a color hierarchy that illuminates the contrast between white and black nations: one embodying privilege, opportunity, and comfort; the other, deprivation, repression, and struggle. If passing for white becomes the backwash and by-product of miscegenation and one of its obvious consequences, it is possible to view it as an aspect intrinsic to the society when mulattoes first appeared. As reflected in the literature, mulattoes were in a unique position to create an impassioned portrait of the presence and the power and the possibility of human interaction. These "white" black individuals found quasi-acceptance, despite their challenges to white supremacist society.[17]

Both the historical phenomenon of passing and the literature of passing illustrate myriad concerns and characteristics of black individuals who passed for white and the duration of the deception. First, the reasons involve escape from oppression, socioeconomic mobility, interracial courtship and marriage, curiosity, the desire for the thrill, and revenge; some passed for investigative purposes, as in Walter White's probe of lynchings. Most of the passing was part-time and involved individuals who passed for white by day and returned to blackness at night. Many individuals with "invisible blackness" passed to secure comfortable accommodations in transportation, in restaurants, and in rest rooms. However, as the literature illustrates, the primary motivation was economic. Often light-skinned black individuals passed at work during the day; or they traveled north as white, for enhanced economic opportunities, then returned to the South and became black again. As the literature shows, geographic mobility was critical in passing. In order to pass successfully, individuals often had to move away from their black families, their black communities, and their black friends.

Second, passing involves a complex set of perplexing social and psychological issues: self-division, co-conspiracy with people who conceal the passer's blackness, trepidation about the possibility of giving birth to a dark-skinned child, interracial conflict against intraracial confrontations, and opportunism against sacrifice. In all of the novels considered here, mirrors and windows significantly represent the escape from a fixed racial identity and/or the exposure of a racial identity. Last, we discover that racial ambiguity can be mirrored by gender ambiguity.

Connected to these myriad concerns and characteristics, their duration and complicity, the literature of passing strongly suggests how the socioeconomic, physical, and psychological violence of white supremacy—supported by legal and extralegal Jim Crow restrictions—worked to keep black people in their "place." Chesnutt and Johnson provide narratives of passing within the structures of legal decisions. Accordingly, three legal actions frame their thematic structures and narrative discussion of black people's quest for socioeconomic agency.

First, the Fugitive Slave Act of 1793 (the first of a series passed) generated a wave of terror and violence that made both national and state governments responsible for the capture and return of runaway slaves. This law further stipulated that anyone who harbored or helped runaway slaves or interfered with the legal process was subject to imprisonment or fines. William and Ellen Craft reveal in their slave narrative, *Running a Thousand Miles for Freedom* (1848), how this legislation motivated them to leave America and escape to Canada. These two Georgia slaves (husband and wife) were fiercely determined to escape the South and steal their freedom. Because Ellen's skin was as light as William's was dark, Ellen disguised herself as a white male slave master in ill health, supposedly going north for medical treatment accompanied by William, his (her) dark property. Their success in passing onward to freedom (eight days after the plan was thought of, they were free) was a result of their boldness and creativity when confronted by whites. William relates their subversive strategy:

> Knowing that slaveholders have the privilege of taking their slaves to any part of the country they think proper, it occurred to me that, as my wife was nearly white, I might get her to disguise herself as an invalid gentle man, and assume to be my master, while I could attend as his slave, and that in this manner we might effect our escape.[18]

Through racial masquerading, gender role reversal[19] (the wife became the "man" and master and the husband the "boy"), and the component of cross-dressing on Ellen's part, they not only thwarted the Fugitive Slave Act of 1850 but used the fallacy of the socially constructed "white is superior" myth to work for their transformations, their escape, and their subsequent freedom.[20] Quite simply, Ellen Craft changed her race, her gender, and her class. Marjorie Garber comments on the Crafts' psychologically performative act of passing from slavery to freedom:

> The wife's transvestism and the husband's sartorial class-jumping (read as race-jumping: "dressed like a white man") occupy the same discursive space, act out the same aggressions and repressions. And this chain of substitutions takes on an extra poignancy when the figure of crossing is literally traversing a border, when the crosser, and the cross-dresser, is a runaway slave.[21]

Unlike Frederick Douglass, a fugitive who in the role of a trickster figure brilliantly schemed to become literate, William and Ellen Craft were illiterate and unable to write a pass. Unlike the creative Henry "Box" Brown, who passed from slavery into freedom (from Richmond to Philadelphia by the Adams Express Company) inside a coffin,[22] everything centered on Ellen Craft's body as a text inscribed with "whiteness." As Hazel Carby points out, Ellen's "whiteness" suggests a paradoxical literary representation: "The mulatto figure is a narrative device of mediation; it allows for a fictional exploration of the relationship between the races while being at the same time an imaginary expression of the relationship between the races."[23] Accordingly, in their brazen escape from slavery the Crafts successfully, in Audre Lorde's term, used the "master's tools" to subvert the Fugitive Slave Act.

Second, the U.S. Supreme Court's decision in *Dred Scott v. John Sandford*, in

March 1857, asserted that the white founding fathers had never intended people of African descent to be viewed as equal to whites. This legal theory claimed blacks were of "an inferior order" and "so far inferior that they had no rights which the white man was bound to respect." Neither Dred Scott nor any other person of African descent had any rights and privileges that were binding on white American society.[24] Additionally, escaped slaves could be pursued into free states, arrested, and returned to slavery. The legacy of this legal decision reduced black people (slave or free) to an inferior status. We discover the legacy of the *Dred Scott* decision, with its diabolical obiter dictum, in Charles W. Chesnutt's *The House Behind the Cedars,* where, according to Judge Archibald Straight, this legal decision suggests the socioeconomic possibilities available to black people.

Almost forty years later, the *Plessy v. Ferguson* decision of 1896 established a more restricting classification of race and its relationship to African American citizenship. Homer Plessy challenged the Jim Crow statute in the state of Louisiana that required racially segregated seating on trains in interstate commerce. Plessy's contention was that because he was only one-eighth Negro and could pass as white, he was entitled to ride in the seats reserved for whites. Using "judicial notice," the Supreme Court swiftly ruled against Plessy. Eschewing any definitive ruling on the racial or genetic definition of a Negro, the Supreme Court assumed, in accordance with common knowledge, that a Negro is any person with any African ancestry. This decision helped to develop and confirm the culturally and socially accepted "one-drop theory" of racial classification for black people, a theory that derived from a long-discredited notion that each race has its own blood type, which is correlated with physical appearance and behavior. It was in the South that it became known as the "one-drop rule," because of the belief that a single drop of "black blood" made a person black. It was also referred to as the "one-drop ancestor rule"; many courts labeled it "the traceable amount," and some anthropologists called it the "hypo-descent rule," which maintains that racially mixed individuals are assigned the status of the subordinate group.[25] Gradually, this definition would become the nation's definition of blacks, generally accepted by both blacks and whites. In James Weldon Johnson's *The Autobiography of an Ex-Coloured Man,* this legal decision frames the protagonist's movement from blackness to whiteness. Interestingly, Virginia made it "a felony to willingly falsify a statement as to color."[26] Thus, legal decisions become a grounding point from which to examine legal restrictions on black people and the literature of passing as a response to hegemonic dictates.

Charles Waddell Chesnutt's *The House Behind the Cedars,* James Weldon Johnson's *The Autobiography of an Ex-Coloured Man,* F. Scott Fitzgerald's *The Great Gatsby,* and William Faulkner's *Light in August* illustrate black characters from the perspective of a subjugated race in a white society and address the complex issue of passing to interrogate racial boundaries. Within this intricate drama of individuals passing for white there are issues of denial (family and culture), criminality, performance, and, most important, the psychological conception and construction of one racial identity. As W. E. B. Du Bois suggests in *The Souls of Black Folk* (1903), the construction of black identity or consciousness suggests a complex act of dual-ity. Du Bois states: "It a peculiar sensation, this double-consciousness, this sense of always looking at one self through the eyes of others, of measuring one soul by the tape of a world that looks on in an amused contempt and pity." According to Du Bois's theory of "double-consciousness," black people struggle with two iden-tities, one black and the other American (meaning white).[27] This modulation between these two worlds is critical in a racist society where whiteness has too often been associated with freedom/subjectivity and blackness has been associated with slavery/Otherness.

The Tragic Black Buck offers an analysis of the physical, psychological, socio-economic, and cultural costs to those black people who attempt to move beyond the margins of racist mythology and economic subjugation. As Frantz Fanon re-minds us in *Black Skin, White Masks* (1952), if there is an inferiority complex (black people desire to be white), it is the outcome of a double process: the first primar-ily economic and the second the process of internalization of this inferiority.[28] Fanon, a Marxist psychiatrist, emphasized in his writings the psychological and economic violence of white supremacy. Fanon's compelling desire was to analyze and eradicate the racist relationship between blacks and whites. Fanon writes, "I believe that the fact of the juxtaposition of the white and black races has created a massive psycho-existential complex. I hope by analyzing to destroy it."[29] As the lit-erature of passing dramatically reveals, skin color, hair texture, and language, more than any other factors, determine one's possibilities in the passing game.

The most important aspect in passing for white is skin color. Often, it is the first physical attribute we see, and American culture places superior psychological and socioeconomic value on whiteness. As Joseph R. Washington Jr. argues, those who pass "are not legally or morally white, they are white because they choose to be so and they are able to choose because they are dominated by diffused white genes."[30] In contrast, too often American popular culture, religion, science, law, and politics work together to assign a permanent pejorative value to blackness. Using the term "white racial narcissism," establishes the connection between color and power. Whiteness, often associated with being a "true" American, becomes defined as pure, innocent, and virtuous.[31] Blackness, on the other hand, becomes defined as soiled, dirty, and sinister. The linguistic pathology related to color reveals that blackness too often represents negativity. Within America racist society, too often these values have been associated with derisive definitions of race.[32] America's heg-emonic iconography has always placed whiteness on a pristine pedestal of beauty and superiority.[33] This "race talk," as Toni Morrison argues, cultivates an "explicit insertion into everyday life of racial signs and symbols that have no meaning other than pressing African Americans to the lowest levels of the racial hierarchy."[34]

The preeminent criterion for passing, as revealed in the literature, is for one to be as white or light as possible. The scholarship of the sociologist Edward Reuter in 1918, along with that of E. Franklin Frazier in 1939, confirms that mulattoes out-distanced darker blacks economically and socially. Furthermore, their works confirm that American society accepts the racist and hegemonic notion that lighter skin suggests higher intelligence and greater innate ability.[35] Hence, the notion of "mulatto supremacy" perpetuates the notion that blackness is inferior. As Toni Morrison explicates in *Playing in the Dark* (1992), there appears to be a tacit agreement among literary scholars that because American literature has been the preserve of white male genius and power, blackness usually becomes marginalized and demonized.[36] Nonetheless, within the black community, light-skinned individuals are sometimes labeled and attacked with pejorative signifiers. Some of these signifiers are "red-bone," "high yella," "yellow bitch," "white honky," "honky white," "white nigger," "nigger white," "octoroon," "quadroon," "half-breed," and "mongrel." In a literary context, "tragic mulatto" is perhaps the most frequently used pejorative signifier in reference to light-skinned black individuals. For black people living under the doctrine of white supremacy, skin color determines reality in America far more than anything else. Black people's use of skin-bleaching cosmetics and the ritual of bathing in bleach[37] are perhaps the most obvious examples of a psychologically negative and physically harmful black aesthetic.

For black people, hair texture also significantly determines identity formation. In America, long, flowing straight or curly hair is the epitome of conventional pulchritude. This long hair (meaning all Caucasian-type hair) is characterized as "good hair," "righteous mass," "nearer my God to thee," and "kind hair," whereas short and nappy (meaning all black-type hair) is depicted as "bad hair," "naps," "tight head," "jarhead," and "kitched."

Like white skin, straight hair privileges those who desire to pass into a system where whiteness is deemed superior to blackness. Madam C. J. Walker rejected the label "hair-straightening queen" and resented accusations that her products were intended to make black women look white; nonetheless, in 1910, she became the first self-made black American millionaire in history by perfecting hair treatments and skin products that transformed black women who were dissatisfied with or ashamed of their hair.[38] Although both skin color and hair texture are often related to whiteness, this does not always suggest self-hatred in black people. Albert Murray reminds us that black people use bleaching agents primarily for facial splotches and that Africans used a series of processes on their hair long before they came in contact with Europeans.[39] Accordingly, hair straightening by black people might be regarded as stylistic and not simply pathological.

This literature also denotes how white society uses language to define an individual. As illustrated in Mark Twain's *The Tragedy of Pudd'nhead Wilson* (1894), to speak "proper" or standard English can position one closer to whiteness, whereas the "black dialect" can relegate an individual, regardless of race, to the margins. Although more subtle than skin color and hair, language constitutes a critical ingredient in the racial masquerade.

This masquerade mirrors the historical and literary performance of those black people who cross racial lines. Becoming white, these black people attempt to remove themselves from the margins. Reflecting the realization that passing suggests healthy schizophrenic possibilities or the antithesis, perhaps Paul Laurence Dunbar's poem "We Wear the Mask" captures the psychic duality:

> We wear the mask that grins and lies
> It hides our cheeks and shades our eyes,—
> This debt we pay to human guile;
> With torn and bleeding hearts we smile,
> And mouth with myriad subtleties.[40]

For black people who are considered dark and in the margins of darkness, the exclusive property and instrument of white males who live in the light, "passing" becomes a penetrating metaphor for racial and class possibilities.

Juxtaposed to these aspects are the antithetical political, cultural, and legal constructs within white America that make this movement beyond racial borders problematic. The dynamics of race, class, gender, and geography associated with the metaphor and metonymy of black individuals passing for white raise the following critical questions:

1 How have the writers of these narratives—women, men; black and white— used the conventions of "passing" narrative (or "tragic mulatto" narrative) to create innovative and sometimes subversive narrative structures?

2 How have the desires and motivations for passing changed over time?

3 How have questions of gender, class, and geography complicated those of blackness and/or whiteness? These are large issues, but the literature strongly suggests significant contrasts between a man's experience and that of a woman. In addition, passing for white often goes beyond the ocular analysis because a higher economic position facilitates one's accessibility into white society. Additionally, there are very different realities associated with passing in the South compared to the North. How are these large issues used by the different writers to illustrate the complex nature of passing?

4 How does the literature of passing explore the psychological impact of white supremacy on the inner lives of both black and white people? The critical concern here is how interracial conflict influences intraracial confrontation. What ultimately emerges in this fictional mediation of passing and race is a complex representation of America in which there is no such thing as blackness and whiteness.

These passing narratives offer a profound challenge to or an internalization of the hegemonic white "master narrative" and authoritatively shape and refigure America's racial boundaries and attitudes concerning skin color, hair texture, and language, recommencing and augmenting the African American frontier of literary ascension. In a social and literary context, the Harlem Renaissance, a significant period of literary ascension, centers our understanding of this passing literature. In *The New Negro* (1925), the editor, Alain Locke, uses diction suggestive of those blacks who attempt to cross racial boundaries. He describes the "New Negro" as a "changeling," his psychological and spiritual transformation as a "metamorphosis."⁴¹ Locke's diction adequately conveys the racial "crossing over" of many blacks during the early twentieth century and the preoccupation with this subject among many black writers of the Harlem Renaissance.

During the Harlem Renaissance, when black people were "digging up their roots" and celebrating their African heritage, it seems appropriate that "passing for white" was dissected under the literary microscope. That numerous black writers such as Nella Larsen, Jessie Redmon Fauset, Langston Hughes, and George Schuyler focused on the phenomenon of passing suggests that these writers were themselves "passing" to a higher level of literary and social recognition in white society. Moreover, despite the bitter and satirical tone of these black writers, they evinced a conscious commitment to confront white supremacy and the sinister self-hating seeds planted in the psyches of many black people by such white nationalistic narratives as D. W. Griffith's *The Birth of a Nation* (1915).

These self-hating seeds have given birth to certain "tests" that signify on passing and construct hierarchies of skin color and hair texture within the black community. At the turn of the century, three tests seeking to restrict dark-skinned individuals were popular. The "paper bag" test required that one place one's arm inside a brown paper bag; only if the skin on the arm was lighter than the color of the bag would the prospective member be accepted into a church or social society. Some churches painted their doors a light shade of brown, and anyone whose skin was darker than the door was kindly asked to seek his or her religious services elsewhere. Throughout churches in Virginia, Philadelphia, and New Orleans, a fine-toothed comb was hung on a rope near the front entrance. If a person's hair was too nappy and snagged in the comb, entrance was denied.⁴² Intrinsically, skin color and hair texture have no meaning. Yet, America's racist society has given them political, psychological, and economic significance. Once skin color and hair texture are rendered meaningful, a hierarchal order is established. Subsequently, many black people have also given these physical aspects meaning, establishing intraracial hierarchal structures that reinforce white supremacy.

The interracial conflict endemic to white supremacy has produced intraracial conflict among some blacks where subjectivity is based on physical features. Mulatto aristocracy clubs such as the Bon Ton Society, in Washington, D.C., and the Blue Vein Society, in Nashville, Tennessee, were formed during Reconstruction, when Southern cities were flooded with the "sot free," black persons freed by the Emancipation Proclamation. To be admitted to the Blue Vein Society, one had to be fair enough for the spidery network of purplish veins at the wrist to be visible to a panel of expert judges.⁴³ One of the Blue Vein Society rhymes states: "Oh! Stan back, black man, / You cain't shine; / Yo' lips is too thick, / An' you hain't my kin."⁴⁴ By constructing a barbed-wire fence of color and class, these color-conscious groups absurdly mimicked whites by excluding their darker cousins from their ranks.

Throughout this book, I scrutinize the overlapping and interconnecting terms "miscegenation," "mimicry," and "masquerade," which are critical both for their historical significance on racial amalgamation and for the critical literary analysis of the legal, cultural, and social representations and constructs of race and attitudes regarding skin color, hair texture, and language. Additionally, these terms provide the psychoanalytic port from which to navigate and negotiate these complex textual waters. Consequently, my definitions of miscegenation extend and elaborate the work of Frantz Fanon and Jacques Lacan. Although they ground their theories in countries other than the United States, their basic tenets easily cross boundaries and flow into our textual waters.

There exists a distinction in the use of these three critical terms by our four writers. Because the desire for socioeconomic agency is uppermost in the lives of many black people, Chesnutt and Johnson put greater emphasis on mimicry and masquerade and view miscegenation as the vehicle for the masquerade of passing. On the other hand, Fitzgerald and Faulkner, with strong concerns about "blood," consistently place the theme of miscegenation at the center of their narratives. In essence, Chesnutt and Johnson are concerned primarily with socioeconomic agency, whereas Fitzgerald and Faulkner, harboring white supremacist beliefs, have anxiety about miscegenation.

With terror in their eyes, many brutalized African women who "crossed the waters" departed the slimy bowels of slave ships impregnated by white members of the crew. Miscegenation (a term that did not find common usage until after the Civil War and was coined by David Goodman Croly and G. Wakeman in 1864),[45] rooted in America's bloody soil of slavery and the pathology of constitutional racism, has been the historical landscape that makes passing for white possible. Like passing, miscegenation suggests a complex duality. Yet the dynamics of racial contact and sexual interest were stronger than prejudice, theory, culture, law, or belief. The involuntary migration of twenty Africans to America began in 1619; the first mulattoes were born shortly afterward. In the sexual relationships between blacks and whites during the colonial years, "miscegenation" was most common among black slaves and white indentured servants. Although the colonial leaders constructed laws to ban miscegenation, by the time the United States was founded, more than 60,000 persons of mixed black and white heritage lived in this new land.[46] Because of the doctrine of white supremacy and also out of economic concerns, colonial governments enacted legal measures to prohibit intermarriage. While this ensured that the children of enslaved black women would follow the condition of their mothers, mulatto children of white women were free but were generally bound to long terms of indentured servitude. Also, while there was widespread miscegenation between white males and black women, miscegenation between black men and white women was generally met with severe hostility. This duality resulted in the restriction of miscegenation to white men and black women; relations between black men and white women became America's greatest taboo, the one that, transgressed, often led to the lynching of black men. Gunnar Myrdal points out this double view of miscegenation among whites: "The astonishing fact is the great indifference of most white Americans toward real but illicit miscegenation. . . . The illicit relations freely allowed or only frowned upon are, however, restricted to those between white men and Negro women. A white woman's relation with a Negro man is met by the full fury of anti-amalgamation sanctions."[47]

It is critical to note that miscegenation is a physical act that requires sexual contact but does not demand intermarriage. In addition, it is critical to recall that, in that absurdist world of mixed races, miscegenation continued beyond the binaries of blacks and whites and whites and mulattoes. Miscegenation also may be said to occur when there is intimacy between unmixed Africans and mulattoes and between mulattoes and other mulattoes. Under the Jim Crow system, sexual contact between blacks and whites was severely restricted. Still, as F. James Davis argues, "Mulatto-mulatto and mulatto–African black mixing continued, of course, and accounted for most of the miscegenation."[48]

Despite these complicated problems, in the literature on passing, there exists a similar dichotomy in which the sexual relationships between blacks and whites mirror the period of black people's enslavement. Additionally, the paradox of this amalgamation is that black people, through the racial, religious, and scientific dogma of white supremacy, were labeled heathen, savage, and inferior. During black people's enslavement and afterward, miscegenation, spreading like a prairie fire, was closely intertwined with a racial socioeconomic structure. As Barbara Christian argues, the "tragic mulatta" figure becomes the vehicle for cultural transference and a constant place of alienation.[49]

A bitter and strange fruit associated with miscegenation is the taboo of incest. In the predatory, tooth-and-claw environment of slavery, most black women had little defense against the sexual advances of white males; some white slave masters also had sexual relations with their mulatto daughters. Unlike Faulkner, who focused on miscegenation, signifying on slavery, Chesnutt and Johnson connected the issues of miscegenation and incest.

Mimicry, our second critical term, recalls that, in order to pass for white, individuals found it necessary to imitate the practices of the white-dominated culture and to attempt to make their blackness invisible. Mimicry is present in the adornment, speech, and behavior of these racial chameleons. Many mulattoes during slavery were trained servants who had received education and training in certain skills, and this brought them closer to whites and their culture. This led many whites to view them as superior to dark-skinned blacks and led some mulattoes to internalize this superiority and take great pride in their white heritage. With this notion of superiority in place, it was easier for those blacks who passed to enter foreign territory. Jacques Lacan points out the "warlike" aspects of this process: "Mimicry reveals something in so far as it is distinct from what might be called an itself that is behind. The effect of mimicry is camouflage. . . . It is not a question of harmonizing with the background, but against a mottled background, of becoming mottled—exactly like the technique of camouflage practiced in human warfare."[50] As argued earlier, mimicry suggests the duality of a profound challenge and the internalization of hegemonic dictates. It is a "double consciousness" or duality that can be traced back to slavery's "house nigger" and "field nigger" binary, where the former was often seen as imitating the white master. Clearly, some "house niggers" did mimic their white masters while at the same time passing critical information to those blacks who worked the fields. Additionally, these "house niggers" were in a unique position to facilitate the attainment of information and skills that helped them pass for white. As Homi K. Bhabha suggests, mimicry is a complex affair of duality connected to power:

> Mimicry is, thus the sign of a double articulation; a complex strategy of reform, regulation and discipline, which "appropriates" the Other as it visualizes power. Mimicry is also the sign of the inappropriate, however, a difference or recalcitrance which coheres to the dominant strategic function of colonial power, intensifies surveillance, and poses an immanent threat to both "normalized" knowledge and disciplinary powers.[51]

This desire for an agency of empowerment is both resemblance and menace, a desire that constantly articulates the racial differences constructed by the legal, cultural, and social restrictions inherent to white supremacy.

Mimics can be considered "image-makers" who chronically imitate white mannerisms in their desire for a feeling of similarity or closeness to whiteness. The life of a mimic is consequently one endless duplication of white society. By aping the speech, behavior, and physical features of whites, mimics cross over to wear the mask of whiteness and become the unfortunate victims of the nervous insecurity that plagues all impostors. Yet, for those who pass, strategically this mimicry can be very close to mockery. Nathan Hare connects mimicry by black people to desire:

> the mimic conforms to white norms, in the expectation that the elimination of all ostensible difference between the races will eradicate the socio-economic discrimination now suffered by his race. Having unconsciously accepted the eternal superiority of the white world, he naturally proceeds to imitate his transcendent supermodel.[52]

Some deceptive individuals who disavow mimicry and who pass for white are the site of interdiction—the representation of those who desire whites' love and acceptance.

Like miscegenation and mimicry, masquerade is rooted in the slave experience and signifies on the prevarication and performative aspects of passing. When we consider Frederick Douglass's and W. E. B. Du Bois's references to the "sorrow songs" and the masking of discourse during black people's enslavement, we can better understand the deep roots of the phenomenon of passing. The "sorrow songs" such as "Steal Away," "Go Down Moses," and "Let Us Break Bread Together" were used frequently for clandestine communication among fellow captives or between captives and free blacks and sympathetic whites working to facilitate black people's escape or revolt. Lawrence Levine argues that these songs state as clearly as anything else the manner in which the sacred world of the slaves was able to fuse the precedents of the past, the conditions of the present, and the promise of the future in one connected reality. In this respect there was always a latent and symbolic element of protest in the slaves' religious songs that frequently became overt and explicit.[53] This latent and symbolic element is indicative of the phenomenon of passing, which is an improvisational art form in which the body as a textual landscape is transformed into its racial antithesis.[54]

The speech acts of enslaved blacks were also coded with double meaning to negotiate a double audience in order to beguile white masters and communicate with other blacks. On one hand, their speech expressed contentment; on the other, their speech expressed their political desire for freedom. With encoded vernacular, blacks in their daily interactions communicated information about secret meetings, plans to escape, and schemes to revolt (as they did in the spirituals, slave songs, blues, and trickster tales). This dissimulation and ingenuity not only enabled one to protect oneself but also suggests how prevaricating a psychological device of empowerment was. This agency of empowerment interconnects chameleonlike behavior,[55] language, criminality, naming/unnaming, and the need for co-conspirators in the passing charade.

The complex charade of blacks passing for white suggests an equally complex methodology. Although there is little theoretical work that directly addresses passing, theories on race abound. Long-discredited biological theories of racial superiority, dominant during the 1920s, are not discussed. More relevant is Theodore Allen's psychocultural theory, which claims that racism and racial slavery were the inevitable consequences of British culture and the search for a colonial identity.[56] The works of Carl Degler, Winthrop Jordan, and Gunnar Myrdal, representative of the psychocultural approach, consider only the marginally critical importance of economics associated with race and thus are of limited value here. White slave owners were concerned mainly with maximizing profits. As Lerone Bennett argues, "It was not at all unusual for a white master to force a white woman servant to marry a black male servant. Nor was it unusual for a white master to give a black man a position of authority over white male and white female servants."[57] Yet this amalgamation brought problems, such as rebellions and escapes, that led white masters to conclude that a "white" racial identity as a social buffer was needed.

Frantz Fanon's theories about economics trace the psychological and social phenomenon in which the oppressed internalize the values and beliefs of the oppressor (mainly white). This internalization, Fanon argues, creates an Other, who, desiring agency, mimics and masquerades as a white person. In very simple terms, this process involves movement from the class of the slaves to that of masters. Although Fanon's theoretical texts provide a critical foundation, they lack the social and historical context that makes passing in America a unique phenomenon. Du Bois's theory of "double consciousness," although it does not directly address passing, suggests the psychocultural, social, and economic tensions black people experience as they attempt to integrate themselves into white society, to pass beyond the black world within "the veil."

With the racial theories of W. E. B. Du Bois, Ralph Ellison, and Frantz Fanon as a foundation, in this book I attempt to connect Jacques Lacan's theory of the phallus as the primal signifier, a representation of power and authority (in this case whiteness), with the desire of blacks to pass for white. By denying their blackness and effectively engaging and internalizing the phallus, protagonists gain agency.

Further, drawing on Peter Brooks's analysis, I suggest that individuals who pass can be conceived of as "desiring machines" whose presence in the narratives creates and sustains narrative movement through the forward march of desire, projecting the self onto the world through scenarios of desire imagined and then acted upon.[58] As revealed in the passing narratives considered here, the realization of desire comes in a sinister form—destruction of the self.[59] Death and desire become intertwined and interconnected because passing suggests living a death-within-life in order to preserve life-within-death.[60] In the literature of passing, from Chesnutt to Faulkner, we can determine that disgust often bears the imprint of desire.

In the first chapter, "The 'Circular Ruins' of Passing: Race, Class, and Gender in Charles Waddell Chesnutt's *The House Behind the Cedars*," I consider Chesnutt's signifying on his theory of amalgamation as he explores the tragic complexity of the passing charade. Published at the turn of the century, this novel speculates on the possibilities of America's future of racial amalgamation. With a title suggestive of a clandestine affair, this literary drama grounds my examination of black individuals who cross over because it illustrates how the dynamics of race, class, and gender intersect. Chesnutt also places emphasis on interracial conflict against intra-racial confrontations. These aspects illustrate the grand desire not to be white but to attain the power and privileges associated with whiteness.

The next chapter, "The Improvisational and Faustian Performance in James Weldon Johnson's *The Autobiography of an Ex-Coloured Man*," examines Johnson's modernistic text. This text identifies and collects from previous texts—notably *Up from Slavery* and *The Souls of Black Folk*, but also the slave narratives—critical tropes in the African American literary tradition. Our protagonist's tragic and comic sojourn across America and into foreign territory highlights the tension between race and nation and racism and nationalism. Here we view cultural and psychological displacement in the process of racial deception. As represented by "fast yellowing manuscripts," the possibility that some black cultural productions such as ragtime music and spirituals will become extinct is very much at risk in the phenomenon of passing.

In my third and signature chapter, "The Tragic Black Buck: Jay Gatsby's Passing in F. Scott Fitzgerald's *The Great Gatsby*," I explore Fitzgerald's characterization of Jay Gatsby as a light-skinned black man passing as white. A close examination of the author's signifying use of race, color, symbolism, and diction suggests that Fitzgerald is playing in and playing with the darkness as it relates to Gatsby's enduring quest for the American Dream, symbolized by wealth, power, property, and especially the white woman, Daisy Buchanan.

My final chapter, "Joe Christmas, a Black Buck with Attitude: The Virulent Nexus of Race and Color in *Light in August*," examines ambiguous constructions of race and skin color. Connecting the taboo of miscegenation to passing, this novel highlights America's persistent and prevailing preoccupation with the "one-drop rule" associated with systemic white supremacist culture. In *Light in August*, William Faulkner explores, as he does in *Absalom, Absalom!* (1936), the notion that white people often do not know a black person when they see one. Faulkner characterizes the "parchment colored" protagonist, Joe Christmas, as "a paradox inside a riddle wrapped in an enigma." Despite Faulkner's depiction of grotesque racism and with markedly little sympathy for the individual who passes, he melodramatically exposes the fallacy of race as a biological and sociolinguistic construction.

These chapters convey the complex phenomenon of passing as an aggressive and repressive performance; these chapters reveal the anti-essentialism of racial identity and challenge the hegemonic criteria of racial identity and racism. As Etienne Balibar argues,

> Racism—a true total social phenomenon—inscribes itself in practices (forms of violence, contempt, intolerance, humiliation and exploitation), in discourses and representations which are so many intellectual elaborations of the phantasm of prophylaxis and segregation (the need to purify the social body, to preserve "one's own" or "our identity" from all forms of mixing, interbreeding or invasion) and which are articulated around stigmata of otherness (name, skin, colour, religious practices).[61]

My enduring concern in this literary project is the cultural construction and representation of race. These passing narratives interrogate America's obsession with racial hierarchies and skin color, hair texture, and language—obsessions that frequently pass beyond America's racial boundaries.[62] As R. Larson adamantly proclaims, "No passing novel can be regarded as anything other than a strong indictment of American life; people are driven to such drastic measures because of American racism and the need for economic survival"[63] (emphasis added). Along with the desire for economic survival and social mobility, the connecting link in these narratives is the Faustian bargains in which the black protagonists make a devilish deal and tragically sell their souls to whiteness. In these passing novels, the artificial lines of racial demarcation create a mixture that is mostly tragedy and some comedy. As tragically and comically dramatized in Wendell B. Harris's film *Chameleon Street,* passing becomes a conflict-ridden process of identity formation and self-image production played out by those adventurous, imaginative, and self-determining black male individuals with the "white" features.

2

"THE CIRCULAR RUINS" OF PASSING

Race, Class, and Gender in Charles Waddell Chesnutt's The House Behind the Cedars[1]

People who belong by half or more of their blood to the most virile and progressive race of modern times have as much right to call themselves white as others have to call themselves negroes [sic].
— CHARLES WADDELL CHESNUTT, *"A Matter of Principle"*

Those who pass have a severe dilemma before they decide to do so, since a person must give up all family ties and loyalties to the black community in order to gain economic opportunities.
— F. JAMES DAVIS, *Who Is Black? One Nation's Definition*

In a journal entry dated July 31, 1875, Charles Waddell Chesnutt makes remarks about his youthful experiences that shed light on his first novel *The House Behind the Cedars* (1900), a narrative meditation on racial mixture and on the motif of black people passing for white. This early note provides a vivid metaphor for harmonizing the Du Boisian paradigm of being black and being American at the same time:

Twice today, or oftener, I have been taken for "white." At the pond this morning one fellow said he'd "be damned if there was any nigger blood in me." *At Coleman's I passed. On the road an old chap, seeing the trunks, took me for a student coming from school. I believe I'll leave here and pass anyhow, for I am white as any of them. One old fellow said today, "Look here Tom. Here's a black as white as you are."*[2] (emphasis added)

Chesnutt, who was so light skinned that he was generally assumed to be white, communicates a profound paradox, a paradox signifying upon the nature of his self-conception.[3] In essence, he is a racial oxymoron, an individual who is what he is not: a white black man, a black white man.

Knowing firsthand the possibilities of passing for white and living on the "color line," Chesnutt wrote many novels, stories, essays, and speeches that concern racial "amalgamation."[4] His solution to "the Negro problem" lay in his adamant assertion that America's racial problems and the prevalence of white supremacy (which he labeled "the unjust spirit of caste") would be diminished if miscegenation flourished: if, so to speak, passing became the norm. In a speech called "Race Prejudice: Its Causes and Its Cure" (1905), Chesnutt addressed the Boston Historical and Literary Association, arguing that if America followed the European example of racial evolution, America's racial anxiety would dramatically lessen.

In 1900, the same year that *The House Behind the Cedars* was published, Chesnutt argued, in a series of articles entitled "The Future America," that a modern America would be formed from America's three "broad types"—white, black, and red. This amalgamation would be "a new people who look substantially alike, and are molded by the same culture and dominated by the same ideas."[5] In a detailed three-step process, Chesnutt laid out his program of racial amalgamation. As a first step, assuming that one-eighth of the population was black, Chesnutt would have this population marry an equal number of whites to produce a first generation of which one-fourth would be mulatto. In the next step, these mulattoes in turn would marry whites to construct a new generation half of which would be quadroons. By the third generation, the whole population would be composed of octoroons, with the pure white people being eliminated and no perceptible traces of black people remaining.

Although Chesnutt surmised that his amalgamation formula would never be realized, it is upon this theoretical foundation and narrative structure that *The House Behind the Cedars* explores the issues of miscegenation, mimicry, and black people who masquerade as white people. Like Frederick Douglass's *Narrative of the Life of Frederick Douglass, an American Slave* (1845), *The House Behind the Cedars* articulates black people's desire for a permanent socioeconomic agency within the parameters of America's veneration of whiteness. The critical difference here is that Douglass's narrative directly challenges white supremacy, whereas Chesnutt's novel indirectly challenges white supremacy. Passing suggests a passive response to white supremacy. By crossing over the color line or passing for white, previously black individuals not only can escape physical, psychological, and socioeconomic oppression and violence; they assertively cast themselves in a racial drama where they clandestinely stand at center stage.

Chesnutt revised *The House Behind the Cedars* (originally called *Rena*) three times between 1889 and 1891. He developed the manuscript into a larger draft by 1895, and eventually a novel by 1899. Although the evolving narrative centers on the concerns of light-skinned individuals like Chesnutt—those who walked the racial tightrope of the color line—*Rena* develops from a mundane love triangle into a sophisticated analysis of America's racial, class, and gender dynamics. The publishers, Houghton Mifflin, recognized the strength of ten years of rewriting and in 1900 published the text under the new title *The House Behind the Cedars*. This novel proved to be Chesnutt's most financially successful book and later served as the basis for a film.[6] Considering Chesnutt's placement in the tradition of American literature as the first major black novelist, there exists little evidence that he was familiar with Frances E. W. Harper's *Iola Leroy or Shadows Uplifted* (1892), a passing narrative that rejects passing as a progressive strategy for black people. *The House Behind the Cedars* suggests the influence of William Dean Howells's *Imperative Duty* (1892) and Mark Twain's *The Tragedy of Pudd'nhead Wilson* (1894). These works closely predate Chesnutt's text and examine black people who cross over to assume a white identity. More than the others, Twain's novel closely resembles *The House Behind the Cedars* in its consideration of the legal,[7] psychological, and economic aspects of black people passing for white. Like Twain, Chesnutt creates fiction that leavens the faults and the foibles of all classes of characters with satire and irony. Both novels conclude with the often tragic repercussions of passing and an indictment of America's racist society.

Anticipating William Faulkner's *Light in August*, Chesnutt in *The House Behind the Cedars* signifies on the notion that Thomas Jefferson, who wrote about freedom and the inferiority of black people,[8] had an intimate relationship with the beautiful mulatto slave, Sally Hemmings. This illicit miscegenation resulted in a number of children, who, among Jefferson's numerous slaves, were the only ones freed in Jefferson's will. Jefferson's behavior, if the story of the relationship with Hemmings is true, suggests the paradoxical paradigm of America's "head and heart" being torn over the issues of race and color.[9] Racial prejudice, Chesnutt believed, is the most sinister feature of the racial conflict in the United States. Also, like the shrewd former slaves who wrote before him, Chesnutt desired to educate whites and to emancipate black people from the "subtle almost indefinable feeling of repulsion toward the Negro, which is common to most Americans."[10] Consequently, the extraordinary life struggles and literary works of Frederick Douglass were important to Chesnutt. He expressed "a profound and in some degree a personal sympathy with every step of Douglass' upward career."[11] Chesnutt's biography of Douglass, published in 1899, suggests his profound respect for Douglass; in it, like many other African American male writers, Chesnutt positions Douglass as a literary father. As George P. Cunningham makes clear:

> Douglass is a central and centering figure in Afro-American discourse and, in some degree, succeeding generations of Afro-American, men as well as women, write under his influence and respond to his figuration of the desire for freedom. . . . Douglass's journey into subjectivity may serve as grounds for theorizing about the Afro-American male as subject and as opening to text that revise, repeat, or enter into dialogue with Douglass.[12]

In his biography of Frederick Douglass, Chesnutt writes: "It was the curious fate of Douglass *to pass through almost every phase of slavery,* as though to prepare him the more thoroughly for his future career"[13] (emphasis added). Enslaved, Douglass is considered an "animal" and a "beast," and as an escaped slave Douglass is considered a criminal. In essence, Douglass has committed the transgression of stealing himself. As the historian Charshee C. L. McIntyre argues, "European Americans created a social structure for free Whites and enslaved blacks and viewed free or freed blacks as unwanted, troublesome and dangerous, and inherently criminal."[14] Of course, the legacy of black people's being criminalized lasted well beyond slavery and Reconstruction. Whereas Douglass "passed" to the North and beyond slavery and took the name of a hero of English fiction and myth, he did not erase his identity as an African American of integrity and action. Chesnutt's literary canon bears witness that black writers responded to Douglass's call and connects the theme of passing to an inchoate desire for freedom in *The House Behind the Cedars*. Thus, a black individual, slave or free, in Jim Crow America endures in a precarious situation.

Although Douglass's rites of passage (obtaining literacy, manhood, and freedom) enable him to escape slavery's physical and psychological torment, he is constantly aware of his tenuous legal status. In Douglass's time as well as Chesnutt's, a black person (regardless of age) was considered by the language of white racism a boy or girl. Consequently, for black individuals to assert their manhood or womanhood, "to act white," to attempt to be white (free, pass, or cross over), or to express equality to whites was, in the eyes of many whites, to commit dangerous and criminal acts that were often met with violence. As Frantz Fanon makes clear, violence against the oppressor, even on an individual level, is the critical incident that "frees the native from his inferiority complex and from his despair and inaction; it makes him fearless and restores his self-respect."[15]

Throughout *The House Behind the Cedars*, we experience echoes of Douglass's passage from slavery to freedom. These echoes suggest that the adventurous black individual who passes for white is in significant ways analogous to the escaped slave; both are on a quest to move beyond America's racist legal and cultural borders. Yet, passing in significant ways surpasses the paradigm of the escaped slave and becomes the ultimate dramatic performance of whitening up.[16] Thus, black individuals who pass and escape into whiteness become a "new people."

The House Behind the Cedars functions as a fictional version of Chesnutt's amalgamation theory, which strongly suggests the private/public and unnatural/natural place of some surreptitious activity.[17] Here, through the maze and morass of miscegenation, the tropes of mimicry and masquerade are established. Through miscegenation, the secluded house becomes an architectural bridge of amalgamation and a paradoxical paradigm of white America's racial anxiety and hidden hypocrisy; it reveals many black people's intraracial conflict regarding skin color, hair texture, and language. Chesnutt's staging of this clandestine drama of racial amalgamation and passing unveils America's deep-seated interracial and intraracial conflicts. These conflicts reveal the economic and psychological realities that motivate some black individuals to cross over to assume a white identity.

In *The House Behind the Cedars*, the masquerade commences with Molly Walden, a "bright" second-generation quadroon with high cheekbones and straight black hair who is seduced by a wealthy and liberal white man who in turn transforms her future. With Molly's father dead and her mother's conspiring silence regarding their relationship, Molly soon lives in her own house, a gift from this wealthy white gentleman. Although free, Molly's impoverished condition changes notably because of her sexual transgression: "Her mother nevermore knew want. Her poor relatives could always find a meal in Molly's kitchen. She did not flaunt her prosperity in the world's face; she hid it discreetly behind the cedar screen."[18] Yet, Molly's economic elevation causes her to cultivate a psychological perspective not dissimilar to that of racist white people. Attending the white Episcopal church, Molly, from her segregated pew (commonly referred to as Nigger Heaven), publicly views a "gentleman" whose religious practices don't interfere with his private pleasures in the house behind the cedar trees. Although black and free, Molly has internalized the hegemonic values of white people: "She did not sympathize greatly with the new era opened up for the emancipated slaves; she had no ideal love of liberty; she was no broader and no more altruistic than the white people around her, to whom she had always looked up; and she sighed for the old days, because to her they had been the good days" (107). As Fanon suggests, a primary motive for the oppressed to internalize the views of the oppressor resides in the social and economic possibilities associated with embracing whiteness and the internalization of blackness as being inferior.[19] Like the "damsel in distress," Molly has been rescued from poverty by a white knight, and she "worshipped the ground upon which her lord walked, was humbly grateful for his protection, and quite as faithful as the forbidden marriage vow could possibly have made her" (105). Unable to be placed on the sacred pedestal of white womanhood, Molly is extremely grateful while enacting the role of secret white mistress. Her personal success prevents her from any altruistic views concerning the masses of black people who, not being economically privileged and light skinned, are unable to embrace whiteness. The light of Molly's fantasy fades with the death of her lord and king, when her large expectations of a legacy never materialize. With two fatherless children, Molly struggles to live in a world where black people are challenging the racist Jim Crow regime.

John (like "Jack" a name common with trickster figures) and Rena Walden, third-generation octoroons and Molly's two remaining children, who lack their white father's name and protection, must attempt to construct their identities and futures in a society where the snarling winds of white supremacy create a perpetual winter in the lives of black people. Yet, having his father's "patrician features" and his mother's Indian hair, John believes there is no difference between himself and the other white boys. While at school, he thrashes the white boy who one day calls him black. When things are reversed, with John being thrashed five or six times, he ceases to utter public declarations of his whiteness. John's embrace of whiteness becomes a private drama and a soliloquy sanctioned by God. "His playmates might call him black; the mirror proved that God, the Father of all, had made him white;

and God, he had been taught, made no mistakes,—having made him white, He must have meant him to be white" (107). John's self-reflecting gaze configures a triangle consisting of his view of himself, God's validation of his whiteness, and the opposing view of his playmates. Here, as in other passing narratives, the mirror becomes a major trope where one's private gaze can supplant, subvert, and supersede the public gaze. Jacques Lacan describes the moment when a child recognizes its own image in the mirror as critical for the constitution and projection of the ego.[20] Two aspects of Lacan's analysis are relevant here. First, John imagines his mirror image to be more complete, more unblemished than the way he experiences his own body. Second, this recognition transforms John into an alienated subject. Interrogating Lacanian theory, the film scholar Laura Mulvey argues: "Recognition is thus overlaid with mis-recognition: the image recognized is conceived as the reflected body of the self, but its interpretation as superior projects this body outside itself as an ideal ego, the alienated subject, which, re-introjected as an ego ideal, gives rise to the future generation of identification with others."[21] Within the context of white supremacy and its hegemonic "one-drop theory," John's affirmation of whiteness is an interpretation that positions him as an "alienated subject." Additionally, as Fanon reminds us, "The eye is not merely a mirror, but a correcting mirror. The eye should make it possible for us to correct cultural errors."[22] Here it is important to understand the potential of the mirror both to disclose and to distort. This contradictory and conflicting condition duplicates the psychological trauma imposed and inscribed by systemic white rule. John's self-correcting gaze constructs an internal psychological and emotional representation of whiteness and a corresponding denial of blackness that will later facilitate his permanent immersion into the sacred white world. His movement from a racial "wasteland" to the "sacred woods" of the white world is facilitated by the books that his white father has left behind at the house.

Unlike his illiterate mother, John becomes fascinated with his (unnamed) father's books. These literary texts plant the seeds of possibility and promise that can catapult John beyond the racial, socioeconomic, and geographic restrictions of the house behind the cedars. Through reading, John vicariously follows the fortunes of Tom Jones and Sophia; he weeps over the fate of Eugene Aram; he penetrates with Richard the Lionheart into Saladin's tent and flies through the air on the magic carpet or the enchanted horse (108). This genre of reading places emphasis on the danger, thrill, and excitement, associated with passing for white. It is from Bulwer's novel that John reads the story of Warwick the Kingmaker, a name he will later choose when he becomes a new man (20). Thus, John attempts to escapes the signifier of black buck.

In many slave narratives such as Douglass's, former slaves changed their names to appropriate their new identities. Douglass recalls his transformation: "Mr. Johnson had been just reading the 'Lady of the Lake,' [by Walter Scott] and at once suggested that my name be 'Douglass.' From that time until now I have been called 'Frederick Douglass'; and as I am more widely known by that name than by either of the others, I shall continue to use it as my own."[23] John's literacy, which expedites his ascendancy, responds to Douglass. Yet, unlike Douglass, who states that "learning to read had been a curse rather than a blessing,"[24] John finds that his ability to pass for white reflects the importance of class and color. This textual immersion suggests that John is sublimating his aggression in defense of his God-sanctioned whiteness. In every society there exists a channel, an outlet through which the forces accumulated in the form of aggression can be legally released healthfully. Fanon suggests a textual connection between this aggression and identity formation. He argues:

> This is the purpose of games in children's institutions of psychodramas in group therapy, and in a more general way, of illustrated magazines for children—each type of society, of course requiring its own specific kind of catharsis. The Tarzan stories, the sagas of twelve year-old explorers, the adventures of Mickey Mouse, and all those "comic books" serve actually as a release for collective aggression. The magazines are put together by white men for little white men.[25]

Furthermore, the father's texts relate that John tastes the "Tree of Knowledge." Whereas the mother's embrace is sensual, John's embrace is textual. This "tree" as a phallic symbol becomes a metaphor for representations of whiteness, representations of authority, and representations of power and possibility. Moreover, this "tree of knowledge" delineates the differences between white social, economic, and political possibilities and power on the one hand and a wretched and oppressed black existence on the other. Although a youngster, John consciously chooses the former. Thus, John develops an aggressive attitude toward hegemonic economic and social structures to go with an intense identification and sacrificial dedication to the hegemony of whiteness.

John's color-based status becomes established by genealogy and geography. Molly and the location of the house behind the cedars at the outskirts of the black community make John black. Yet, with the "blood of his white fathers, the heirs of the ages" (109) crying for their own, John's intense desire to move beyond these racial borders, where color determines character, leads him to the office of Judge Archibald Straight. It is here that the near-white John Walden becomes white. Additionally, it is here that the text formulates triangular configurations—four of them in all—that channel desire and sustain narrative movement.

While Judge Straight reads an article about the "hopeless intellectual inferiority of the negro, and the physical and moral degeneration of mulattoes, who combined the worst qualities of their two ancestral races" (110), John, "with all the features of a white man," barefoot with a straw hat in his hand, walks in to declare his inchoate desire to be a lawyer. Significantly at odds with this "tree of knowledge," John seeks the realization of his white genealogy. He desires to transform the fantasy of whiteness into fact. At this time in history, the legal profession is restricted to white men. With John's desire manifesting, extending, stretching, and projecting itself, the text suggests that his aspiration to be a lawyer implicitly implies his whiteness.[26] But, one step beyond this, within Jim Crow America, the black man as a freely choosing human being is fantasy, as well. John's desire intersects racial and class boundaries because this profession implies socioeconomic opportunities unavailable to black men.

John's desire for subjectivity formulates our initial triangle of desire because, unknown to him, he has come to an old friend and companion of his dead white father, who desired to provide for his illicit progeny, John and Rena Walden. Judge Straight recalls his old friend's desire: "Archie, I'm coming to have you draw my will. There are some children for whom I would like to make ample provision. I can't give them anything else, but money will make them free of the world" (112). He dies unexpectedly, before the will can be drawn. Having mentioned this desire to the dead man's family, Judge Straight encounters vehement hostility and the suggestion that "it was a pity the little niggers were not slaves—that they would have added measurably to the value of the property" (112). Gazing intently at John, who like Douglass does not know the name of his white father, the Judge realizes the intersection of a father's and a son's desires. This matrix of desire,[27] which combines the past, present, and future, positions of John as a person who is not ashamed of his mixed ancestry but who resents the barriers erected by systemic racial prejudice. Yet, despite Judge Straight's sympathies, he knows the cultural and legal constructs that make John's aspiration to be a lawyer an impossible proposition.

Citing the *Dred Scott v. Sandford* decision of 1857, Judge Straight judiciously informs John that "one drop of blood" makes the whole man (or woman) black. Taking up the article Judge Straight reads, "negroes are beings 'of an inferior order, and altogether unfit to associate with the white race, either social or political relations, in fact so inferior that they have no rights which the white man is bound to respect and that the negro may justly be reduced to slavery for his benefit" (113). Although the decision does not define a "negro," it assumes that there exists some traditional means of making that judgment. For the Judge and for American society, this decision, more than any other, dictates the limited social, political, and economic possibilities open to black people. To a lawyer, this scene and its diction reflect the critical significance of the legal profession as a linchpin of white supremacy used to deny humanity to black people and to facilitate the sanctioning of Jim Crow law.

In candid language the denotations and connotations of white, meaning freedom and black, meaning oppression, becomes established. Responding to the racist discourse, John states, "I am white," and, exposing his arm, declares, "and I am free, as all my people were before me" (113). Sagaciously, John reasons that passing for white is his remedy to the demeaning legal discourse. Using ocular analysis as his argument, John correctly suggests that one's race is mainly determined by observable features (skin color, hair texture, and other physical features). His theory is that if one appears to be white, one is white unless there exists some contradictory knowledge or evidence.

The dialogue between Judge Straight and John highlights the opposing definitions of what constitutes "race." For Chesnutt, color, often meaning race, is the critical deterrent to black people's achieving agency. Arguing the irrelevance of color, Chesnutt states:

Why should a man be proud any more than he should be ashamed of a thing for which he is not at all responsible? Manly self-respect, based upon one's humanity, a self-respect which claims nothing for color and yields nothing to color, every man should cherish. But the Negro in the United States has suffered too much from the race pride of other people to justify him in cultivating something equally offensive for himself.[28]

Chesnutt's analysis is in accord with W. E. B. Du Bois's racial theory of that era. Du Bois asserts:

So far at least as intellectual and moral aptitudes are concerned we ought to speak of civilizations where we now speak of "races. . . . Indeed, even the physical characteristics, excluding the skin color of a people, are to no small extent the direct result of the physical and social environment under which it is living. . . . These physical characteristics are furthermore too indefinite and exclusive to serve as a basis for any rigid classification or division of human groups.[29]

Judge Straight and John concur that the legal aspects are less a concern with regard to race than is the way people think—how they individually comprehend and construct race. Clearly, the distinct morphological characteristics of skin color, hair texture, and physical features propel racial classification. This prejudicial cultural agreement reveals America's spurious notion of legally defining and constructing racial categories. Thus, even though Judge Straight consults his legal texts to determine that South Carolina classifies a person as white only when the person's admixture of African blood does not exceed one-eighth, one's reputation and reception into white society are significant factors.

John realizes that by transplanting himself to South Carolina, he can change the theory of his whiteness to a legal fact. Here Chesnutt conveys the importance of geography in the passing phenomenon. In "What Is a White Man?," Chesnutt points out the critical importance of South Carolina:

It is certainly true that the color-line is, in practice as in law, more loosely drawn in South Carolina than in any other Southern State, and that no inconsiderable element of the population of that state consists of these legal white persons, who were either born in the state, or attracted thither by this feature of the laws, have come in from surrounding states, and forsaking home and kindred, have taken their social position as white people. A reasonable degree of reticence in regard to one's antecedents is, however, usual in such cases.[30]

Hence, in order to be successful in assuming a white identity, one must remove oneself from the geographical location where family, friends, and others (white people) can establish one's racial ancestry. Also, by allowing John to read and study his law books, Judge Straight—contrary to his name—bends the law and becomes a co-conspirator expediting John's desire to pass as a white lawyer. Judge Archibald Straight, John's dead father, and John construct the initial triangle of desire that formulates three subsequent narrative configurations.

Upon turning eighteen, John asks his mother for a sum of money and, forsaking home and kindred, leaves the narrow walls of "niggerhood" to escape into the white world. Before he escapes, John gives his sister, Rena, a dime with a hole in it for a keepsake.[31] When asked about her son, Molly replies, "He's gone over on the other side" (116). The language of absence and death is also that of passing for white.

Both Molly's references to death and the dime (as a symbol of incestuous desire) are critical to the issue of black people passing for white. Like a magnet, John is attracted to whiteness, and in order to effectively and permanently pass for white, John must disavow any association with his family, friends, and anyone else who can identify him as a black person. He must purge all manners of speech, dress, and conduct that might be associated with blackness and embrace whiteness. The monetarily worthless dime suggests a bribe for his sister's silence and cooperation regarding his deception of passing. Chesnutt conveys a connection between death and desire. John, as a "machine of desire," represents the simultaneous act of death and rebirth. A death to his blackness gives birth to his whiteness. Because John does not know his father's name, there is an unconscious desire in John to assume his role. Chesnutt's language suggests the play of substitution and reversal where the signified has moved into the place of the signifier. Yet, by passing, John refigures the absent (dead) white father, who becomes symbolically absent, as well. Hence, the dime, emphasizing circular movement, symbolizes John (Walden) Warwick's becoming a configuration of his dead father's and Judge Straight's desires; John returns to the house behind the cedars ten years later.

During slavery, many white men were clandestine and cautious in their illicit relations with black women. John's anxiety-laden behavior upon returning to the house behind the cedars, analogous to that of a white slave master, resembles the behavior of a criminal. Chesnutt's description of John (Walden) Warwick sharply contrasts with his "barefoot" encounter with the Judge: "He was dressed in a suit of linen duck—the day was warm—a panama straw hat and patent leather shoes" (1). John's shoes are a particular signifier of success. Other than the "straw hat," John has transformed himself by changing his name from Walden to Warwick, changing residence from North Carolina to Clarence, South Carolina, and changing his racial identity from black buck to white gentleman.

As John strolls through his old hometown, the converging past and present suggest John's new life and the tragic future. John passes the curfew bell that at nine o'clock during the days of slavery would warn all "Negroes," slave or free, that it was unlawful to be outside. Chesnutt's ironic contrasts are vivid. For example, a colored policeman now exists in the old constable's place, next to Judge Straight's office, a colored man whistles as he varnishes a coffin, and, at Liberty Point, John recalls it as the place of slave auctions. Chesnutt's reference to Liberty Point, along with the "old Jefferson Hotel, once the leading hotel of the town" (4) where political meetings were held and political speeches made, ironically suggests the leader Thomas Jefferson. Chesnutt's description of John's success in passing echoes Jefferson's discourse: "Once persuaded that he had certain rights, or ought to have them, by virtue of the laws of nature in defiance of the customs of mankind, he had promptly sought to enjoy them" (53–54). Yet, John's remembrances (analogous to the rumors of Jefferson's affair with a slave woman, Sally Hemmings) don't allow him to acknowledge his past openly. Although he recognizes "Aunt Lyddy, the ancient negro woman who had sold him gingerbread and fried fish, and told him weird tales of witchcraft and conjuration" (3), John refuses to speak to Aunt Lyddy or to give her any sign of recognition. Like Sir Walter Scott's Ivanhoe, John Warwick returns after ten years to find himself a stranger in his hometown of Patesville. Better, like a modern-day Robin Hood, John returns as a criminal attempting to steal blackness (in this case, Rena) and to transform it [her] to whiteness. The text suggests that John's white racial identity and upper-class status make any identification with his past and his blackness dangerous and out of character.

Equally dangerous, the text foreshadows John's incestuous gaze upon a young woman whom he later discovers is his sister, Rena. As John's and Rena's paths converge, "The girl's figure, he perceived, was admirably proportioned; she was evidently at the period when the angles of childhood were rounding into the promising curves of adolescence" (5). Later, after seducing Rena away from their mother, John extends his incestuous gaze beyond the boundaries of a brother-sister relationship: "His [John's] feeling for her was something more than brotherly love,— he was quite conscious that there were degrees in brotherly love, and that if she had been homely or stupid, he would never had disturbed her in her stagnant life of the house behind the cedars" (44). Here, Chesnutt intertwines miscegenation and mimicry. John, assuming the role of an arrogant white father, graciously seeks to protect and elevate his progeny. Although Rena is not homely, she is naive in the art of masquerading as white. Also, like Molly, who bemoans the old days and more so, John has internalized the racial prejudice because of his success in passing. Yet, John's motives reflect a psychological intersection of anxiety and desire. He believes there is relief in having about him someone who knows his past, but he realizes that his social position could "collapse like a house of cards" (45) if his blackness were to be discovered.

Chesnutt suggests rules for successful passing. They include limited communication with one's black relatives, complete breaks with one's black friends, no discussion of race matters, and avoidance of the limelight.[32] Obviously, John's daring act of self-invention is at odds with these guidelines; like his iconoclastic white father, John challenges racial and class boundaries.

Like his mother's white lover, John quite consciously uses a divide-and-conquer strategy; he manipulates his mother and Rena to achieve his objectives. Thus, our second triangle of desire is formulated. Like some of the men in Chesnutt's other stories, John seeks a surrogate wife. On the first attempt to return to the house, when he "incestuously" encounters Rena, John cautiously declines to make his presence known. He realizes that he has made the right decision when he discovers that Molly's neighbors, Peter Fowler and his son, Frank, are observing him. On his second attempt, "like a thief in the night" (20), John surreptitiously makes his way to the house behind the cedars to fulfill his objectives. Engaging in the subterfuge of having a message from Molly Walden's son, John gains entrance to the house. After more affectation and pretense, our "bearded young gentleman" finally reveals to his mother that he is her son. Molly's response—"It like the dead comin' to life. I thought I'd lost you forever" (12)—reinforces the notion that those black individuals who pass for white have entered the world of the deceased or have "passed away." Yet, ironically, John believes that Rena lives a dead or "stagnant life" in this secluded house. Chesnutt's diction reveals that John mimics and mirrors Molly's deceased "king" and the phallic representation of an enchanted white world:

> No king could have received more sincere or delighted homage. He was a man, come into a household of women,—a man of whom they were proud, and to whom they looked up with fond reverence. For he was not only a son,—a brother—but he represented to them the world from which circumstances had shut them out, and to which distance lent even more than its usual enchantment, and they felt nearer to this far-off world because of the glory which Warwick reflected from it. (13–14)

Here Chesnutt connects the white John Warwick and the romantic literary texts that have guided and produced him. John becomes the lord of illusions. Once on the throne as a representation of the white father, John proceeds to manipulate and gain his mother's trust in order to convince her to let Rena, who still has the dime John gave her, join him in the white world. In essence, John desires Rena to be beautiful, to make her a queen in the made-up romance in which he dwells. And, as king, John will oversee and regulate Rena's mimicry and masquerade.

With the skill of a trial lawyer, John psychologically manipulates his mother and Rena. His revelations about his past ten years and his subtle suggestions concerning the present are calculated to produce desire in Rena and guilt in his mother. By first revealing that he has a little son, Albert, and that his white wife is dead, John produces an account of taking "a man's chance in life" (12) that reads like a slave narrative: "with a stout heart an abounding hope he had gone out into a seemingly hostile world, and made fortune stand and deliver. *His story had for the women all the charm of an escape from captivity, with all the thrill of a pirate's tale*" (15; emphasis added). John's didactic discourse describing his journey from "slavery to freedom" and his present status as a prominent member of the South Carolina bar, with wealth, power, and prestige, has produced in Molly and Rena the desired effect. Molly "drank [it] in with parted lips and glistening eyes," whereas Rena listened as "the narrow walls that hemmed her in seemed to draw closer and closer, as though they must crush her" (15). Now, with his dead wife's connections, her good family name, and their son, John becomes the ultimate representation of the socio-economic possibilities of passing. Intensely gazing upon Rena, and knowing the art of negotiation, John is less concerned with informing them of his past than with seducing Rena away from his mother and the house.

Although wealthy, John feels incomplete because he does not have someone of his own blood to love and look after his son. More important, there is no one of blood to constantly validate his "making it" in the white world. Secret smiles from a black friend or family member would establish the success of a black Horatio Alger. In Molly's reply to John's desire, Chesnutt reveals how passing creates tragic realities that separate John's white world and Molly's secluded life in a black community: "She would have given all the world to warm her son's child upon her bosom; but she knew this could not be" (16). Blackness has fixed Molly. Earlier, John comments that Rena's hair has the "wave" that his mother's hair lacks. This comment connects with John's desire to have someone of his own "blood" to raise his child. Because Molly is "stained" with the mark of an "Ethiopian," it becomes clear to Molly that John has been slyly suggesting that Rena, unlike her mother, has the right phenotype, hair texture, and physical features to join him in passing for white. Here, Chesnutt suggests how the visible features of hair and skin color are critical in one's ability to pass. Whereas Molly's hair becomes associated with "bad hair," Rena's hair is "good hair." Rena's "ivory complexion" and "rippling brown hair" make her an object of desire for John and a candidate for passing. Thus, through this intraracial dynamic, Molly, who "bore the mark of the Ethiopian" (122), assumes an inferior and marginal status, whereas Rena, being nearer to whiteness, assumes a superior status.

Distraught at the prospect of Rena's joining John in the white world, Molly sobbingly pleads with him to reconsider. Initially, John accedes to her request, but in Rena's absence he returns to the subject and, by playing upon the mother's guilt, he succeeds in wearing her down. John reminds his mother that Rena has no future behind the cedar trees with her and that "nothing but death can remove that stain [Molly's blackness], if it does not follow us even beyond the grave" (17). Again the juxtaposition of death and desire is repeated. Because Molly and the house are identified with blackness, Rena, despite her fair complexion, will have a limited future. With a mixture of sympathy and sarcasm, John continues to contrast the wonderful white life Rena could have by passing with her stagnant black life in Patesville. Using the information his mother has given him about the local black folks, John produces a discourse that illustrates two racially different worlds of possibility:

> It's a pity that she couldn't have a chance here—but how could she? I thought she might marry a gentleman; but I dare say she'll do as the rest of her friends—as well as Mary B., for instance who married—Homer Pettifoot, did you say? Or maybe Billy Oxendine might do for her. As long as she has never known any better, she'll probably be as well satisfied as though she married a rich man, and lived in a fine house, and kept a carriage and servants, and moved with the best in the land. (18)

Like Molly's description of her white lord, John's father, the words "gentleman" and "rich man" here invoke the high status of a white man. Even the names Homer Pettifoot and Billy Oxendine are very satirical and suggestive of a wretched class position, and they are possibly the names of black servants who, rather than marrying her, will do Rena's bidding if she marries a wealthy white man. Not unlike Charles Dickens, Chesnutt suggests the personality and economic status of many of his characters by their names. Further, John perspicaciously insinuates that Rena should pursue the same course of action that Molly has pursued with her white "lord." The critical difference is that if she passes for white, Rena will have a legally sanctioned marriage and respect from her friends, and her children will not be stigmatized and stained by the labels "illegitimate" and "nigger," as John and Rena have been. With John, Rena can escape her mother's "scarlet letter."

Realizing that her life has not been honorable, Molly feels tortured by John's piercing remarks. In essence, John shrewdly suggests that his mother has been living a sordid life of sin and shame. By making subtle references to Molly's adulterous and illicit relationship with a married white man, John makes Molly acquiesce. "It had been conquered by her son. It beckoned to her daughter. *The comparisons of this free and noble [white] life and the sordid [black] existence of those around her broke down the last barrier of opposition*" (19; emphasis added). Understanding firsthand the tangible economic and social possibilities of a miscegenation embrace, Molly decides to allow Rena to cross over. Molly mournfully understands that by allowing Rena to pay John a visit, "she would never come back except, like her brother under cover of night. She must lose her daughter as well as her son, and this should be the penance for her sin" (21). Here, Chesnutt conveys a shameful synthesis of fornication, adultery, and miscegenation.

The price for Molly's willful act of illicit miscegenation reveals that her children are more often hindered than helped by the circumstances of their birth. Mulattoes or light-skinned individuals are too often rejected by white people and black people alike. Publicly rejected by his white schoolmates, John privately assumes a white identity. Rena, with the "narrow walls" threatening to pulverize her, becomes seduced by John as the white father figure and the phallic signifier of whiteness. Having triumphantly effected his own metamorphosis, John offers Rena his protection, his surname, Warwick (although false), and provisions for a future that her white father, with all his good intentions, could not or did not provide. In contrast to this world of possibility, Chesnutt uses Judge Straight's discourse as a foreshadowing technique. For example, when the Judge learns that John has seduced Rena into joining him, he states: "My young friend John has builded, whether wisely or not, very well; but he has come back into the old life and carried away a part of it, and I fear that this addition will weaken the structure" (30). Judge Straight connects gender to passing; Rena is viewed as inferior; not only is she unlikely to pull off this racial ruse, but also she will "weaken" John's kingdom. On another occasion, the Judge issues a "passing" warning that connects geography to the law. He states: "In equity he [John Warwick] would seem to be entitled to his chance in life; it might have been wiser, though, for him to seek it farther afield than South Carolina. It was too near home, even though the laws were with him" (24). Thus, this triangle of desire involving Molly, John, and Rena, like the first, results in another child (Rena Walden), born from a miscegenation relationship, who becomes a "desiring machine" and a desired figure that must mimic and masquerade as a white person.

In order for Rena's mimicry and masquerade to be successful, John (Walden)

Warwick, a creature of his own creation, understands that she must be transformed and transmuted before she can be introduced to and sanctioned by his upper-class white world. Early on, John suggests to his mother that, because she is not as steeped textually, Rena needs preparation before she can ride up the hill that he has climbed so painfully (18).

Rena's movement into the white world is assisted by Frank Fowler. Frank is the son of Peter and Nancy Fowler, who, while slaves, were set up by Molly's lord to provide service to his quadroon concubine. Frank, described as "a dark-brown young man small in stature, but with a well-shaped head an expressive forehead and features indicative of kindness, intelligence, humor and imagination" (25), figures critically in our two subsequent triangles of desire. Because Frank accidentally injured Rena's arm while working with a sharp steel tool and years later saves Rena from a watery death, and because of the sharp disparities in their color and class positions, Rena and Frank have developed a mistress-slave relationship. "When he had made the scar upon her arm, by the same token she had branded him her slave forever; when he had saved her from a watery grave, he had given his life to her" (117). Despite Frank's devotion to and concern for Rena, he will become, like Molly, a permanent outsider stained by America's hegemonic color and class divisions.

Frank, a "faithful friend of the family" mourning Rena's departure, reveals the extent of his devotion: "Ef you ever wanter come home, an can't git back no other way, jes' let me know, an I'll take my mule an' my kyart an' fetch you back, ef it's from de een' er de worl'" (27). Although Frank's diction suggests the depths of his devotion, it also conveys the sharp distinctions associated with a splendid house with servants and a carriage, a distinction that Molly views as the "height of the ridiculous." Molly's desires for Rena, like John's, have nothing to do with Frank and his mule-driven cart. "Her daughter was going to live in a fine house, and marry a rich [white] man, and ride in her carriage. Of course, a negro would drive the carriage, but that was different from riding with one in a cart" (27). The irony of Molly's statement is that she could not visit Rena's home except in the role of a servant. So, here again, Molly has internalized the hegemonic values and beliefs of racist and wealthy whites. The possibility of a black man being wealthy, having a beautiful house, and having white or black servants is ludicrous to Molly. Although Molly (whose diction is not unlike Frank's) does not view herself as white and cannot pass, she identifies with whiteness and believes her "blood and breeding" make her superior to black people of a darker hue and lower economic status. For Molly, only representations of whiteness are associated with wealth, power, and affluence. For Molly, wealth means whiteness, having a carriage means whiteness, and having a "negro" servant means whiteness. It is Frank whom Molly "accosted" to bring Rena's baggage down to the wharf. Thus, for Molly, Frank as a representation of blackness becomes useful only to the extent that he can perform slavelike functions. Molly maintains her prejudiced and elitist attitude, despite the fact that, unlike herself, Frank, a skilled tradesman, can read and write. In Molly's eyes, Frank's dark phenotype and lower-class status make him inferior. Yet, Rena's friendship with Frank provides a narrative subplot because of Frank's romantic desires for Rena.

With this relationship in the background, Rena moves up the hill to embrace John's white world. Again recalling Douglass's *Narrative*, Chesnutt, in the chapter titled "Down the River," paradoxically describes Rena's and John's escape from blackness. For Rena, the voluntary "middle passage" begins. Once they are aboard the ship, the contrasts are distinctive. While Rena Walden secludes herself in the darkness of her stateroom, John Warwick, having left the shade of the cedars, moves with comfort and ease in the luminous sunshine of the white world. Also, while Rena takes her meals behind closed window blinds, John openly dines with the captain and other white passengers. As a South Carolina lawyer, John finds immediate prestige and honor. And, when asked, "Did your people lose any niggers?" (29). John responds in a fashion that reflects the intensity to which he has internalized and mastered his guise. As if at a meeting of the Pale Faces or the Knights of the White Chameleon (two of the numerous racist organizations that flourished in the South), John, positioned on the pedestal of whiteness, "grandly" mimicking a white slave owner, prevaricates, "My father owned a hundred [slaves]" (29). This is quite an ironic prevarication, considering the passionate desire of his father's relatives to have reduced John and Rena ("the little niggers") to chattel status. For John, there are no limits to his whiteness, and he has mastered the means of taking advantage of it. Beyond the curtain of the cedars, John Warwick, the chameleon and trickster figure, enjoys the freedom and the prerogative to pursue boldly his objective of inaugurating Rena into his Faustian pact with whiteness and this white world of Clarence (a pun on "clearance"), South Carolina. This is the soul-selling agreement that has helped to position John Warwick in a "fine old plantation house, built in colonial times, with a stately colonnade, wide veranda, and long windows with Venetian blinds. It was painted white, and stood back several rods from the street, in a charming setting of palmettoes, magnolias, and flowering shrubs" (43). Obviously, passing for white has paid off marvelously for John; his mansion stands in sharp contrast to the "small" house behind the cedars. John's prestigious mansion and enhanced class status (planter) are metaphors for the grand possibilities associated with passing, and they are critical to Rena's seduction.

While in their private room in Wilmington, John informs Rena of his master plan for her future. First, true to the master-slave paradigm of naming and unnaming, Rena Walden will become Rowena Warwick.[33] Second, Rowena will attend a boarding school in Charleston for a year. After her successful transformation, she will assume her place as mistress of John's regal residence. John and Rowena's drive through the town recalls Douglass's experience in New Bedford. Douglass's *Narrative* states:

> I visited the wharves, to take a view of the shipping. Here I found myself surrounded with the strongest proofs of wealth. Lying at the wharves, and riding in the stream, I saw many ships of the finest model, in the best order, and of the largest size. Upon the right and left, I was walled in by granite warehouses of the widest dimensions, stowed to their utmost capacity with the necessaries and comforts of life.[34]

The echoing and contrasting passage in *The House Behind the Cedars* is as follows:

> There for the first time Rena saw great ships, which, her brother told her, sailed across the mighty ocean to distant lands, whose flags he pointed out drooping lazily at the mastheads. . . . The market, a long, low wooden structure, in the middle of the principal street was filled with a mass of people of all shades, from blue-black to Saxon blonde, gabbling and gesticulating over piles of oysters and clams and freshly caught fish of varied hue. (29–30)

Consequently, in both narratives, the ships and the abundance of wealth become metaphors for the passage from slavery to freedom. And these ships ironically comment on and connect John and Rena to their enslaved black ancestors. Also implicit here is the concept that the ships and their white captains and crews enslaved John's and Rena's African ancestors.[35] Yet, the "mass of people of all hues" suggests Chesnutt's analysis of the possibility of racial harmony. This triangle of desire, involving John, Rena, and Molly, culminates with an old and phlegmatic world being left behind and a new and promising white world approaching, one in which Rowena Warwick, propelled by John's desires and her own, will become a proper object of desire.

Once in Clarence, South Carolina, John, our permanent impersonator, introduces Rowena Warwick, "fresh from boarding school," to upper-class white society; this introduction creates a sensuous triangle of desire that has significant socioeconomic possibilities. Yet, despite Rowena's schooling and grooming, she remains, like James Baldwin, a "stranger in the village."

While at a tournament, which recalls Walter Scott and the feudal days of chivalry, Rowena encounters George Tyron. George, as one of the "knights, masquerading in fanciful costumes" (31), becomes attracted to the racially masquerading Rowena. Having completed her year's residence at the boarding school learning "the ways of white folks," Rowena is carefully inaugurated into elite white society. With John's tutelage, Rowena has her debut, or coming-out ceremony, at the feudal tournament. By accidentally dropping a "little square of white lace-trimmed linen," Rowena attracts the attention of George, who gallantly captures the linen with his lance before it touches the ground. Coincidentally, this incident also captures the attention of Frank Fowler, who, while intensely looking for his childhood friend Rena, is hit in the head by a flying fragment from the lance of one of the knight. While Frank binds a "red bandanna" to his bleeding head, George binds Rowena's white linen to his lance. Ironically, George Tyron of North Carolina is John's good friend and his client.

In referring to George's chivalry, John connotes and foreshadows a dual masquerade: "If George were but masked and you were veiled, we should have a romantic situation,—you the mysterious damsel in distress, he the unknown champion. The parallel, my dear, might not be so hard to draw, even as things are" (35–36). John's statement suggests a projection of his incestuous desire onto George, his symbolic brother figure. A parallel of two "foreigners" is drawn, and the lives of Rowena Warwick and George Tyron intersect when George dauntlessly wins

here, witness 'is seductive [handwritten marginal note]

the tournament and selects Rowena as the "Queen of Love and Beauty." Thus, George Tyron, a geographical "stranger" who wins the tournament, and Rowena Warwick, a racial "stranger" new to the white world who becomes queen, will jointly share the limelight at the tournament's culminating masquerade ball. In contrast to Rowena, with her "first fruits" of social success, Frank, with his bandaged head, wistfully gazes after John and Rowena's departing carriage.

Costumed with the assistance of Mrs. Newberry and escorted to the masquerade ball by George, Rowena reveals a double consciousness that resides more in the blackness of her secret past than in the seemingly luminous whiteness of her present: "Her months in school had not eradicated a certain self-consciousness born of her secret. The brain-cells never lose the impression of youth, and Rena's Patesville life was not far enough removed to have lost its distinctness of outline. Of the two, the present was more of a dream, the past was the more vivid realty" (40–41). Obviously, Rowena's education, designed to transform her "mind and manners," has had a marginal effect, and, unlike John, she will find passing for white to be her greatest challenge. It's ludicrous to think that a year in a boarding school would have intellectually transformed Rowena, who never took to books the way John did. Her "education" may have taught her to walk regally and perform socially in a white world, but it has done nothing to develop the sharp wit and reason she will need to pass for an upper-class white woman. Likewise, literacy would have allowed Rowena to contemplate the dream projections of a white world and to engage the discourse of the dominant culture. As a representative of a "Southern belle," Rowena lacks the skills of analysis and synthesis needed to be like John, a master of deception. Her "education" is sharply contrasted with John's admiration for his father's books, the education received from his mulatto teacher, Judge Straight's assistance, and the law degree earned. Because women during this period were not expected to have a good education, it seems that Rowena's ability to pass is strongly linked to John's guidance and direction, and if Rowena attempts to think for herself, disaster is likely to occur.

With the support of Mrs. Newberry (a name that signifies on Rowena's "born-again" status) and with George in the guise of "devoted knight" at her side, Rowena, with her heart "in her mouth" most of the time, successfully manages the masquerade within a masquerade. John's discourse confirms this deception when he informs Rena that "the masquerade is over, let us sleep, and tomorrow take up the serious business of life. Your day has been a glorious success" (42). Yet, as Rowena moves into John's white world, acting and living a lie, and as George's love-struck desire increases, she tearfully reflects on her mother and her past life. Past and present (domesticity and passing) intersect to create Rowena's uncertain future. In a "Mirror, mirror on the wall, who is the fairest of them all" scene, Rowena's uncertainty converges in her self-critical gaze:

> She stood before an oval mirror brought from France by one of Warwick's wife's ancestors, and regarded her image with a cold critical eye. She was as little vain as any of her sex who are endowed with beauty. She tried to place herself, in thus passing upon

her own claims to consideration in the hostile attitude of society toward her hidden disability. There was no mark upon her brow to brand her less pure, less innocent, less desirable, less worthy to be loved, than these proud women of the past who had admired themselves in this old mirror. (51)

Paula Giddings comments that "blacks found postwar America a hall of mirrors, where they saw their reflection first from one angle, then from another."[36] In this regard, Rowena is unable to find a cultural mirror that corresponds to her image of herself. Her Lacanian moment is sharply at odds with that of John, who arrogantly believes that God has sanctioned his whiteness. This illustrates that Rowena experiences a very different kind of Lacanian moment. Because her vision must be connected to domestic possibilities, rather than to vocational or public service, Rowena's commitment inexorably leads back to her mother, Molly. It also illustrates the critical moment where race and gender collide and where the possibilities of passing favor men. Whereas the mirror and the literary texts propel John forward, Rowena is textually unarmed, and, with her hesitant gaze, her future in whiteness becomes unpredictable, if not doubtful.

As Rowena strengthens her pose, her romantic relationship with George intensifies. Yet, both are involved in compromising relationships. While Rowena's commitment to her brother, his achievements, and her nephew force her to conceal the knowledge that she passes for white, George has an on-going friendship with Blanche Leary, a "vivacious blonde" who desires marriage. Despite these compromising situations, Rowena and George passionately engage in conversations and social encounters that lead to George's marriage proposal and Rowena's acceptance. At this point, Rowena becomes disconcerted about telling George the truth of her racial heritage. John's paternalistic advice to Rowena confirms both his chauvinistic attitude and his impression of the white father. First, John condescendingly inquires, "How long have these weighty thoughts been troubling your small head?" (54). Addressing Rowena as if she were his progeny, John gives additional guidance in order to impress upon Rowena the high stakes involved in the fraudulent game of passing: "We are under no moral obligations to inflict upon others the history of our past mistakes, our wayward thoughts, our wayward thoughts, our secret sins, our desperate hopes, or our heart-breaking disappointments. Still less are we bound to bring out from this secret chamber the dusty record of our ancestry" (54). When the nurse brings his son, Albert, who "crowed with pleasure and put up his pretty mouth for a kiss" (56) from Rowena, John uses this tender moment to continue his verbal reprimand by asking accusatory and guilt-provoking questions: "Very well; would you not be willing, for his sake [George's], to keep a secret—your secret and mine, and that of the innocent child in your arms? Would you involve all of us in difficulties merely to secure your own peace of mind? Doesn't such a course seem just the least bit selfish?" (56) John's suturing use of the word "selfish" is an ironic psychological projection. First, being selfish or putting oneself first is inherent to the charade of passing; Rowena would not be with John if she were not motivated by the wish for personal gain. Second, John's ten years of absence, without any communication or offer of financial support to his mother and Rena, represent a significant act of selfishness. Hence, John's challenge to Rowena, combined with John's sounding out of George on the question of ancestry, does give Rowena some temporary peace. More important, John's conversation with George reveals how passing is a process of self-creation. Discussing Rena and himself, John informs George that *"You must take us for ourselves alone—we are new people"* (57; emphasis added). Of course, this reinforces Chesnutt's theory of a raceless future America and the possibility of a black person, such as Douglass, who repeatedly reinvents himself. But, when Rena's repeated dreams of her mother's sickness are confirmed by a letter, she rushes back to blackness (the house behind the cedars).

Through a series of coincidences in Patesville, and despite the gallant attempts by Frank to protect her white identity, George discovers the truth of Rowena's black ancestry. Chesnutt stages this cataclysmic and melodramatic scene like the end of a masquerade ball when guests must remove their masks. While with Doctor Green, George, through "colored glass bottles in the window" of a drug store, views a young woman remarkably similar to his Rowena. Dismissing this possibility because Doctor Green has told him the woman is black, George is horrified when he comes face to face with Rena (Rowena). The effect of George's critical gaze is emotionally devastating:

> When Rena's eyes fell upon the young man in the buggy, she saw a face as pale as death, with staring eyes, in which love which once had reigned there, had now given place to astonishment and horror. She stood a moment as if turned to stone. One appealing glance she gave,—a look that might have softened adamant. When she saw that it brought no answering sign of love or sorrow or regret, the color faded from her cheek, the light from her eye, and she fell fainting to the ground. (94)

Later, in the solitude of his hotel room, George, with his emotions swinging like a pendulum, reveals that this shocking discovery "transformed [Rowena] into a hideous black hag. With agonized eyes he watched her beautiful tresses become mere wisps of coarse wool, wrapped round with dingy cotton strings; he saw her eyes grow bloodshot, her ivory teeth turn to unwholesome fangs" (98). Rowena's crossover dreams become a nightmare in the psyche of George Tyron. Like the scene that contains the description of the coin with the hole, this scene suggests James Weldon Johnson's protagonist viewing himself transformed into a hideous and black monstrosity when he reveals his African ancestry to his white fiancée. This nightmare functions as a device to explicate the primitive, irrational aspect of racial prejudice. The bottom of this triangle falls out, bringing anxiety to John Warwick and hope to Frank Fowler. Yet, George's reaction does not surprise us when we recall his earlier validating response of "With all my heart sir," to Doctor Green's bombastic racist discourse. With its echoes of Thomas Jefferson's racial discourse, Doctor Green had stated:

They may exalt our slaves over us temporarily, but they have not broken our spirit, and cannot take away our superiority of blood and breeding. In time we shall regain control. The Negro is an inferior creature; God has marked him with the badge of servitude, and has adjusted his intellect to a servile condition. We will not long submit to his domination. I give you a toast, sir: The Anglo-Saxon race: may it remain forever, as now, the head and front of creation, never yielding its rights, and ready to die, if need be, in defense of its liberties. (91–92)

Like other narratives of passing, Doctor Green's manicured racism draws on the myth of Ham to promote and validate his theory of white supremacy.

With George's knowledge of Rowena's blackness, John wonders whether his life of deception will be revealed and whether his legal position and social standing will disintegrate. Frank, however, can renew his desires for Rena now that she has been found out and it is unlikely she will reenter the white world. George becomes a co-conspirator when he writes a letter to John and decides not to reveal that Rowena and John are passing for white. John assuages his conscience and shows his gratitude for Frank's assistance and co-conspiracy by buying him a new mule, harness, and cart. Here John is giving away not flawed currency but significant means of production that will keep Frank Fowler in the fields. John's payoff reaffirms the significant intraracial and class distinctions between the two men. This triangle of desire involving John Walden (Warwick), Rena (Rowena) Warwick, and George Tyron, with Frank Fowler constantly in the background, leads to the text's most tragic triangle of desire.

The final triangle of desire involves Rena (Rowena), George Tyron, and Jeff Wain; again, Frank Fowler, like a sturdy cedar tree, stands in the background. Rejecting John's ardent pleas to go "far away from the South and the Southern people, and start life over again" (122) and to give passing another try, Rena vehemently vows never to leave her mother and considers what her future will be in a black community. This triangle highlights the legacy of white supremacy with regard to the intraracial conflict among some black people and the significance of gender and the traumatic effects in the passing phenomenon.

Before John fades into the background, his last attempt at seduction sheds light on the significance of gender. In an effort to assuage Rena's failed attempt at passing, John causes Rena to weep "hysterically" when he urges her to pass again. In a real sense, passing for white means to live in a perpetual state of hysteria.[37] Rena's hysteria represents a divided self—a desire to be what she is not. Connecting black people to Jewish people with regard to passing, Sander Gilman maintains that this hysterical effect is common to some Jewish individuals. Occurring twice as often in Jewish males, this anxiety results from the "struggle for life in the city which causes the madness of the male Jew." The Jew, Gilman continues, "can pass, can become white, perhaps even is white."[38] Individuals of both groups engage in equivocation and transform themselves in order to achieve socioeconomic possibilities. Yet, despite the ideological equivalences, Fanon reminds us that there is a significant difference in the often savage response to Jewish people's and black people's desire for socioeconomic agency. Fanon states:

No anti-Semite, for example would ever conceive of the idea of castrating the Jew. He is killed or sterilized. But the Negro is castrated. The penis, the symbol of manhood, is annihilated, which is to say that it is denied. The difference between the two attitudes is apparent. The Jew is attacked in his religious identity, in his history, in his race, in his relations with his ancestors and with his posterity; when one sterilizes the Jew, one cuts off the source; every time that a Jew is persecuted, it is the whole race that is persecuted in his person. But it is in his corporeality that the Negro is attacked. It is as a concrete personality that he is lynched. It is as an actual being that he is a threat.[39]

John, with his invisible blackness, believes he has moved beyond the realm of violence when he suggests continuing the masquerade and sending Rena north to a school to obtain a "liberal education" with the possibility of marrying someone better than George. John's discourse suggests an attempt to correct the mistake of having failed to provide Rena with a sound education. Rena represents a failed Galatea whom John is vainly trying to salvage. But Rena firmly responds, "I shall never marry any man, and I'll not leave mother again. God is against it; I'll stay with my own people" (121). This complex response connecting marriage and passing reveals the traumatic effect of George's rejecting gaze and Rena's difficulty in rejecting her mother and her black ancestry. Unlike John's, Rena's discourse recalls Iola Leroy, the female protagonist in Francis Harper's *Shadows Uplifted*, who rejects passing and suggests a nationalistic perspective on racial separation, the desire to advance the causes of black people. Ironically, John's response, "God has nothing to do with it, God is too often a convenient stalking-horse for human selfishness" (121), is antithetical to his earlier justification for passing, that God "must have meant him to be white." John becomes the ultimate opportunist, changing his guise (language) to fit the situation. Despite John's tenacity, sagacity, and duplicity, the possibility of John's being found out and subjected to the rage of whites is very real.

As Valerie Smith points out, male slave narratives like Douglass's portray black men who embody not only "the journey from slavery to freedom, but also the journey from slavery to manhood." Smith notes, "By mythologizing rugged individuality, physical strength and geographical mobility, the narratives of men enshrine cultural definitions of masculinity."[40] Slave narratives, like passing narratives, confirm the gender disparities. Rena confirms this perspective when she states, "A man may make a new place for himself—a woman is born and bound to hers" (121). Again, Chesnutt exposes the gender disparities where men have a wide vision embracing significant socioeconomic opportunities and women's social conditioning chains them to domesticity. Thus, John, the racial magician whose latest performance (Rena's disappearance into whiteness) has failed, eventually disappears for good.

With Rena rejecting the possibility of trying to pass again, Jeff Wain represents the possibility of Rena's engaging in an "uplift the black race" mission as a school-teacher. As George struggles with his feelings of fading passion and of having been deceived, Jeff Wain enters our racial drama. Rena's failed attempt at passing transforms her from a person who despises darker people because they are not as white as she is and not as economically privileged into a person who has sympathy for others' faults and who can appreciate their good qualities.

In numerous ways, Jeff Wain refigures John Warwick. His color, physical features, and class status, along with his offering Rena a teaching position, are all looked upon very favorably by Molly Walden. Although Jeff is described as a mulatto who is unable to pass, his description encompasses the three critical aspects (color, hair texture, and language) that often construct racial hierarchies within the black community: "His complexion was of a light brown—not quite so fair as Mis' Molly would have preferred; but any deficiency in this regard, or in the matter of the stranger's features, which, while not unpleasing, leaned toward the broad mulatto type, was more than compensated in her eyes by very straight black hair, and as soon appeared, a great facility of complimentary speech" (133). Although Molly is seduced by these physical features, Rena's interests now reside only in giving service to the black community. Equally disturbing is Jeff's hegemonic discourse juxtaposing Rena's physical appearance to the learning process. Jeff states, "a lady er her color kin keep a lot er little niggers straighter 'n a darker lady could." "Dem niggers won't have no other teacher after dey've once laid eyes on you: I'll guarantee dat" (134–135). Jeff's use of the racist signifier "nigger," along with his preference-by-pigment philosophy, profoundly constructs the intraracial conflict among some black people that supports notions of white supremacy. As Aldon Lynn Nielsen maintains, "Racist terms, summarized by the epithet 'nigger,' survive as frozen metaphors within American speech; thus whites who have never had any contact with blacks in their lives may still exhibit an essentially racist mode of thought, one which privileges them while demoting an invisible other to a secondary status."[41] When black people employ racist discourse and use this pejorative signifier the effect is similar, but, unlike with white people, the contact is often frequent. Consequently, this discourse suggests a desire to construct a separate caste position among those who view themselves as neither black nor white. These hegemonic aspects of identity formation are mirrored in the "Blue Vein Society" or "quadroon ball"-like[42] social affair that honors Jeff Wain. Here the tragic triangle of desire is constructed.

The dual purpose of this "quadroon ball" is to pay honor to Jeff Wain and to bid farewell to Rena, who decides to teach at a black school where Wain is chairman of the school committee. In accord with Molly's preference-by-pigmentation philosophy, the social affair is restricted to light-skinned individuals. "Mis' Molly's guests were mostly of the bright class, most of them more than half white, and few of them less. In Mis' Molly's small circle, straight hair was the only palliative of a dark complexion" (141).

Echoing the days of slavery, the only black person in the room, Uncle Needham, who "seldom played for colored gatherings," extracts melodies from his fiddle. Excluded from the party but allowed to sit on the "back porch and look at the dancing and share in the supper," Frank gazes at Rena through a window. Additionally, Frank's gaze discerns Jeff as a "grinning hypocrite masquerading" who will bear watching. Coincidentally, when Rena finally agrees to dance with Jeff, George Tyron, with "head and heart" in turmoil, passes by the house behind the cedars and also gazes through an open window. Having rationalized his racist philosophy, George has come with the desire to "make her [Rowena] white." But, hearing the same tune that opened the masquerade ball in South Carolina and seeing Rowena (Rena) in the arms of a "grinning mulatto, whose face was offensively familiar to Tyron," George find his rage and revulsion returning. Chesnutt positions all the prominent male figures (except John) with their gazes on Rena. The windows, like the mirrors, place further emphasis on the divided and fractured nature of these individuals and on the fact that these men seek to become whole by embracing Rena. Consequently, this scopophilic desire characterizes men as active individuals who look; women are passive, desired objects to be looked at.

Rena as a representation of whiteness, an object of desire, and the most divided individual, is constantly under the dissecting male gaze (John's, George's, and Jeff's) as they attempt to construct her identity. As John's initially incestuous gaze is transformed into a desire to obtain a mistress for his home and caretaker of his son, George, like Rena's father, surrenders ideas of marriage and instead desires Rowena as his mistress. Meanwhile, Rena's "clear eye, when once set to take Wain's measure, soon fathomed his shallow, selfish soul, and detected, or at least divined, behind his mask of good nature a lurking brutality which filled her with vague distrust" (165). All three individuals construct masklike faces in their attempts to achieve agency. John masquerades as a white man whose father lost a "hundred slaves," George, romantically involved with Blanche Leary, masks his immoral intentions toward Rowena, and Jeff Wain, with equally immoral intentions, masquerades as a single man with wealth and a large plantation. With the last name "Wain," Chesnutt signifies on the diminishing position of Rena's psychological state, as well as foreshadowing Frank and his wagon. Like a true knight, Frank stands alone with a gaze that is loving and protective. By constructing these triangles of desire, Chesnutt relates that Rena's psychological breakdown occurs not because of her immorality but because she is morally superior to those for whom purity of blood becomes entangled with hegemonic and racist notions of human worth. Additionally, within these triangles of desire, Chesnutt constructs mirror doubles. George Tyron is John Warwick's double, and Blanche Leary is Rowena Warwick's counterpart. On a literary level, these two doubles provide balance to the narrative, but, more important, they advance Lacan's theory of the mirror stage. Despite the effect of Rowena's exposure, John's mirror construction (status) remains stable in the white world, whereas Rowena's construction (status) becomes destabilized by her ties to domesticity and the dissecting male gaze. This dissecting gaze continuously forces Rowena back upon the gender roles of domesticity.

Our final triangle of desire reaches a crescendo when both Jeff and George, with dishonorable and questionable motives, attempt to seduce (rape) Rena. With one of her students, Plato, bribed with half a dollar by George to abandon her, Rena, secluded in the forest, finds George advancing upon her, "flushed with anticipation," and also Jeff, with "evil passions which would stop at nothing" (181). In contrast to these objectifying gazes, Rena's gaze is one filled with terror. While Jeff's desire can be viewed as pure lust, George, as an incestuous agent of John Warwick, refigures John's white father's seduction of Molly Walden. This is borne out when we consider that Blanche Leary (her name suggests that George should have been leery of those who appear to be white) is waiting for George's marriage proposal. Rena's submission to George would echo and refigure Molly's miscegenation and illicit union. Hence, George's movement from romance to rape configures an incestuous and miscegenation triangle of desire. Although Rena escapes, hysteria overwhelms her, and it is Frank Fowler with his mule, in his honorable, knightly role, who later discovers her, distraught and disoriented. The triangles of desire round out, and the circle is complete. Rena's journey to the white world terminates where it began, in the house behind the cedars. A piece of crepe marks this final place of refuge, the place of Rena (Rowena) Walden's death and of her symbolic return to the womb. Rena's death echoes back to the man varnishing a coffin at Liberty Point. Too often, for black people, freedom is found at death's door. Chesnutt's characterization of Rena's dramatic escape and ensuing death suggests the rebellious lyrics of enslaved Africans: "And before I be a slave [or a concubine to a white man or black man] I'll be buried in my grave / And go home to my God and be free." As Heather Hathaway points out, "miscegenation creates, yet destroys, the family."[43] Mixed blood generates a simultaneous confirmation and denial of genealogy, yet the social and exogamy taboo against acknowledging this tie forbids that same relationship.

The death of Rena Walden, although stereotypical within the self-destructing tragic mulatto paradigm, suggests that Charles W. Chesnutt's vision and theory of racial amalgamation are beyond the realm of America's persistent veil. *The House Behind the Cedars* can be considered a protest novel in which the author's sympathies reside with those who pass because of racial restrictions. Directly addressing the reader, Chesnutt argues against the stigma that characterizes black blood as evil:

> Had they [Rena and John] possessed the sneaking, cringing, treacherous character traditionally ascribed to people of mixed blood—the character which the blessed institutions of a free slaveholding republic had been well adapted to foster among them; had they been selfish enough to sacrifice to their ambition the mother who gave them birth, society would have been pleased or hum-bugged and the voyage of their life might have one of unbroken smoothness. (86–87)

Although Chesnutt's intrusive statement appears somewhat early in the text, we discern that he is consistently sympathetic to those black individuals who opt for going over to the other side.

Yet, as Rena passes away, she murmurs to Frank, "my good friend—my best friend—you loved me best of them all" (195). This death scene ironically confirms Chesnutt's theory of racial amalgamation. The alternative, having Rena survive and unite with the dark-skinned Frank Fowler, would be antithetical to the creation of a new and universal people who will look substantially alike. As Sally Ann

H. Ferguson maintains, Frank Fowler's name denotes a sexual pun that suggests the impossibility of Rena and Frank's union. Ferguson comments: "While Frank's first name characterizes him as a candid and loyal friend to light-skinned Rena Walden, beleaguered protagonist in the tale, the sound of his surname implies that Frank would somehow 'foul her.'"[44] Despite Chesnutt's portrayal that character, not color, is critical, the dark-skinned Frank represents and confirms Fanon's theory of the terrifying phallus, an obstacle to those who can assimilate into American society. Ironically, Chesnutt opposed black intraracial breeding and advocated miscegenation, mimicry, and masquerade, despite the often tragic possibilities. Equally important, Chesnutt illustrates, through the paradoxical paradigm of passing, that the insanity and inhumanity of the pervasive doctrine of white supremacy negatively affects both black people and white people, regardless of their class positions.

In a real and tragic sense, all of Molly Walden's children and her grandchild have "passed away," leaving her isolated and secluded behind the curtain of cedar trees with only memories of passing desires. The story is tragic in the sense that, more often than not, American society has failed to embrace its black descendants with fairness and reciprocity. As Patricia J. Williams deftly argues: "Blacks are the objects of a constitutional omission that has been incorporated into a theory of neutrality. It is thus that omission is really a form of expression, as ridiculous as that sounds: racial omission is a literal part of original intent; it is the fixed, reiterated prophecy of the Founding Fathers."[45] Yet, the novel is triumphal in that Rena Walden and Frank Fowler represent the real heroes in this narrative. Rena is heroic for her willingness to be truthful and for her devotion to her mother. Also, Rena heroically displays her commitment to serve the black community, and she ultimately develops a consciousness free of color hegemony. Hard-working and altruistic, Frank loves Rena for her kindness and sincerity and not for her illusionary representation of whiteness. Hence, with Rena's (Rowena's) death, *The House Behind the Cedars* comes full circle (all triangles in the circle cascade), with the ruins of passing representing the failed American future of racial amalgamation. As, indeed, Rena's trip home in Frank's cart suggests, John Warwick's continued passing for white is perhaps no less tragic than Rena's death; he has bucked the Jim Crow system. John's son Albert, unlike the "fly in the buttermilk," will know only a heritage of whiteness and believe in the notion of ethnic purity. Concerning ethnic purity, Chesnutt states:

> Frankly I take no stock in this doctrine. It seems to be a modern invention of the white people, to perpetuate the color line. It is they who preach it, and it is their racial integrity which they wish to preserve—they have never been unduly careful of the purity of the black race. . . . Are we to help the people to build up walls between themselves and us, to fence in a gloomy backyard for our descendents to play in?[46]

The tragic conclusion of *The House Behind the Cedars,* Charles Waddell Chesnutt's pithy moral treatise on black individuals who pass for white, suggests that black people must gloomily accept the reality that for too many whites, democracy and racial oppression are not conflicting ideals; passing or going over to the other side tragically represents the ultimate performance for those who seek to enhance their economic and social possibilities in America's color-conscious racial wasteland. Ironically, cedar is a sturdy wood that resists to decomposition and decay, yet, in Molly's house, secluded among the cedars, the passing phenomenon has produced deception and death. Passing and masquerading, as a flight or an escape to the white world, do not work; the costs are extremely high and virulent.

Charles Waddell Chesnutt justifies a theory of amalgamation, but the novel *The House Behind the Cedars* presents the limits of that possibility. The narrative presents those limits because Chesnutt's knowledge of Mark Twain and Frederick Douglass has confirmed his own sense of limitation. In this light, *The House Behind the Cedars* becomes a story of "passing" that turns on the inevitable exposure or breakdown that racial recognitions bring.

3

THE IMPROVISATIONAL AND FAUSTIAN PERFORMANCE IN JAMES WELDON JOHNSON'S *THE AUTOBIOGRAPHY OF AN EX-COLOURED MAN*

The Negro's only salvation from complete despair lies in his belief, the old belief
of his forefathers, that these things are not directed against him personally,
but against his race, his pigmentation. His mother, aunt or teacher long ago
carefully prepared him, explaining that he as an individual can live in dignity,
even though he as a Negro cannot.
— JOHN HOWARD GRIFFIN, *Black Like Me*

While in France, a young white man with a supercilious tone that suggests that he expects an "authoritative denial" queries the Ex-Coloured Man: "Did they really burn a man alive in the United States?"[1] Our nameless protagonist and narrator does not recall what he "stammered out" as a response and reveals he would have been relieved if he could have responded: "Well, only one" (100). The stunning question and the cowed response reveal that James Weldon Johnson's *The Autobiography of an Ex-Coloured Man* (1912) is constantly toying with the ambiguity and the alternatives of both the often tragic and the comic nature of life. Living and passing as an American white man in Europe, the Ex-Coloured Man is staggered by the question, but his evasive response is so absurd that it is almost comical.

Johnson's paradoxical juxtaposition of tragedy and comedy raises critical concerns of race/nation and racism/nationalism. Although psychologically the Ex-Coloured Man views himself as white, the French man views him as a(n) (black?) American, who regardless of race should have knowledge of whether black people are being lynched. This racial and national tension highlights the double consciousness of the protagonist. More specifically, when our protagonist successfully passes, he is characterized as comic. To the extent that he accepts racial exposure, there are tragic implications. While America (often meaning white America) ideologically extends democracy to all its citizens, too often America's extreme nationalism, tied to the notion of white supremacy, during the late 1800s and early 1900s caused black people to experience socioeconomic exclusion and violence. The Ex-Coloured Man's craven response to the savage racial violence is to escape and to assume a white identity. Accordingly, the act of passing for white negotiates these two binaries. Using the tragic/comic literary nexus,[2] Johnson self-consciously explores the racial, cultural, regional (mainly urban), and (inter)national places where black and white people intersect. Thus, in *The Autobiography of an Ex-Coloured Man,* passing for white represents the comic aspects of the charade, whereas both the denial of and exposure of his blackness represent tragic aspects. This novel is also unique is terms of its point of view: a first-person narrative, yet in terms of genre it is not autobiography.[3]

Thematically, black music—ragtime piano—provides the intersection between the tragic and the comic realities for both black people and whites in America. Symbolically, Johnson uses ragtime music to represent or highlight the historical and literary tropes of miscegenation, mimicry, and masquerading. Throughout *The Autobiography of an Ex-Coloured Man*, Johnson uses ragtime music as a hybrid form of rhythm in which the accompaniment is strict two-four time and the melody, with improvised embellishments, is in steady syncopation to signify on the phenomenon of black individuals assuming a white identity. When we consider that ragtime is a sophisticated mix of black and European musical forms with complex multiple rhythms, Johnson's connection of musical amalgamation and the critical elements of miscegenation, mimicry, and masquerading to popular culture become quite explicit. Discussing the history of ragtime piano, Rudi Blesh and Harriet Janis point out:

> Piano ragtime was developed by the Negro from folk melodies and from the syncopations of the plantation banjos. As it grew, it carried its basic principle of displaced accents played against a regular meter to a very high degree of collaboration. . . . The treatment of folk music, both white and Negro, according to African rhythmic principles (for in the African drum corps one or more drums play in off-beat rhythms over the regular meter of another drum) produced a completely new sort of music. It also produced a music truly American.[4]

In essence, Johnson illustrates that ragtime music as a miscegenation (American) collaboration[5] can mimic and masquerade as an African American or as a European cultural production. Unlike the other authors considered here, Johnson places emphasis on ragtime music to illustrate that black cultural productions can be lost in the charade of passing.

In sharp contrast to Chesnutt's problematic theory of amalgamation, according to which black people would, step by step, disappear into whiteness, Johnson suggests that black people amalgamate in a manner that would allow them to maintain their distinct racial and cultural qualities. Like Du Bois, Johnson recognizes the distinctive cultural contributions black people make to American society. In his autobiography *Along This Way* (1933), Johnson trenchantly argues in favor of a theory of amalgamation in which black people would retain their uniqueness:

> if I could have my wish, the Negro would retain his racial identity, with unhampered freedom to develop his own qualities—the best of those qualities American civilization is much in need of as a complement to its other qualities—and finally stand upon a plane with other American citizens. . . . *But what I may wish and what others may not wish can have no effect on the elemental forces at work; and it appears to me that the results of those forces will in time, be the blending of the Negro into the American race of the future.*[6] (emphasis added)

This blending of "elemental forces" suggests both miscegenation and racial masquerading. These proclivities, as Johnson appropriately implies, are difficult to restrict by either separate and unequal legal or illegal sanctions. Despite these "blendings," in Johnson's future America, black people would not disappear; rather they would "add a tint to America's complexion and put a perceptible permanent wave in America's hair" (412). Johnson's observation rightly insinuates that, despite America's racial and economic violence, many African Americans who can pass do not desire to disappear into whiteness, yet desire to leave their perceptible and permanent mark on America culture.

Also in *Along This Way*, Johnson reveals three astonishing experiences, which inform our discussion of *The Autobiography of an Ex-Coloured Man* (1912), about a black man who in a Faustian deal sells his "birthright" and passes for white. Rejecting the title *The Chameleon*,[7] suggested by his brother, John Rosamond Johnson, Johnson explores the psychological, social, and cultural dynamics of a black man struggling with his black and white identity. As the literary scholar Arthur P. Davis points out, the genre of the lynching-passing fiction has always held a dual fascination for black and white Americans:

> Passing-for-white has always intrigued the American reader, black and white. The latter group has often been terrified as well as fascinated by the possibilities of Negro blood cropping up in their families or to put it more precisely, the knowledge of the presence of black blood (for example, Sinclair Lewis's *Kingsblood Royal,* and Robert Penn Warren's *Band of Angels)*. The Negro, on the other hand, has liked the theme, primarily because it shows the absurdity of putting such great importance on race in America when actually one cannot tell a Negro from a white.[8]

These three particular experiences add dramatic force to Davis's insightful argument and to the critical importance of Johnson's novel both as an ironic statement of black male subjectivity and as an indictment of America's race relations.

In the first incident in *Along This Way*, Johnson discusses his friend William Pickens, an exceptional Yale student who is black yet "frequently and involuntarily passes for white." In the deepest parts of the South, while conducting business on the phone, Pickens never fails to receive a "Yes, sir" (114). The tonality of the voice is the vehicle for his masquerading as white. It must have been thrilling as well as profitable for Pickens to perfect the verbal performance of masquerading as a white man. At the same time, black individuals who appear and sound "white" profit financially in a racist society where whiteness is revered. Here, body and speech intertwine to expedite the charade of signifying on whiteness.

The second of Johnson's experiences to inform a great deal of *The Autobiography of an Ex-Coloured Man* relates to the experiences of Johnson's childhood friend and colleague Judson Douglass Wetmore. In *Along This Way,* Johnson surreptitiously refers to Wetmore as D—Eugene Levy, an extremely light-skinned individual who crosses the color line and passes for white.[9] Johnson and Wetmore were both about eight years old when they met; they were "unlike each other in more ways than one" (33). Whereas Johnson's brown skin and features identified him as black, Wetmore's light skin and features made him appear to be white. Johnson describes Wetmore as "extremely good looking, having, in fact, a sort of Byronic beauty. . . . Neither in color, features, nor hair could one detect that he had a single drop of Negro blood" (76). Due to family conflict (mainly with his father), Wetmore left home; like Johnson, he would become a lawyer. Johnson notes that, when he visited Wetmore's law office, all of Wetmore's clients were white. Later, Johnson's friend married a Jewish woman, who knew of his blackness, yet whose parents were unaware of his black ancestry. This long-term and close relationship suggests that Wetmore's experiences provided a wealth of information for Johnson's novel.

The third experience is Johnson's traumatic near-lynching experience in Jacksonville, Florida, at the hands of a crazed mob of gun-toting white males with their bloodhounds. When a light-skinned black woman came to his office to seek his advice on an article she was writing, Johnson suggested that they go to the nearby Riverside Park. On the train to the park, a white conductor called local white residents to inform them that a black man had gotten off the train with a "white" woman. In describing this incident, Johnson juxtaposes a state of pastoral peace with one of terror, which suggests the brutal reality of Richard Wright's poem "Between the World and Me."[10] Johnson recalls his pleasant meeting with the woman, shattered when "They surge round me. They seize me. They tear my clothes and bruise my body. . . . As the rushing crowd comes yelling and cursing, I feel that death is bearing in upon me. Not death of the empty sockets, but death with the blazing eyes of a frenzied brute" (167). The societal transgression: Johnson, a black man, being in the company of a white woman in a rather secluded park, a serious violation of Southern etiquette. Johnson's lack of trepidation delivers him from the neck-breaking coils of the lynching-rope and castration and from being left dangling like rotten fruit from a tree. All charges are dismissed when Johnson informs the legal authorities that the black woman is not white. Afterward, through a powerfully perceptive and brazen statement, the woman throws a further ironic twist to this tale. Before escorting this white-looking black woman back to the Boyland Home for Colored Girls, Johnson states: "She laid on the

Major's (Major B—) head the sins of his fathers and his father's fathers. She charged him that they were the ones responsible for what had happened" (169). Being with a black woman who was mistaken for being a white woman almost cost James Weldon Johnson his life.

This last incident is important in a number of ways. First, the woman's comments present a synthesis between the past and the present that connects the rape of black women to the lynching-burning of black men. Both are systematic rituals of sexual and racial violence. As Katrin Schwenk contends, the complexities of lynching and rape are encoded in the general critical discourse of African American literature.[11] Inherent in these issues are the myths of the black male as rapist and the black woman as sexual seducer in contrast to the virtuous white woman and the white male as protector. In dialogic terms, blackness becomes defined as a pejorative concept, while whiteness defines a superior concept. Lynching and rape become critical to a cultural narrative that ensures racial, gender, and class hegemony.[12]

Second, the near-lynching confirms Davis's point that there is creative slippage between the seemingly discrete racial categories of black and white. Too often in America, racial identity based on ocular analysis is assumed and not questioned. This slippage strongly confirms that the mythic notion of race is not a biological but a social construction based largely on ocular evidence. Furthermore, the incident suggests the place where miscegenation, mimicry, and masquerading intersect. As a product of miscegenation, the black woman could have equivocated and mimicked and masqueraded as white in order to save herself from the armed and bloodthirsty white lynch mob.

Last, the traumatic incident, with its strong smell of death, has long-term psychological repercussions. Would this near-white woman be afraid to associate with or marry a dark-skinned man? Would Johnson be fearful of accompanying or marrying a light-skinned black woman? In essence, would this interracial conflict generate additional intraracial conflict? For a black man living in the South, any association with a white woman could spell danger and even death. Johnson reveals the terrifying effect of his experience: "I would wake often in the night-time, after living through again those frightful seconds, exhausted by the nightmare of a struggle with a band of murderous, bloodthirsty men in khaki, with loaded rifles and fixed bayonets. *It was not until twenty years after, through work I was engaged in, that I was able to liberate myself completely from this horror complex*" (170; emphasis added). As for the white-looking black woman safeguarded by the perception of the white throng as a white woman, we can only surmise what long-term traumatic psychological effect the near-lynching produced in her.

It should be noted that Johnson, like his friend Walter White,[13] who wrote about passing in his novel *Flight* (1920), investigated America's bloody history of lynchings and race riots. White's investigations of lynching resulted in his exhaustive study, *Rope and Faggot* (1929). Both men, while working for the NAACP, took considerable risks to bring attention to the savage and sadistic crime of lynching and to the too often deadly racial conflicts between black people and white people.

Johnson's lynching poem, called "Brothers," explores the physical and psychological place where lynching and the often unfounded accusation of rape[14] intersect. Sardonic and sarcastic in tone, the poem concludes: "Brothers in spirit, brothers indeed are we?"[15] In another poem, "White Witch," Johnson warns his black brothers about miscegenation: "Look not upon her beauty bright / For in her glance there is a snare, / And in her smile there is a blight."[16] *The Autobiography of an Ex-Coloured Man*, like Mark Twain's *The Tragedy of Pudd'nhead Wilson*, explores this sexual and racial conflict and captures the almost debilitating trepidation associated with being a black man in Jim Crow America.

Like Charles W. Chesnutt, who lived through the time of the Black Codes, James Weldon Johnson, who lived during the Race Riots of 1919 and named that time the "Red Summer," was a man of diverse talent and interests. Born in Jacksonville, Florida, on June 17, 1871, Johnson was raised in a privileged and cultivated family.[17] Johnson was so privileged that he was nursed by a white nanny. Like Chesnutt, Johnson, during the fall of 1896, began reading law in his spare time and passed the bar examination some twenty months later. Both men were aware of the critical legacy of the *Dred Scott v. Sandford* decision, which defined all black persons in a similar manner: inferior, bound by no rights a white man need respect, and objects for inhuman treatment. In fact, in 1900, the year that *The House Behind the Cedars* was published, 106 black people were reported lynched; in 1912, the year Johnson's novel was published, there were 61 reported lynchings.[18] Black people's struggle against and reaction to racial violence and injustice are an enduring motif in African American literature.

Whereas Douglass's *Narrative* and *The Autobiography* represent "extralegal records" because the narrators are always outside the realm of American justice, Du Bois's *The Souls of Black Folk* represents the constant modulation of Johnson's narrator between the black world and the white. Yet, there are both black and white intraracial dynamics represented. For example, as Sterling A. Brown points out, Johnson novel is important because it is "the first to deal with the Negro life on several levels, from the folk to the sophisticated."[19]

It is important to add the influence of Booker T. Washington and his autobiography *Up from Slavery*. Johnson knew and was friendly with Washington, but in *Along This Way*, he suggests that his intellectual position came closer to Du Bois's position. Johnson's references to Washington are directly didactic and subtly critical; he literally rewrites the genres of slave narratives and autobiography.[20] Johnson illustrates that passing for white and masquerading represent a journey up from the legacy of slavery. Despite the strong similarities between *The Autobiography of an Ex-Coloured Man* and *Along This Way*, Johnson, unlike Chesnutt, never passed for white,[21] but he understood the dynamics and the numerous reasons why some light-skinned black people seeking greater socioeconomic agency in a white supremacist culture would take this step.

In Johnson's *The Autobiography of an Ex-Coloured Man*, our protagonist and narrator, after witnessing the fiendish Southern lynch-burning of his "dark double," decides to go North, change his name, disguise himself (grow a mustache), and permanently assume a white identity. Implicit in this decision is the narrator's permanent abandonment of black culture, or, more specifically, ragtime music. Divulging his thoughts, he describes the necessity of passing and masquerading and rationalizes being a traitor to his race:

> *I argued that to forsake one's race to better one's condition was no less worthy an action than to forsake one's country for the same purpose.* I finally made up my mind that I would neither disclaim the black race nor claim the white race; but that I would change my name, raise a mustache, and let the world take me for what it would; that it was not necessary for me to go about with a label of inferiority pasted across my forehead. (139; emphasis added)

Here, Johnson, adding race and country and racism and nationalism to the protagonist's later comment connecting "money" to passing for white, suggests that to be an American is to be self-centered and materialistic and that race is a factor that can preclude economic agency. Further, as our protagonist constantly modulates (mimics) between the black world and the white world on numerous occasions before this revelation and with a growing disdain for black people and identifying with whites, his attitude—"let the world take me for what it would"—appears disingenuous. Throughout this mimicking, his musical ability has sustained him economically. And his growing disdain for black people becomes mirrored in his growing disdain for his black musical heritage. Furthermore, the growing of a mustache suggests the criminality that is intrinsic to his acts of deception and his racial masquerading. The deceptive and disguising mustache suggests a change in the white father figures—(one real, the other symbolic)—as phallic symbols of both wealth and power, which places us at the site of miscegenation.

Miscegenation, mimicry, and masquerade become centered on the economic, psychological, and physical violence of systemic white supremacy. Published anonymously,[22] this text, with its first-person point of view, operates within the sizable shadow of the slave narratives. Accordingly, in at least two regards, *The Autobiography* signifies and represents, in Henry Louis Gates's term, a "talking text."[23] Johnson's novel, representing a black man's flight from economic bondage, speaks to the black slave's physical flight from bondage to freedom. As the historian James Olney argues, there are certain aspects of a slave narrative that make it an "authentic" text. Among the many aspects that Olney gives is this: one or more prefaces or introductions written by a white abolitionist friend of the narrator or by a white amanuensis/editor/author who is actually responsible for the text, in the course of which preface the reader is told that the narrative is a "plain unvarnished tale" and that naught "has been set down in malice, nothing exaggerated, nothing drawn from the imagination." Indeed, the narrative, it is claimed, understates the wretched horrors of slavery; it usually encompasses a sketchy account of parentage, often involving a white father; descriptions of a cruel master, mistress, or overseer; descriptions of successful attempt(s) to escape; and reflections on slavery.[24]

By making an analogy between the slave experience and the experience of those who pass for white, Johnson aptly signifies on many of those aspects that Olney describes as characteristic of the slave narrative. In fact, Johnson's depiction of the paradigm of passing goes beyond those established by the earlier writers of the literature of passing. For example, compared to Charles W. Chesnutt's novel *The House Behind the Cedars*, *The Autobiography of an Ex-Coloured Man* places more emphasis on the importance of the legacy of black people's enslavement (slave culture), the minstrel tradition, the protagonist's geographical mobility (national and international) in this racial charade, and the cultural costs when black people pass for white. As Eric J. Sundquist maintains, Johnson's fictive autobiography

> is about "passing" in several other senses as well—the passing of slave culture, the manifold geographical passages that have defined African-American life from its beginnings, and the passing of vernacular culture into the transfigured, assimilated idioms as so-called high culture. All these connotations of passing are melded together between the smug, calculating narrator and Johnson himself, who, as his later essay "The Dilemma of the Negro Author" (1928) would make clear, was acutely aware that the black writer was constrained in his subject matter by both sides of the color line: he could not choose white subjects; he must not embarrass African Americans by choosing certain delicate black subjects; and he was hard pressed to avoid capitulation to the popular stereotypes of minstrelsy.[25]

The preface to *The Autobiography* adheres to the first criterion set forth by Olney, whereas the body of the text addresses the remaining issues set forth by Olney and Sundquist.

Just as the abolitionists William Lloyd Garrison and Wendell Phillips lent "authenticity" to Douglass's *Narrative,* the publishers, Sherman, French & Company, acted like abolitionists when they validated and gave authenticity to Johnson's novel. In fact, the preface was dictated to them almost verbatim by Johnson.[26] Johnson drew on W. E. B. Du Bois's diction and metaphoric use of language to seduce the reader. Mimicking Du Bois's writings, one statement from the "authenticating preface" reads:

> It is very likely that the Negroes of the United States have a fairly correct idea of what the white people of the country think of them, for that opinion has a long time been and still is being constantly stated but they are themselves more or less a sphinx to the whites. It is curiously interesting and even vitally important to know what are the thoughts of ten millions of them concerning the people among whom they live. In these pages it is as though a veil had been drawn aside: the reader is given a view of the inner life of the Negro in America, is initiated into the "freemasonry," as it were, of the race. (xxxiv)

Accordingly, as the literary scholar Robert B. Stepto explains, *The Autobiography*, as a "generic narrative," is, like the Douglass and Du Bois narratives, a "coherent expression of personalized response to systems of signification and symbolic geography occasioned by social structure."[27] Yet, unlike in Chesnutt's narrative, the systems of signification in Johnson's narrative become centered on the protagonist whose musical ability and geographic mobility bring a broader national (American) and international (European) perspective to the phenomenon of black people passing for white.

In the first paragraph of *The Autobiography,* the narrator reveals the secrecy, criminality, thrill, and chicanery associated with those black people who pass for white. The Ex-Coloured Man discloses:

> I am divulging the great secret of my life, the secret which for some years I have guarded far more carefully than any one of my earthly possessions; and it is a curious study to me to analyze the motives which prompt me to do it. I feel that I am led by the same impulse which forces the un-found-out criminal to take somebody into his confidence, although he knows that the act is likely, almost certain, to lead to his undoing. I know that I am playing with fire, and I feel the thrill which accompanies the most fascinating pastime; and, back of it all, I think I feel a sort of savage and diabolical desire to gather up all the little tragedies of my life, and turn them into a practical joke on society. (1)

First, the narrator, with an objective and psychoanalytic tone, appropriately suggests that the "great secret" of passing for white in America's racist society is as much the ultimate act of signification on whiteness as it is the ultimate act of denial of his African American ancestry (blackness). Hence passing is a paradoxical performance, one which challenges the legal, economic, and social tenets of white supremacy, at the same time that it conversely reinforces the pervasive notion of white superiority. The significance of this paradox illustrates that the unique cultural productions of black people will disappear when individuals masquerade as white.

Second, the narrator connects passing to criminality. Often intrinsic to passing are acts of deception and equivocation. The results of this deception and prevarication may be somewhat innocent for the unaware, but when it comes to friends and lovers the experience can be extremely disconcerting. Furthermore, as a byproduct of miscegenation, the element of criminality suggests the numerous legal sanctions against black and white amalgamation.

Third, by associating crossing over the color line with "playing with fire" and feeling "the thrill," Johnson suggests the exhilarating excitement of being an impostor and a chameleon. Also, the reference to "playing with fire" suggests the danger of being lynched. Here one obtains a sense of power and privilege by escaping the margins of racial prejudice and placing oneself at the center of a racist discourse.

Last, the playing of a "practical joke" implies that passing for white can be a prevaricating performance through which a person can indirectly enact revenge on those individuals who have caused him or her anguish. This masking performance is fundamental to America hegemonic iconography. As Ralph Ellison makes clear:

> the Negro masking is motivated not so much by fear as by a profound rejection of the image created to usurp his identity. Sometimes it is for the sheer joy of the joke; sometimes to challenge those who presume, across the psychological distance created by race manners, to know his identity. Nonetheless it is in the American grain. . . .

America is a land of masking jokers. We wear the mask for purposes of aggression as well as for defense; when we are projecting the future and preserving the past. In short, the motives hidden behind the mask are as numerous as the ambiguities the mask conceals.[28]

Throughout *The Autobiography*, with constant signifying on the tropes of the slave narratives, Douglass, and Du Bois, all of these critical aspects of passing reveal the seminal importance of Johnson's novel.

Like Chesnutt's novel, Johnson's confessional paragraph illustrates that miscegenation initiates the tangled mesh of mimicry and masquerading. Also, like Douglass's first chapter, Johnson's first chapter is textually structured with binaries in opposition.[29] Tragically and consistently ironic, this racial drama opens with the slave narrative trope of "natal alienation": vague remembrances by the protagonist of his Southern home (Georgia) and of his white father. Although the Ex-Coloured Man says he has distinct memories of his mother and father, the remembrances of his father are materialistically reduced to shiny shoes or boots, a gold chain, and a great gold watch. The shoes are significant because it is the protagonist's slavelike task to fetch his white father's slippers whenever he comes to visit his mother. These "shiny" (here a pun on the racial word "shine") shoes also suggest an offensive analogy to the protagonist's dark-skinned friend "Shiny." Textually, this naming suggests that Shiny's black presence is acutely visible, whereas the Ex-Coloured Man's presence fades. This black boy, Shiny, who refigures Booker T. Washington and foreshadows the speech-making protagonist in Ellison's *Invisible Man* (1947),[30] is the most intelligent student in the class, yet "in spite of his standing as a scholar, he was in some way looked down upon" (9). Some of the white students would often repeat, "Nigger, nigger, never die / Black face and shiny eye" (10). Additionally, Shiny's name represents the paradox of the word's meaning, both good and bad. Again, as Ellison relates, this word play is intrinsic to a racist perspective. Ellison states:

> The essence of the word is its ambivalence, and in fiction it is never so effective and revealing as when both potentials are operating simultaneously, as when it mirrors both good and bad, as when it blows both hot and cold in the same breath. Thus it is unfortunate for the Negro that the most powerful formulations of modern American fictional words have been so slanted against him that when he approaches for a glimpse of himself he discovers an image of humanity.[31]

Like former slaves coming to terms with their humanity, the protagonist has distinct remembrances of his mother but "faint recollection of the place of birth" (2). Concerning his home, the Ex-Coloured Man recalls "a hedge of vari-colored glass bottles stuck in the ground neck down." According to Robert Farris Thompson, these bottles represent an example of African culture surviving in the New World. As Robert B. Stepto asserts, Thompson believes that the multicolored bottles are analogous to the

> light-giving or light-reflecting objects such as mirrors and automobile headlamps in tombstones in southern black cemeteries. . . . These objects express the "flash of the

spirit," the "spirit embedded in glitter"; they "rephrase" the African (and more specifically, in many instances, Kongo custom of "inserting mirrors into the walls of pillars of tombs" and of "displaying a mirror embedded in the abdomen" of statues "as a sign of mystic vision."[32]

Consequently, when the protagonist digs up the bottles to determine whether they grew like flowers, he is unknowingly desecrating and discovering his African (black) heritage. The "terrific" whipping he receives becomes fixed in his mind.

This "terrific" physical whipping is analogous to the shocking psychological whipping the protagonist endures when he ironically discovers that he is black (a "nigger") and not white. Robert E. Fleming argues that the most notable irony "is reserved for the narrator's comments about himself. It is significant that passages which deal with his reactions and feelings are characterized by a neoromantic style, by sentimental and rather inflated diction. The narrator views himself in romantic terms, as a tragic hero whose flaw is the black blood he has inherited from his beloved mother."[33] For example, one day the principal enters his class and, after talking to the teacher, asks for the "white scholars to stand for a moment." When the protagonist stands, his teacher asks him to be seated for the present and to rise with the others (the black students). The protagonist relates, "I sat down dazed. I saw and heard nothing. When school was dismissed, I went out in a kind of stupor" (11). Johnson's ironic use of diction suggests that he almost experienced a "blackout" because he was no longer in the white group. Until this point he had been led to believe and was convinced that he was white. Earlier, when a fight had broken out between the white students and the black students, he had sided with the whites who were throwing rocks at the [niggers] black students. When he goes home, he tells his mother that one of the "niggers" has struck a boy with a slate. Although his mother sharply reprimands him for using this racist and pejorative signifier, she never tells him his racial identity. Additionally, his white teacher, who has dresses made by the protagonist's mother, obviously knows he is black but allows him to think that his white skin cloaks his blackness. Later, while living as a black man in Harlem, he discovers that the use of the racial signifier "nigger" is complex. For example, when he hears, "Nigger, dat cue ain't no hoe-handle," he understands that this word is analogous to the word "fellow" and a term of endearment. He also discovers that "its use was positively and absolutely prohibited to white men" (67). Consequently, despite the use of the derisive signifier "nigger," his mother and the teacher are co-conspirators in the fraud of allowing our protagonist to believe that he is white.

The fraud is deepened when the other black students, revealing their co-conspiracy, acknowledge that "We knew he was colored," whereas the white students, revealing their astonishment, say: "Oh, you're a nigger too" (11). Comforted by "Shiny," the black student, and "Red Head," a white student, the protagonist goes home to confront his mother. Finding his mother busy with a client, the protagonist confronts his mirror, looking for answers. Upon finding the courage to gaze, he reveals:

I looked long and earnestly. I had often heard people say to my mother: "What a pretty boy you have!" I was accustomed to hear remarks about my beauty; but now, for the first time, I became conscious of it and recognized it. I noticed the ivory whiteness of my skin, the beauty of my mouth, the size and liquid darkness of my eyes, and how the long black lashes that fringed and shaded them produced an effect that was strangely fascinating to me. I noticed the softness and glossiness of my dark hair that fell in waves over my temples, making my forehead appear whiter than it really was. How long I stood there gazing at my image I do not know. (11–12)

This long autoerotic and Lacanian moment in which the protagonist finally recognizes and attempts to come to terms with his own image is problematic because of the deception by his black mother and his white teacher. Unlike John Walden in *The House Behind the Cedars,* our protagonist finds it difficult to project his ego. Despite his fascination with his whiteness, he at this point realizes that the derogatory stamp of blackness is permanent and irreversible. Also at this point, the protagonist illustrates what Fanon maintains—that a black person is "driven to discover the meaning of black identity. White civilization and European culture have forced an existential deviation on the Negro . . . what is often called the black soul is a white man's artifact."[34]

At this moment, his Du Boisian double consciousness begins. The narrator-character immediately searches his mother's face for defects. He notices that her skin is almost brown and that her hair is not as soft as his and "that she did differ in some way from the other ladies who came to the house; yet, even so, I could see that she was very beautiful, more beautiful than any of them" (12). Here the mother becomes the Other to her son. When he asks, "Mother, mother, tell me am I a nigger," and then asks, "Well, mother, am I white? Are you white?" his mother responds that she is not white but that he has "the best blood of the South." Like Molly Walden in *The House Behind the Cedars* and Roxy (no surname) in *The Tragedy of Pudd'nhead Wilson,* this black woman, hypnotized and drugged by whiteness, has internalized the notion that white is superior and believes the fallacy that the "best blood" comes from an upper-class white biological source. Also, like Molly (whose white suitor dies), the Ex-Coloured Man's mother is a kept women whose life is severely changed when her white suitor decides to marry a white woman. The Ex-Coloured Man's quadroon mother, by denying his blackness and acknowledging his whiteness, projects her marginal and confused status onto her son. Yet, the narrator strongly identifies with his mother as mutual victim as he comes to discern that his father's denial of paternity is crucial to the racist Southern culture. As Simone Vauthier makes clear: "if black, which is nonwhite, can look non-black, nay white, then the opposition white/non-white shows up as problematic. . . . The social structure insofar as it determines status according to 'race', i.e. color, is jeopardized. . . . The place of the white individual within the race-based social scheme and hence his very identity are threatened by the mere existence of a white Negro."[35]

As the protagonist recalls that fateful day in school, he states, "I have never forgiven the woman who did it so cruelly. It may be that she never knew that she gave me a sword-thrust that day in school which was years in healing" (12). Here Johnson's language moves from the general to the specific. Whereas the first sentence leads us to question which woman (mother or teacher) he is referring to, the second indicts his white teacher. This diction reveals that our narrator harbors resentment toward his mother for his reduced racial and class position at school and a lowered self-conception. Later, his prophecy of his mother's death reinforces this consideration. He is jealous of the love his mother has for his father, yet he resents her "tainted blood." Because he desires to be white like his father, this love and hatred for the mother suggest the psychological binaries of the Oedipus and the Electra complexes.[36] Furthermore, this statement about the "woman" meets Olney's criterion that the slave must describe the cruel treatment he has received from a master, mistress or overseer. Ironically, aspects of his relationships with his mother, father, and teacher are characterized as cruel. Our protagonist is transformed from a white student to a black student, who, along with the dominant white society, will view blackness as being inferior.

Before that traumatic day in school, the Ex-Coloured Man recalls having some spent of the "happiest hours" of his childhood. He recalls his mother playing some old Southern songs, which she sang, and his "particular fondness for the black keys" (5). Unknowingly, our protagonist reveals his rootedness to black culture; his rootedness to a black heritage and his mother's songs echo Douglass's discussion of the Sorrow Songs. Although the protagonist has been led to believe that he is white, his black heritage has always been in the background; now blackness will be the basis of his identity formation. Hence, his relationship with his mother becomes a symbolic representation of blackness: "She would hold me close, softly crooning some old melody without words, all the while gently stroking her face against my head; and many a night I fell asleep. I can see her now, her great dark eyes looking into the fire, to where? No one knew but her. *The memory of that picture has more than once kept me from straying too far from the place of purity and safety in which her arms held me*" (5). Here, the Ex-Coloured Man's phrasing and introspective analysis spiritually and culturally place blackness at the center of a discourse at odds with the dominant culture. This picture represents the controlling force in the novel's persistent binary representation of blackness and whiteness.

Another binary in opposition is the protagonist's aversion to washtubs, where his skin is scrubbed until it aches. This bathtub incident echoes the spiritual song "Wash Me White as Snow"; it suggests his mother's attempt to remove all traces of sin as blackness. Moreover, this bathtub scene is suggestive of the bleach baths that some black individuals used in order to whiten themselves or pass. A critical factor in passing is the notion of "being born again," a major concept in the most important religion in the justification of enslaving black people. In this regard, blackness becomes associated with the myth of Ham and the "original sin." As a result, the protagonist views himself as "a perfect little aristocrat," yet refers to himself as "a pampered pet dog" (5) when his mother opens the piano. As in the first chapter of Douglass's *Narrative,* we have in *The Autobiography* the bifurcation of whiteness/ blackness, human/ animal, knowledge/ignorance, the master-slave relationship, and wealth/scarcity. As Henry Louis Gates argues, these binaries suggest "an ordering of the world based on a profoundly relational type of thinking, in which a strict barrier of difference or opposition forms the basis of a class rather than, as in other classification schemes, an ordering based on resemblances or the identity of two or more elements."[37] Like our decoding and deciphering of Douglass's *Narrative*, we find in Johnson's novel a constant juxtaposition of these binaries to signify on the presence and absence of qualities associated with blackness and whiteness. This double consciousness is evident in the protagonist's Du Boisian analysis of his psychological transition:

> And so I have often lived through that hour, that day, that week, in which was wrought the miracle of my transition from one world into another; for I did indeed pass into another world. From that time I looked out through other eyes, my thoughts were colored, my words dictated, my actions limited by one dominating, all-pervading idea which constantly increased in force and weight until I finally realized in it a great, tangible fact. (14)

Being black, he now believes that it is impossible to return to his pampered and privileged white identity. The irony of this "fall from grace" is that the Ex-Coloured Man psychologically assumes both a white identity and a black identity. This duality suggests that Johnson constructs the binaries only to deconstruct and explode them later in the narrative. Through his mimicking, the Ex-Coloured Man's identity becomes repeatedly fragmented and fractured by racial and class dynamics. As a result of this fragmentation, the Ex-Coloured Man assumes a white identity and disregards black culture.

Whereas the last criterion that Olney mentions is the slave's reflections on slavery, in the next two sections of this chapter, I, by way of contrast, consider the Ex-Coloured Man's reflections on his escape from blackness and his embrace of whiteness. His use of ragtime music as the vehicle for this escape has less to do with self-hatred than with the wretched social and economic restrictions that are antithetical to the white life of privilege and possibility.

Having painfully accepted the seemingly irreversible fact of his blackness, the protagonist attempts to make the best of his "inferior" status. It is here that Johnson explodes the binaries he has constructed as he illustrates our protagonist mimicking both black people and white people in his quest for identity. The process of accepting other black people becomes extremely difficult for the Ex-Coloured Man. In fact, except for Shiny, who represents another "dark double" and the "token nigger," he has "a strong aversion to being classed with them" [the other black students] (15). Like some racist whites, he views Shiny as special, different, and, therefore, superior to other black people. In essence, Shiny is "the exception that proves the rule" of white superiority. Psychologically and emotionally, he finds himself freer with elderly white people than with whites near his own age. This freedom with elderly whites suggests that he instinctively recognizes that it is the adults that he must convince first if he is to pass. Despite his acceptance of his blackness, emotionally he is a white Negro with delusions of racial transformation.

Textually, the Ex-Coloured Man's psychological state foreshadows his complete cultural immersion in whiteness.

Not surprisingly, his imagination and heart become fired with passion for a girl with "dark hair wild framing her pale face" (20). Yet, this passion for a fellow musical student is juxtaposed with a profound dread that this young white girl might discover his feelings. Although this is an innocent relationship, the dread suggests the anxiety associated with miscegenation. More important, when his youthful passion fades, the protagonist states that "I should never love another woman, and that if she deceives me I should do something desperate" (21). Here, Johnson connects the narrator's musical interest to his desire to embrace whiteness. Ironically, this statement foreshadows the protagonist's deception when he permanently embraces whiteness.

The irony deepens when he embraces his white father for the last time. As in the time of slavery, when his father becomes engaged to a woman of "another great Southern family," the protagonist and his mother are sent away to Connecticut. During slavery, the master's children from an illicit relationship with a slave woman were often sold, so as not to bring embarrassment and shame to their white owners. The same shame is implicitly illustrated when the father "laboriously" drills a hole in a ten-dollar gold coin and places it around his son's neck. (Of course, this moment is remarkably similar to the one in which, in Chesnutt's novel, John gives Rena a dime with a hole in it.) This worthless and flawed coin symbolizes the inconsequential nature of their father-son relationship and the white man's materialistic values. Here the father gives the semblance of wealth, yet withholds it. Jim Crow culture, along with his own guilt and shame, will not allow him to acknowledge overtly his "illegitimate" progeny. Recalling this critical moment, the protagonist states, "I have worn that gold piece around my neck the greater part of my life, and still possess it, but more than once I have wished that some other way had been found of attaching it to me besides putting a hole through it" (3). These words illustrate his strong interest in material things and imply a desire for a holistic relationship with his white father. It never develops. This "gold" coin reinforces Douglass's statement: "gold and silver—the only standard of worth applied by slave-holders to slaves!"[38] The devalued gold coin and the chain permanently tied to his "property" (progeny) profoundly confirm the hegemonic master-slave paradigm.

This paradigm becomes more evident when the protagonist's father comes to Connecticut to pay his final visit and is moved and impressed with his son's musical abilities; he sends the Ex-Coloured Man a piano. Again Johnson connects the Ex-Coloured Man's musical interests with whiteness; again the protagonist expresses resentment and regret over material acquisitions. He states, "I had left my father; but, even so, there momentarily crossed my mind a feeling of disappointment that the piano was not a grand" (28). He is not accepted as a son; he is, instead, a bastard who lacks public acknowledgment by his father.

Although the piano is not a "grand," the Ex-Coloured Man has already perfected his musical skills to the extent that he becomes the "infant prodigy." He goes on to compare himself to other children and states that he learns to play not by counting out exercises but by trying to "reproduce the quaint songs which my mother used to sing, with all their pathetic turns and cadences" (18). His mother's music (black music) is viewed as unsophisticated and wretched. This disparaging discourse foreshadows his desire to use his musical talent for exploitative ventures; it foreshadows the concept that ragtime music is superior because it is a mixture of black and white music. It is also through the music that the Ex-Coloured Man meets and describes a young girl who foreshadows his white wife: "her pale face and her slender body swaying to the tones she called forth, all combined to fire my imagination and my heart with a passion . . . somehow, lasting" (20).

When his father disappears and his mother dies, our protagonist decides to return South in an attempt to discover his blackness. If we could locate a paradigm that characterizes the narrator's actions as the Ex-Coloured Man travels in America and Europe, it would be early in the first chapter, where he gives us an excellent example of his approach-avoidance conflict. He reveals: "I remember with what pleasure I used to arrive at, and stand before, a little enclosure in which stood a patient cow, how I would occasionally offer her through the bars a piece of my bread and molasses, and how I would jerk back my hand in half fright if she made any motion to accept my offer" (2–3). The horse has been a traditional symbol of power and the ruling class, but the cow symbolizes weakness. The cow is a paradoxical symbol in that it represents both maternity as a source of nourishment and a frightening beast. The passage also suggests the master-slave dialect as well as the human-animal binary where the protagonist with his "bread and molasses" is in a position of power and authority, as he seduces and in "half fright" denies gratification. The cow becomes a metonymy for the Ex-Coloured Man's weakness. Until he permanently embraces whiteness, this consistent pattern illustrates the Ex-Coloured Man's cowardly behavior.

Echoing Du Bois, Johnson describes the Ex-Coloured Man's journey to the South. Whereas Du Bois's southern journey leads to an emotional and spiritual connection with the souls of black folk, the Ex-Coloured Man recoils in horror at the abject poverty and wretched conditions of black people. Too often he is unable to see beyond the veil of Jim Crow economic and social oppression. At this point in the narrative, he seems to believe that black people are—to invoke the vernacular—"My race but not my taste," "My skin-folks but not my kin-folks." For example, when our protagonist finds lodgings in Atlanta, he longs for his sanitary and unsullied past:

> I glanced around the apartment and saw that it contained a double bed and two cots, two washstands, three chairs, and a time-worn bureau, with a looking-glass that would have made Adonis appear hideous. I looked at the cot in which I was to sleep and suspected, not without good reason, that I should not be the first to use the sheets and pillow-case since they had last come from the wash. When I thought of the clean, tidy, comfortable surroundings in which I had been reared, a wave of homesickness swept over me that made me feel faint. (38–39)

With race and class intersecting, this scene not only associates these filthy and cramped conditions with the lives of black people but also recalls the protagonist's Lacanian mirror moment and suggests that, like an ostracized white-God figure, he has been cast underground into a hellish black condition. Because his limited financial resources cause him to discover how lower-class black people live, the Ex-Coloured Man is biased in the conclusions he draws. Although the porter reassures him that the black people he encounters are of the lower class, their "unkempt appearance, the shambling, slouching gait and loud talk and laughter of these people," he relates, "aroused in me a feeling of almost repulsion" (40). Despite these adverse social conditions, our protagonist becomes enthralled with the "fullness and freedom" of Southern black people's diction. "Lawd a mussy!" "G'wan man!" "Bless ma soul!" "Look heah chile!" These hearty expressions and their laughter, generated from "the pits of their stomachs," our narrators concludes, keep black people "from going the way of the Indian" (40). The significance of this represents a paradox. It seems contradictory for a person who has internalized the "superior" values and beliefs of whites and who will go on to pass for white and to mimic whites to be excited about the unique vernacular of black people. Additionally, here, vernacular indicates the vitality of black people; it is an excellent example of Johnson's concept of "blendings" while maintaining one's distinction.

This paradox represents the fundamental problem of black people seeking agency in racist America. On the one hand, the blood and bones of black people have been the foundation for the enormous wealth of white America, yet, on the other, black people are too often viewed as being innately inferior. The uniqueness of black diction—along with the folk tales such as those of Joel Chandler Harris, the Cakewalk, ragtime music, spirituals, slave songs, and Jubilee songs—will be the seductive elements[39] that will at some point influence our elusive Ex-Coloured Man's attempt to embrace blackness.

In Atlanta, the Ex-Coloured Man is told that "you could go in any place in the city; they wouldn't know you from white" (41) by a Pullman car porter, a young black man who not only assists our protagonist in negotiating Atlanta but also helps himself to all of his money, hidden in his trunk. Years later, he discovers this individual wearing his favorite black and gray necktie. Consistent with his vacillation with the cow and the notion of "ragged time" (this is the idea of a musical meter that is ragged, torn apart into conflicting rhythms by syncopation), the Ex-Coloured Man fails to act. Despite his "strong suspicions," he states that "My astonishment and the ironic humor of the situation drove everything else out of my mind" (61). This statement is particularly ironic when we recall the tears that come to his eyes when the porter lends him fifteen dollars (his own money) and he concludes that "there were some kind hearts in the world" (46).

Unable to attend Atlanta University because his money has been stolen, he is convinced by the porter to go to Jacksonville. In an experience that recalls Henry "Box" Brown's twenty-six-hour journey from Richmond to Philadelphia and from slavery to freedom inside a coffin and Linda Brent's seven-year self-confinement in a tiny space in her grandmother's shed, our protagonist relates:

> I spent twelve hours doubled up in the porter basket for soiled linen, not being able
> to straighten up on account of the shelves for clean linen just over my head. The air
> was hot and suffocating and the smell of damp towels and used linen was sickening.
> At each lurch of the car over the none-too-smooth track I was bumped and bruised
> against the narrow walls of my narrow compartment. (46–47)

As this coffin-basket experience parallels traditional slave narratives, so it suggests
and signifies on the process by which those of fair complexion passed as white and
sometimes posed as their own masters. Often light-complexioned slaves masqueraded as servants on their way to meet their owners. It also suggests the brazen, colorful creativity and danger of men posing as women and women posing as men.
This creativity by blacks foreshadows Johnson's portrayal of minstrelsy, where, as
Ann Douglas convincingly maintains, the "routines of mimicry and role-playing
developed in the days of slavery, at the heart of American entertainment. Blacks imitating and fooling whites, whites imitating and stealing from blacks, blacks reap-
propriating and transforming what has been stolen, whites making another foray on
black styles, and on and on: this is American popular culture."[40]

In Jacksonville, our protagonist becomes introduced to the cigar-making trade,
where "the color line is not drawn" (49). He learns to make cigars, smoke, swear,
and speak Spanish. In a short time, he learns to speak Spanish better than any of
the Cubans at the factory. When he becomes a "reader" (a person who reads to the
other workers to lessen the monotonous work of rolling cigars), the Ex-Coloured
Man expresses his class bias. He states: "My position as 'reader' not only released
me from the monotonous work . . . and gave me something more in accord with
my taste, but also added to my income" (54). This places emphasis on the importance of language in the masquerade of assuming another identity. The Ex-
Coloured Man's superior position releases him from the "time and trouble" of giving music lessons. Johnson's use of the word "released" suggests that literacy and
reading are critical to his passing to an elevated class position. Further, the protagonist makes the connection between his musical ability and class mobility. He self-
servingly states: "Through my music teaching and my not absolutely irregular attendance at church I became acquainted with the best class of colored people in
Jacksonville" (54).

At this point in the narrative, music is defined not as a cultural artifact but as an
economic asset and a means to black upper-class subjectivity and foreshadows his
embrace of whiteness. Like a white anthropologist and sociologist who is finally
"getting the practice," his musical ability facilitates his acquaintance with the "best
class of colored people in Jacksonville." Accordingly, he formulates a theory of the
three classes of black people in America.

The first group consists of desperate individuals; included in this class are ex-
convicts and barroom loafers. He says, "They cherish a sullen hatred for all white
men, and they value life as cheap." He has "heard more than one of them say: 'I'll
go to hell for the first white man that bothers me'" (56). In the second class of
black people are those connected to whites through domestic service. He theorizes

that "These may be generally characterized as simple, kind-hearted, and faithful; not overfine in their moral deductions, but intensely religious. . . . Between this class of the blacks and the whites there is little or no friction" (57). The last group comprises well-to-do and educated black people. Concerning this group he concludes that, "if a colored man wanted to separate himself from his white neighbors, he had to acquire some money, education, and culture, and to live in accordance" (57). Clearly, we can surmise that our protagonist, drugged with privilege, identifies more with this class than with the others. Ragtime music is the cultural production that aligns the Ex-Coloured Man with education and money. Additionally, the Ex-Coloured Man believes that this final group of blacks mirrors and mimics whites. He speculates "that the white people somehow feel that colored people who have education and money, who wear good clothes and live in comfortable houses, are 'putting on airs,' that they do these things for the sole purpose of 'spiting the white folks,' or are, at best, going through a sort of monkey-like imitation" (58). The tragedy for this group, the Ex-Coloured Man recounts, occurs when they are compared to the first group. This group also has the distinction of forming its own "society as discriminating as the actual conditions will allow." These social circles are connected throughout the country, and a person in good standing in one city is readily accepted in another. Johnson perceptively refers to the Blue Vein Society, of Nashville, and the Bon Ton Society, of Washington, D.C. (formed during Reconstruction), in which membership is based not only on superior class position but on physical (phenotype) and psychological resemblance to whiteness. The detached tone and attitude of the Ex-Coloured Man conveys that his time in Jacksonville has been one of racial research and has not involved a true attempt to understand and embrace black people. When he escapes to the blackness of New York, his perspective will be somewhat the same.

With noticeable similarity to his description in his poem "The White Witch," Johnson describes New York in racially paradoxical terms. As the Ex-Coloured Man steams up into New York Harbor, his rhetoric represents this city as a symbol of desire and death:

> She sits like a great witch at the gate of the country, showing her alluring white face and hiding her crooked hands and feet under the folds of her wide garments—constantly enticing thousands from far within, and tempting those who come from across the seas to go no farther. And all these become the victims of her caprice. Some she at once crushes beneath her cruel feet; others she condemns to a fate like that of galley slaves; a few she favors and fondles, riding them high on the bubbles of fortune; then with a sudden breath she blows the bubbles out and laughs mockingly as she watches them fall. (65–66)

By using the Statue of Liberty as metaphor and metonymy, Johnson constructs the horror and the hopes of black people in America.[41] Like F. Scott Fitzgerald's robust "green breast," in *The Great Gatsby* (1925), Johnson's Statue-guarded city has the double possibility of nourishing or neglecting those who suckle. For many black people, the American Dream has too often been a horrid nightmare and a "wasteland" with heavy physical and psychological penalties. Those black people who are able to pass through the color-coded territory have been favored with limited social and economic rewards for their racial betrayal. Yet, there exist the possible guilt and constant trepidation about being exposed. New York, as a "fatally fascinating thing," like some white women who lure some black men to their doom, will be the final frontier in America where the Ex-Coloured Man will attempt to embrace his blackness.

This New York or "Club" section, where our protagonist attempts a closer connection to his black heritage, is significant in two ways. First, Johnson suggests an intricate connection among passing, minstrelsy (mimicry), and ragtime music. Second, we ascertain the Ex-Coloured Man's deep-seated feelings about miscegenation.

While in a club, he hears music whose "barbaric harmonies, the audacious resolutions, often consisting of an abrupt jump from one key to another, the intricate rhythms in which the accents fell in the most unexpected places, but in which the beat was never lost, produced a most curious effect" (72). This is ragtime music, a metaphor for both the narrator's double consciousness and the possibility of passing or racial improvisation. It is also a cultural production whose history mirrors the economic exploitation of the many black individuals who created this improvisational art form. As the narrator recounts, white men steal black music and pass it off as their own. He explains: "Several of these improvisations were taken down by white men, the words slightly altered, and published under the names of the arrangers. They sprang into immediate popularity and earned small fortunes, of which the Negro originators got only a few dollars" (73). This not only confirms Ann Douglas's analysis of black people who imitate whites and whites who steal from black people but also suggests that the exploitation of black people has shifted from physical poaching to cultural poaching. The irony of this situation is extended when the narrator, after living white in Europe, attempts to become like a colonizing white man in his desire to "voice all the joys sorrows, the hopes and ambitions of the American Negro, in classical musical form" (108). His postcolonial diction here suggests the transformation (passing) of black culture into an European art form. Within America's culture of white supremacy, the stage and the genre of entertainment have generally been safe places for black people (trickster figures) to mimic whites and for whites to mimic black people. Of course, this mimicking suggests minstrelsy, where whites in black face and black people in blacker face, working through fear, found the freedom to signify on and to challenge the dominant culture. As Eric Lott notes, the performance stage has been the site of fascination and fear:

> the intensified American fears of succumbing to a racial image of Otherness were everywhere operative in minstrelsy, continually exceeding the controls and accounting, paradoxically, for the minstrel show power, insofar as its "blackness" was unceasingly fascinating to performers and audiences alike. This combined fear of and fascination with the black male cast a strange dread of miscegenation over the minstrel show, but evidently did not preclude a continual return to minstrel miming.[42]

As a white Negro, the Ex-Coloured Man can be considered a minstrel performer who illustrates his "strange dread of miscegenation." While at the club, he notices a white widow in the company of a black man who is generally known as a "bad man." He goes on to state that this black man is a "surly, despot who held sway over her deepest emotions" (89) and that "his ugly look completely frightened me" (90). Earlier, his "fear and fascination" with regard to their relationship are explicit: "I shall never forget how hard it was for me to get over my feelings of surprise, perhaps more than surprise, at seeing her with her black companion; somehow I never exactly enjoyed the sight" (79). Psychologically and emotionally, his diction suggests the ideology of a racist white man who harbors deep hatred for a despotic black man who violates the social (sexual) boundaries of America's white supremacist society.

When our protagonist gets caught in the middle of this relationship of miscegenation, which leads to the death of the white widow (via a bullet to the throat[43]), he is saved by a white father figure—a nameless millionaire. He describes their Faustian relationship: "this man sitting there so mysteriously silent, almost hid in a cloud of heavy-scented smoke, filled me with a sort of unearthly terror. He seemed to be some grim, mute, but relentless tyrant, possessing over me a supernatural power which he used to drive me on mercilessly to exhaustion. But these feelings came very rarely; besides, he paid me so liberally I could forget much" (88). At the millionaire's apartment, in the "midst of elegance and luxury," he falls asleep while waiting for his master. Unlike the sweating and anxiety-laden Bigger Thomas, sitting in the Dalton's affluent home in Richard Wright's *Native Son* (1940), the Ex-Coloured Man becomes so comfortable that he falls asleep. This Faustian relationship mirrors the one with his nameless white father. Instead of a flawed gold coin and an inferior piano, the protagonist's ability to play music again illustrates the master-slave relationship. The Ex-Coloured Man reveals that, while playing for the white man, he becomes "so oppressed with fatigue and sleepiness that it took almost superhuman effort to keep my fingers going; in fact, I believe I sometimes did so while dozing" (88). As Joseph T. Skerrett Jr. puts it, the millionaire is a "Mephistophelean figure, satanically suggesting to the narrator an attitude that would as well ease his conscience as it would enable him to avoid the pain and suffering of a commitment to his black identity."[44] When the virulent trouble comes, the millionaire decides to take the Ex-Coloured Man to Europe instead of his valet, Walter. Before he immerses himself in the white world of Europe, he vividly recalls the widow's "beautiful white throat with the ugly wound. The jet blood pulsing from it had placed an indelible red stain on my memory" (91). Ironically, this "red stain," the result not of the bloody sacrifices of his black ancestry but of the covetous desire of some whites, marks the end of the Ex-Coloured Man's failed quest to embrace blackness and initiates his escape into whiteness.

While traveling in Europe, the Ex-Coloured Man lives the life of an upper-class white man. He states that his benefactor "bought me the same kind of clothes which he himself wore, and that was the best; and he treated me in every way as he dressed me, as an equal, not as a servant" (95). Although the narrator believes he is "an equal," he unknowingly reveals that his statement that he is "dressed" by his benefactor indicates his inferior, slavelike status. The only "hardship" in this prestigious lifestyle occurs when his benefactor wakes the Ex-Coloured Man up "in the early hours of the morning" to play something. Of course, this confirms the real Faustian purpose of his being in Europe. He is there as a musical servant to do his white master's bidding. This musical performance begs the question "What shall it profit a man if he gains the whole world and lose his own soul?"

While in Paris, he encounters his former "master," his white father. One evening, he goes to a production of Faust and, while gazing at a young white girl seated to his left, he tragically discovers that the girl is his sister, accompanied by his father and his wife.[45] "Here" he states in anguish, "here in your very midst, is a tragedy, a real tragedy" (98). Like his sister, he is on his first trip to Paris, but his sister is brought by her father, whereas the Ex-Coloured Man is brought by a surrogate white father. Like the shocking discovery of his blackness, his cowardly behavior recalls his childhood as he "walked aimlessly about for an hour or so," with his "feelings divided between a desire to weep and a desire to curse" (99). Both desires suggest the agony and anguish of his blackness, which is the reason for his father's rejection of him, and his desire to be in his sister's place of privilege and possibility (whiteness). His being unrecognized by his father transforms the Ex-Coloured Man into an Invisible Man. As the scholar Arthur P. Davis argues, this opera scene becomes dramatically analogous to the school scene where the narrator discovers his blackness. Davis states: "Such dramatic but restrained episodes point up far more strongly the tragedy of the American race situation than sensational and brutal scenes of violence."[46] One's being able to look white is not enough for those persons (in this incident his father) who have knowledge of one's blackness.

This opera scene is significant in that it echoes the interweaving of miscegenation and incest. Like John Warwick's incestuous gaze directed at Rena Walden in *The House Behind the Cedars*, the Ex-Coloured Man gazes at the young girl whom he discovers to be his half-sister. Johnson's implicit suggestion here is that if the white father were not present, an incestuous affair might have happened. Hence, when the Ex-Coloured Man desires to weep and curse, it is possible that, as Ralph Ellison suggests, "maybe [his] freedom lies in hating" blackness. Further, the "Sins of the Father" and the Oedipal complex are fully exposed in the opera scene. In *Totem and Taboo,* Sigmund Freud suggests a connection between miscegenation and incest and black and white relationships. Freud advances the idea that the critical objectives of taboo are the "guarding [of] chief acts of life—birth, initiation, marriage and sexual functions, and the like, against interference" and the "securing of unborn infants and young children" and that the desecration of a taboo results in the "taboo itself [taking] vengeance."[47] The Ex-Coloured Man represents the desecration of the taboo that occurred between his white father and his black mother. Yet, true to his behavior (and unlike in the Oedipal paradigm), our narrator seeks no vengeance. This aspect is critical in viewing his passing for white as a passive (cowardly) performance. Rather than challenging his white father as a phallic representation of power and authority, he desires an embrace.

The protagonist's desire to turn his blackness into whiteness is enhanced when he realizes that he has been turning classic music into ragtime music, and he is shocked when a "big bespectacled, bushy-headed man" turns ragtime music into classical music. This succinctly confirms Eric Sundquist's point about the passing of vernacular culture into so-called high culture. Also, this becomes the motivation for the Ex-Coloured Man's desire to return to the South. With the mentality of a white colonizing explorer, he decides "to live among the people, and drink in my inspiration firsthand. I gloated over the immense amount of material I had to work with, not only modern ragtime, but also the old slave songs—material which no one had yet touched" (104). His white benefactor responds by telling the Ex-Coloured Man that "by blood, by appearance, by education, and by taste" (105) he is a white man. Here a white man informs a black man that he can successfully pass for white; he has passed beyond the boundaries of race/nation and racism/nationalism. Equally important, he informs the narrator that at this point in his life it would be a serious economic and psychological handicap to attempt to become a Negro composer. Recalling Mr. Auld's strict directions to his wife that learning would make Frederick Douglass unfit, the millionaire, commenting on the antithetical nature of an educated black man, states: "I can imagine no more dissatisfied human being than an educated, cultured and refined colored man in the United States" (106). Additionally, with his "authority of skin," the millionaire employs the terms and logic constructed by the dominant oppressing culture. As Fanon elaborates: "Western bourgeois racial prejudice as regards the nigger and the Arab is racism of contempt; it is a racism which minimizes what it hates. Bourgeoisie ideology, however, manages to appear logical in its own eyes by inviting the sub-men to become human, and to take as their prototype Western humanity as incarnated in the Western bourgeoisie."[48] Although the Ex-Coloured Man wonders whether he is going back to help those he considers his people (black people) or to distinguish himself, he concludes that music offers him a better future. Leaving his "friend" (father), he believes that, except for his mother, the millionaire, or the master-slave relationship, has been the greatest influence in his life.

Having the appearance, education, and tastes of a white man, the Ex-Coloured Man embarks on a brief journey that will permanently position him in white society and enhance his white profile. There are critical aspects to this passage into whiteness. First, he interacts with those individuals who either offer no serious challenge to white supremacy or who openly support it. His attraction to these individuals reveals that he consistently views "life as an outsider might and constantly reverts to white values, attitudes, and responses."[49] Second, the lynching and burning of his "dark double" has a traumatic effect on him. Third, his desire for permanent socioeconomic security becomes a mission. Finally, the Ex-Coloured Man's marriage to a white woman completes his embrace of whiteness. All these aspects convey the circular thought pattern of our protagonist and the narrative structure of *The Autobiography of an Ex-Coloured Man*. This thought pattern (which recalls his behavior with the cow) can be defined as movement from problem perception, away from problem solution (down a diversionary path), and back again to problem perception. Of course, the enduring problem remains: his heritage of blackness in a world dominated by whiteness.

Aboard the ship returning to New York, he meets a black man who has a racial philosophy that makes the Ex-Coloured Man comfortable because it is benign. Like our narrator, this individual is an upper-class, well-educated, sophisticated, and self-centered Negro. His racial philosophy can be summed up as: "I don't object to anyone having prejudices so long as those prejudices don't interfere with my personal liberty" (110). The Ex-Coloured Man views him as the "broadest-minded colored man" concerning the "Negro" question and the race problem. While with this individual in Washington, the Ex-Coloured Man meets and is impressed by black people of education, culture, and means. Here, with an objective tone, expressing white values and beliefs, he theorizes on the adaptability of Negroes: "I have seen the black West Indian gentleman in London, and he is in speech and manners a perfect Englishman. I have seen natives of Haiti and Martinique in Paris, and they are more Frenchy than a Frenchman. I have no doubt that the Negro would make a good Chinaman, with exception of the pigtail" (112). Despite the last tongue-in-cheek comparison, the Ex-Coloured Man views black people mainly in relation to whites. Black people's ability to mimic and mirror the "speech and manners" of whites is very often the criterion for viewing them in a positive light. This cultural imposition and cognitive dissonance (the inability to hold two opposing viewpoints at one time), as Fanon points out, represents the legacy of black people's having internalized white people's belief that blacks are inferior. The Ex-Coloured Man represents an excellent example of the fact that, too often, as Fanon aptly argues, "The black man wants to be like the white man. For the black man there is only one destiny. And it is white."[50] The Ex-Coloured Man, in combat with his own image and having been the "slave" of his two white masters, has enslaved himself in an ideology of Euro-American white supremacy.

This internalization of white supremacy leads the protagonist to conclude that black men marry light-complexioned women and dark women of "stronger mental endowment" marry light-complexioned men not because of inferiority but out of "economic necessity." Or, as he paraphrases, "Have a white skin, and all things else may be added unto you" (113). For some black people who are trying to escape economic violence under white domination, economic agency as it intersects with the "lack of color" becomes the critical factor for material success in America.

The protagonist's "lack of color" transforms him into a sterile Homer Plessy figure as he silently passes for white on a Jim Crow train traveling from Nashville to Atlanta. Making this analogy, Eric J. Sundquist states: "Homer Plessy incarnated the absurd limits to which respect of the color line might be taken in the fact that he himself was also light enough to pass for white, so light that he had to announce to the conductor that he was black so as to test the train car law. Unlike Homer Plessy, Johnson's protagonist does not publicly announce that he is black."[51] As a racial voyeur, he listens to a "fat Jewish-looking man," a professor from Ohio, an old Union soldier, and a Texas cotton planter discuss race and the "Negro question." The Jewish man, realizing that "to sanction Negro oppression would be to sanction Jewish oppression," straddles the racial fence; the professor's position is that of the apologetic coward; the soldier stands "firmly on the ground of equal rights and opportunity to all men"; and the Texan, "fierce, eloquent, and profane in his argument," is a devout racist who believes "anything—no country at all—is better than having niggers over you" (116–117). Johnson, returning to the racism and nationalism theme, uses this "smoking-car argument" to convey that the white man's sexual fears (miscegenation or black male corporeality) are at the root of white supremacy. The Texan asks the soldier the critical questions "Do you want to see a mulatto South? To bring it right home to you, would you let your daughter marry a nigger?" (119). At this point, the soldier and the Texan are in agreement. Ironically, the protagonist, pretending to be white, has contempt for the timid professor, but, not surprisingly, he admires the crudely racist Texan: "Yet I must confess that underneath it all I felt a certain sort of admiration for the man who could not be swayed from what he held as his principle. Contrasted with him, the young Ohio professor was indeed a pitiable character" (120–121). Again, his cowed behavior is that of a "psychological sellout" who has not changed from his adolescent days when he called black people "niggers."

Again, as a voyeur and a "psychological sellout" at the site of the lynching and burning of his "dark double," the Ex-Coloured Man expresses contempt not for the demonic white males engaged in this heinous crime but for the victim. As if hypnotized and powerless to take his eyes from what he does not want to see, our voyeur watches "a man only in form and stature, every sign of degeneracy stamped upon his countenance" (136). By aptly not revealing the "crime" for which this black man is being tortured, Johnson lets us surmise that miscegenation or the "rape" of a white woman is the possible reason. Drawing a crowd of white men, women, and children, with black people in the background, the fiendish ritual makes its sacrifice to the sanctions of white supremacy. This situation is foreshadowed by our protagonist's stammering response of "Well, only one," in Paris when asked about the lynching and burning of black people. Both voyeur and victim are "stunned and stupefied." With the awful stench of burnt flesh—human flesh—in his nostrils, the Ex-Coloured Man confesses:

> A great wave of humiliation and shame swept over me. *Shame that I belonged to a race that could be so dealt with; and shame for my country, that it, the great example of democracy to the world, should be the only civilized, if not the only state on earth, where a human being would be burned alive.* My heart turned bitter within me. I could understand why Negroes are led to sympathize with even their worst criminals and to protect them whenever possible. By all the impulses of normal human nature they can and should do nothing less. (137; emphasis added)

As an "expert" in sociological analysis and the art of psychological projection, the Ex-Coloured Man has no sympathy for the nameless black victim and no outrage at the white men transformed from human beings into savage beasts. Furthermore, his cowed performance is all the more ironic because the Ku Klux Klan as a whole are a bunch of cowards who, masked in white robes and hoods, ride around at night and attack only if the numbers are heavily in their favor. His humiliation and "shame at being identified with a people that could with impunity be treated worse than animals" (139) serve as the catalyst for his assuming a white identity. And, like his spineless father, the Ex-Coloured Man, chained to his father's shame, deserts blackness for the enhanced possibilities that whiteness will bring.

Having crossed over, the Ex-Coloured Man, his mind colonized and socialized to live a luxuriant lifestyle, views affluence and wealth as being analogous to whiteness: "I had made up my mind that since I was not going to be a Negro, I would avail myself of every possible opportunity to make a white man's success; and that, if it can be summed up in any one word, means 'money'" (141). Although the text is not explicit, Johnson's language suggests that the protagonist becomes a white slumlord who profits from lower-class black people. Living some white men's nightmare, the Ex-Coloured Man, like John Warwick in Chesnutt's novel, who boasts about enslaved blacks, frequently smiles at the racist and pejorative remarks directed at "people of color" and says he returns home laughing "heartily over what struck me as the capital joke I was playing" (144).

This "joke" turns into a serious matter and the ultimate gamble when he becomes attracted to another white woman. His description of her reveals how deeply embedded the iconography of whiteness has been internalized: "she was almost tall and quite slender, with lustrous yellow hair and eyes so blue as to appear almost black. She was as white as a lily, and she was dressed in white. Indeed, she seemed to me the most dazzlingly white thing I had ever seen" (144). Johnson's diction suggests that the protagonist has been thoroughly indoctrinated by a white racist standard of beauty.[52] Yet, despite the woman's resplendent whiteness, our chameleon claims that it is her voice that attracts him. With visions of the blonde, blue-eyed, and "dazzling white thing" dancing in his head, our protagonist's desire for her escalates. Like John Warwick, the Ex-Coloured Man fears that his blackness will be found out as his nonchalance and his careless attitude as a white man fade away. His bravado in masquerading fades as his fears of committing miscegenation escalate. And his fears are realized when, in the company of his "dazzling white thing," he encounters his old friend Shiny. Sharp-witted and perceptive, Shiny, instantly realizing that his friend is passing for white, "let drop no word that would have aroused suspicion as to the truth" (148). This reinforces the aspect that other black people are facilitators in this masquerade of passing.

Ironically, it is Shiny's secrecy and silence that give the Ex-Coloured Man the courage to reveal not only his devotion for his white thing but the truth of his black heritage. His black truth is met with a "wild fixed stare" that recalls the repulsive transformation in George Tyrone's image of Rena Walden and that makes the Ex-Coloured Man feel that he "was growing black and thick-featured and crimp-haired" (149). At this point in the narrative, passing for white is no longer a capital joke, a thrill, a revenge on white folks, or a diabolical desire. Love is at stake. Yet, this masking or masklike face has its cost. As the literary scholar Karla F. C. Holloway asserts, a result of self-negating masking is that "we actually, and perversely, privilege the gaze of others. The bodies that emerge when others control our images are disfigured and fragmented."[53]

After weeks of anguishing separation, our miscegenation lovers meet at a party, and, while he is playing Chopin's Thirteenth Nocturne, she whispers his Christian name and three times vows her love for our chameleon. When he sits by his love, and "involuntarily clos[es] it [the Nocturne] with the major triad," the Ex-Coloured Man completely reverses the paradigm of his "particular fondness for the black keys" (5). It is here our Ex-Coloured Man "involuntarily" plays Chopin in the major triad instead of the minor key, using only white keys instead of black ("nigger") keys (152). Abandoning blackness, whiteness has claimed his soul. With visions of the "dazzling white thing" still dancing in his head, the protagonist moves forward with plans of marriage. The marriage of miscegenation, void of the mimicry and masquerade, is analogous to a high-stakes gamble that recalls the Ex-Coloured Man's experience shooting craps, where he recklessly reverses the Hamlet-like paradigm: "Whether it was my [gambling] companion's suggestion or some latent dare-devil strain in my blood which suddenly sprang into activity I do not know; but with a thrill of excitement which went through my whole body I threw a twenty-dollar bill on the table and said in a trembling voice: 'I fade you'" (69). This dare-devil-like marriage produces first a daughter and then a son, with his mother's eyes and features, whose life results in his mother's death. The significance of the Ex-Coloured Man's focusing on these features reveals his hidden anguish about producing a dark-skinned child. Many individuals who pass for white either make a decision not to have children or live in terror during the whole nine months of pregnancy, fearing the birth of a dark-skinned child. Like John Warwick in *The House Behind the Cedars,* the Ex-Coloured Man is extremely fortunate that his progeny don't expose his black ancestry. His wife's death produces, for the first time, more heartfelt yet comic self-criticism and analysis: "Sometimes it seems to me that I have never been a Negro, that I have been only a privileged spectator of their inner life; at other times I feel that I have been a coward, a deserter, and I am possessed by a strange longing for my mother people" (153).

By identifying himself as a coward and a deserter, he profoundly confirms the paradigm of enticing the cow with the molasses-smeared bread and drawing back as the cow approached. Concerning his longing for his blackness, he accurately compares men like Booker T. Washington and "small and selfish" white men like himself. While some black men are transforming history, he makes a little money. True to the Faustian paradigm, his "fast yellowing manuscripts" (ragtime piano music as a representation of a mulatto culture) illustrate that he has sold his soul for a flawed gold coin, a coin that symbolizes his counterfeit, shallow, materialistic white lifestyle. Like those of his "dark double," the Ex-Coloured Man's desires (tragically and ironically) have been symbolically "castrated" and reduced to a "mess of pottage." As a mulatto living incognito in a white world, viewing himself through white eyes and trapped by white values and beliefs, our chameleon becomes an alienated outsider. And, like the trickster figure and quick-change artist

William Douglas Street, in the film *Chameleon Street,* who at the end of the film is led away by police in handcuffs (his wife informs the authorities), the Ex-Coloured Man becomes psychologically imprisoned by the invisible but nevertheless real walls that separate white people from black people. Thus, like Prometheus chained in the Caucasus Mountains, the Ex-Coloured Man becomes chained, in this case to whiteness, but, unlike Prometheus, who is freed by Heracles, our protagonist's psyche experiences the pain caused by the cowardly and shameful betrayal of his blackness. Tricked by his own guile, the Ex-Coloured Man is sapped dry of his mother's musical legacy and of the music in his soul.

James Weldon Johnson's *The Autobiography of an Ex-Coloured Man* goes against the grain of the literary tradition of the stereotypical "tragic mulatto" paradigm[54] in its point of view, its genre, its highlighting of the connection between passing and cultural productions, and in its intertextual resonances. Johnson's irony and chameleonlike language convey the too tragic reality that black people are living in, to use Toni Morrison's expression, a "star-spangled and race strangled"[55] America. Like his literary predecessor, James Weldon Johnson indicts the doctrine of white supremacy and indicates that, too often for black people seeking agency, the American promise (dream) is a worthless prevarication.

More specific, as evidenced by the Ex-Coloured Man's "fast yellowing (mulatto) manuscripts,"[56] Johnson's examination of the passing phenomenon illustrates that when black people go over to the white side, black culture is threatened with extinction. In essence, the Ex-Coloured Man has crossed over and can never get back; his behavior is a tragic betrayal of his black heritage. Using ragtime music as a metaphor for the other three unique cultural expressions of blackness (the Uncle Remus stories, the spirituals or slave songs, and the Cakewalk), Johnson explicates the danger of black people's giving up their cultural heritage for the individualistic, shallow, and often narcissistic reward of assuming a white identity. When black people retain their racial identity, they permanently add their unique and improvisational cultural or "black gifts" to America. And, as James Weldon Johnson astutely argues, "No people that has produced great literature and art has ever been looked upon by the world as distinctly inferior."[57] Johnson implicitly suggests that black people's cultural productions—ragtime music and the slave songs, among others—represent a profound challenge to the often rigid and racist structures of identity politics.

4

THE TRAGIC BLACK BUCK
Jay Gatsby's Passing in F. Scott Fitzgerald's The Great Gatsby

*Memory is a selection of images, some illusive, others printed indelibly on the
brain. Each image is like a thread; each thread woven together to make a tapestry
of intricate texture and the tapestry tells a story and the story is our past.*
— KOSI LEMMONS, DIRECTOR, *Eve's Bayou* (1997)

In this chapter, I intend to make you think about a timeless and widely read novel as
you never have before. F. Scott Fitzgerald's *The Great Gatsby* (1925) tragically explores the paradoxical theme of racial passing: the phenomenon of pale blacks passing for white. Although the class and ethnic tensions in the novel are lucid, literary
scholars have not considered the theme of racial passing. Indeed, the narrative constantly whispers the presence of blackness. Fitzgerald's extravagant protagonist and
antihero Jay Gatsby is the manifestation of his creator's deep-seated apprehensions
concerning miscegenation between blacks and whites, in that Fitzgerald, writing
about the quest for the American Dream, guilefully characterizes Jay Gatsby as a
"pale" black individual who passes for white. By skillfully doing this, Fitzgerald illustrates how intrinsically American literature and the American Dream are racial,
because the construction of whiteness (white privilege and white property) and
socioeconomic prosperity are often predicated on the elimination of blackness. Accordingly, considering America's violent history of racial exploitation and exclusion, who better to define the American Dream and the pursuit of happiness than a
fabulously wealthy light-skinned black individual who is passing for white?

Toni Morrison's literary investigation highlights the sagacious play and critical importance of blackness in white American literature in general and in the narrative strategies and idiom of white American writers such as Edgar Allan Poe, Herman Melville, Willa Cather, and Ernest Hemingway in particular. Morrison argues that "the black presence is central to any understanding of our national literature and should not be permitted to hover at the margins of the literary imagination."[1] While Morrison does not consider Fitzgerald specifically, her study encourages us to see the play of race in most American literature. Not surprisingly, in *The Great Gatsby,* Fitzgerald plays in the dark and plays with the dark, and through Fitzgerald's discourse, Gatsby's "pale" body becomes raced with blackness. Fitzgerald hints, via Gatsby's real name, Jimmy Gatz, that he is part German;[2] in addition, his father, Henry C. Gatz, comes to New York City from a small town in Minnesota to bury his lost son. Even before this racial or ethnic revelation, significant narrative evidence indicates that Jay Gatsby is tragically and comically characterized with regard to black individuals and cultural representations of blackness.[3] These characterizations move us toward conceptualizing Jay Gatsby's blackness more than any other racial or ethnic identity.

Light-skinned or pale black individuals involved in racial passing abound in American literature. The desire for invisibility, the desire to perform "whiteness," resides at the center of the black individual's flight from his or her own body. Jay Gatsby's representation in the novel as a pale passing figure mirrors those of the chameleons John (Walden) Warwick, the nameless Ex-Coloured Man, found respectively in Charles Waddell Chesnutt's *The House Behind the Cedars* (1900) and James Weldon Johnson's *The Autobiography of an Ex-Coloured Man* (1912). Equally significant, Fitzgerald's racial, psychological, and behavioral characterizations of Jay Gatsby foreshadow those of the esoteric bootlegger Joe Christmas in William Faulkner's *Light in August* (1932). In these novels, characterizations of skin color, hair texture, physical features, and language are crucial signals associated with pale black individuals who pass as white.

Like Faulkner, Fitzgerald characterizes Jay Gatsby as a dangerous and impertinent pale black individual; to use his extremist diction, Gatsby represents a black "buck." *The Great Gatsby's* tragic conclusion conveys the protagonist's disappearance in the novel or the possibility of "aphansis," which Jacques Lacan defines in *The Four Fundamental Concepts of Psycho-Analysis* as the disappearance of the subject behind the signifier. Here the racial signifier is "buck," a word that within white supremacist discourse figures the black man as a sexual menace. The sexually racist term signifies a territory between human and animal and thus eschews specificity even while marking it. By closely examining Fitzgerald's signifying play of race, color, and diction, we discover that Jay Gatsby represents a buck of an "indeterminate breed" and is constantly defined as a treacherous threat to the sacred notion of white "purity."[4] Within the captious context of Nordic superiority, black people, Jewish people, and even white immigrants from southeastern Europe are labeled the Other. Yet, within this xenophobic framework, the interracial conflict becomes most climactic when it involves pale black individuals who, by passing for white, threaten white superiority. Essentially, beyond its class and ethnic stratifications, *The Great Gatsby* raises critical questions about racial identity. Thus, my argument here is that, although Jay Gatsby advances himself in terms of socioeconomic subjectivity, he is more significantly characterized as a dangerous "pale" individual, culturally, socially, and legally designated as black, who attempts to pass himself off as a sophisticated and very wealthy white individual. Accordingly, in this inquiry, *The Great Gatsby* represents a timeless narrative of racial passing.

As historical documents and the narratives of passing demonstrate, the possibility of black individuals passing themselves off as white is quite significant. F. James Davis explains that "Passing as white probably reached an all time peak between 1880 and 1925."[5] Repressive Jim Crow political and socioeconomic forces during this period were the primary impetus that led countless numbers of light-skinned black individuals to assume a white identity, either temporarily or permanently. In order for light-skinned blacks to pass as white and to perform whiteness, it is often necessary for them to change their names, to prevaricate, and to deny their families, their culture, and their history. By a paradoxical definition, when black individuals assume a white identity, they challenge the sacrosanct ideology of white supremacy while revealing the fallacy of the social, political, and legal constructions of race. In American society, pale blacks who pass for white represent an extreme example of upward mobility; yet, passing means a denial of blackness even if the individual is not black. For a pale black individual who passes for white, then, "race is always already experienced as a construction, as a performance in which a person self-consciously creates her [or his] own race, as an act of existential self-affirmance, in some specified relation with others."[6]

This paradox of racial provocation and racial pretense suggests the Horatio Alger–like possibilities inherent in the American Dream, a dream that too often implies that becoming an American is quintessentially a masquerade, an impersonation, and an act of self-invention. Consequently, the phenomenon of racial passing is a complex paradigm of identity formation in which individuals of mixed racial ancestry attempt to position themselves within the dominant white supremacist culture. In fact, passing becomes a metaphor for attaining the American Dream.

Like Charles Waddell Chesnutt, who writes about passing and who occasionally passed for white himself, F. Scott Fitzgerald intimately knows the tragedies and the possibilities of an individual who assumes another identity, because Fitzgerald's life was itself a passing narrative. Robert Westbrook relates that Fitzgerald confided in a friend that Sheilah Graham had sobbingly revealed to him that she was "part Jewish" and that Fitzgerald had sympathized with her because

> *as an Irish Catholic at Princeton he knew exactly what it was like to be a despised minority and he hated the whole business. Like Sheilah he had done his best to pass.* With a wardrobe full of Brooks Brothers suits and enough fame as the top American novelist, he had hoped to slip in among the beautiful people—Ginevra King's [Fitzgerald's wealthy and self-absorbed lover while he was at Princeton] world of country club dances. He longed for an Episcopalian heaven where there were no strange words or smells or foreign rituals that set a person apart.[7] (emphasis added)

However, despite Fitzgerald's dreams of a raceless religious realm and his sympathy for Jewish people, he often expresses anti-Semitic and xenophobic attitudes. Westbrook divulges that "There was an old vein in Scott which disliked foreign people. 'I hated Italians once. Jews too,' he confided to a friend in 1935. 'Mostly foreigners. Mostly my fault like everything else. Now I only hate myself.' But with a few glasses of gin, this self-hatred could easily turn outward."[8] Along with his anti-Semitic, nativist, and xenophobic judgments, Fitzgerald expressed decidedly anti-immigration and white supremacist sentiments. Seizing his imperative duty, in a letter to his close friend, Edmund Wilson, Fitzgerald wrote:

> God damn the continent of Europe. . . . Rome is only a few years behind Tyre and Babylon. *The negroid streak creeps northward to defile the Nordic race. Already, the Italians have the souls of blackamoors.* Raise the bars of immigration and permit only Scandinavians, Teutons, Anglo-Saxons and Celts to enter. . . . My reactions were all philistine, anti-Socialist, provincial and racially snobbish. I believe at last in the white man's burden. We are as far above the modern Frenchman as he is above the Negro. [9]
> (emphasis added)

Fitzgerald's racist notion of Nordic superiority echoes Madison Grant's argument in *The Passing of the Great Race or the Basis of European History* (1916). Grant's argument defines the Nordic people of northwestern Europe as being superior to the inferior southern and eastern races of the Alpine and Mediterranean regions and, worst of all, the Jews.[10] Fundamental to Grant's argument is the idea that Western civilization was in a state of incipient decline due to excessive emphasis on materialism and the presence of nonwhites. Implicit in Grant's fear of the passing of the great race was racial passing within the great white race. Also, James R. Mellow reveals that "In his [F. Scott Fitzgerald's] private notes, more often than not, he referred to them [black people] as niggers."[11] Like those of Ernest Hemingway, F. Scott Fitzgerald's Nordic, white supremacist, and white nationalist perspectives were not unique in his time.

We discover in a revealing letter to John O'Hara that, along with his racism, F. Scott Fitzgerald engaged in a Du Boisian self-analysis, affirming his own dual breeding:

> *I am half black Irish and half old American stock with the usual exaggerated pretensions.* The black Irish half of the family had the money and looked down on the Maryland side of the family who had, and really had, that certain series of reticences and obligations that go under the poor old shattered word "breeding" (modern form "inhibitions"). So being born in that atmosphere of crack, wisecrack and countercrack I developed a two-cylinder inferiority complex. So if I were King of Scotland tomorrow after graduating from Eton, Magdalene to guards, with an embryonic history which tied me to the Plantagenets, I would still be a parvenu. I spent my youth in alternately crawling in front of kitchen maids and insulting the great.[12] (emphasis added)

Fitzgerald's description of his own miscegenation genealogy (a midwesterner of Irish and southern origin), or his own "blackness,"[13] suggests the racist discourse where Irish people were often characterized as "white Negroes" or "white niggers." As Vincent J. Cheng argues, the "racial comparison most frequently and insistently made about the Irish during the latter half of the nineteenth-century was with 'Negroes,' especially with Bushmen and Hottentots, generally perceived as the lowest rung on the scale of human races, just barely above apes."[14] Perhaps Fitzgerald's latent racial anxieties and inferiority complex also stem from his relationship to white supremacist culture's preoccupation with its God-given mission, to uphold the racial purity of the old-plantation South.

However, as a literary trickster figure, writing through his racial anxieties, Fitzgerald subverts and deconstructs the dominant white discourse by playing in and with darkness. Considering this phenomenon, Morrison aptly reasons:

> Encoded or explicit, indirect or overt, the linguistic responses to an Africanist presence complicate texts, sometimes contradicting them entirely. A writer's response to American Africanism often provides a subtext that either sabotages the surface text's expressed intentions or escapes them through a language that mystifies what it cannot bring itself to articulate but still attempts to register.[15]

This literary subversion occurs because, despite Fitzgerald's xenophobia, he understands the "rotten" nature of white supremacy, characterized by the vile contempt and moral mendacity of Tom and Daisy Buchanan; he recognizes the limitations and the flagitious absurdities of America's white supremacist culture.

The limitations associated with race are powerfully on display in Fitzgerald's short story "The Offshore Pirate" (1920), a clandestine narrative of racial passing that foreshadows *The Great Gatsby*.

In Fitzgerald's racial characterizations of Gatsby, one feels his own ostracism, passing, and racial anxiety, and these aspects might explain why the characteristics he ascribes to Jay Gatsby are associated with those of a pale black man passing for white. Unlike William Faulkner, who writes in *Light in August* rather unsympathetically about the enigmatic parchment-colored character Joe Christmas, F. Scott Fitzgerald's characterizations of Jay Gatsby, while mysterious, are sympathetic. Jay Gatsby and Joe Christmas, with their histories of family abandonment and poverty, represent everything that is strange, threatening, and Other. On this point, Fitzgerald acknowledges that he "never at any one time saw him [Jay Gatsby] clear myself—for he started as one man I knew and then changed into myself—the amalgam was never complete in my mind."[16] Considering the composition and complexion of the novel, Fitzgerald's signifying use of the word "amalgam" suggests the amalgamation of blacks and whites through miscegenation, the site where racial identity and national identity are either constructed or deconstructed. Textually, Fitzgerald's physical descriptions of Gatsby are equally vague and enigmatic; in fact, Fitzgerald occasionally describes Gatsby as "pale," making his racial identity rather ambiguous. However, as we shall see, the strong possibility exists that Fitzgerald's subversive textuality makes Gatsby into the signifying metaphor of difference, a version of the stock fictional character of the "high-yellow" mulatto who passes for white. As in many narratives of racial passing, Fitzgerald's characterizations of Jay Gatsby's racial ambiguity are also compounded by the matrix of class and gender ambiguity.

F. Scott Fitzgerald places *The Great Gatsby* in New York City during the summer of 1922. This is a dazzling world of the Jazz Age, the Roaring Twenties, and the Boom.[17] Further, as symbolized by the Harlem Renaissance and characterized by black artists and writers who challenge white hegemony and celebrate their blackness, this is a time of enthralling socioeconomic possibilities for blacks. Jay Gatsby as a wealthy black individual exemplifies Ralph Ellison's phrase that the Renaissance captures "the Harlemness of the American predicament." Moreover, Nathan Irvin Huggins points out, "The aura of the postwar decade, epitomized in F. Scott Fitzgerald's 'younger generation' and the Jazz Age, was reflected among negro intellectuals too. They created the 'New Negro.'"[18] Also, Juda Bennett explains: "In many ways, F. Scott Fitzgerald categorizes this emergent discourse [the performing of America through blackness] by labeling the twenties as the Jazz Age—or that period which performs Americanness through black music. To allow for this close reading we must reconnect 'jazz'—which in the teens and twenties had various meanings—to blackness."[19] Fitzgerald connects the improvisational playfulness of jazz music to blackness through Jay Gatsby's romantic desire for Daisy Buchanan.

Along with the Jazz Age and the Harlem Renaissance, this period follows the bloody Red Hot Summer of 1919 when membership in the Ku Klux Klan, a nativist group, was at its peak; the Klan helped pass restrictive legislation that slowed immigration to a trickle. In 1924, the Johnson-Reed Act excluded immigrants of African descent from entry to the United States. This period was also the era of the eugenics movement, whose central claim was that "race and woman must not be left to their own devices."[20] Hence, this was an extremely race- and gender-charged atmosphere in which black people especially were subjected to the pervasive physical, psychological, and socioeconomic violence of America's white supremacist culture.

In *The Great Gatsby*, Jay Gatsby reinvents himself in a clandestine attempt to recreate the past and to embrace the American Dream, as symbolized by his desire for the seemingly white and very wealthy Daisy Buchanan. Not having the resources to marry Daisy, Gatsby attains vast wealth through criminal activities and later attempts to woo her from her husband, Tom. Fitzgerald astutely characterizes Daisy as America itself, with her voice "full of money," with "the kind of voice that the ear follows up and down as if each speech is an arrangement of notes that will never be played again . . . there was an excitement in her voice that men who had cared for her found difficult to forget."[21] Like America's "fresh green breast," Daisy's voice is full of promise. On the other hand, Gatsby is a praetorian dreamer, and "the golden girl," Daisy, is his praetorian object of desire. Simply put, Daisy stimulates his desire; like the Sirens, Daisy is a femme fatale who eventually lures the enraptured Gatsby to his doom. What I am about to argue is that the quality of concealment in *The Great Gatsby* is skillful enough to have caused most people to read over scenes that should be read through. By first examining F. Scott Fitzgerald's narrative structure of racial class discourse directed at Jay Gatsby and then examining his relationship to the presence of blackness and to the theme of miscegenation, we can uncover Fitzgerald's subversive characterizations, codes, and constructs of Jay Gatsby as a great American literary figure of racial passing.

Early in *The Great Gatsby*, Tom Buchanan, as a provocateur for the eugenics movement, the anti-immigration movement, and the Ku Klux Klan, theorizes about the book *The Rise of the Colored Empires* by a man named "Goddard" and superciliously affirms to the participant-narrator, Nick Carraway, Jordan Baker, and his wife, Daisy Buchanan, that, "[t]his fellow has worked out the whole thing. *It's up to us who are the dominant race to watch out or those other races will have control of things.* . . . This idea is that we're Nordics. I am and you are and you are and—" After an infinitesimal hesitation he includes Daisy: "*—and we've produced all the things that go to make civilization—oh science and art and all that*" (17–18; emphasis added). The actual text Tom refers to is *The Rising Tide of Color Against White World Supremacy*, by Lothrop Stoddard, published in New York in 1920. Its supremacist thesis is that superior white men must come together to challenge the threat posed by black, brown, red, and yellow people. Although the source of Tom Buchanan's tremendous wealth is never ascertained, he makes it quite certain that he intends to do anything necessary to maintain his wealth, which is associated with his white privilege and whiteness as property. With his boundless wealth, Tom embodies the absolutely brutal power and brassy arrogance of America's white supremacist culture.

Fitzgerald's use of the name "Goddard" is both literal and figurative. Like the author Lothrop Stoddard, Henry H. Goddard was a white eugenicist who believed that the "grade of intelligence or mental level for each individual is determined by the chromosomes that come together . . . any later influence. . . . Any attempt at social adjustment which fails to take into account the determining character of the intelligence and its unalterable grade in each individual is illogical and inefficient."[22] This hegemonic discourse posits black people as inherently inferior to whites. Figuratively, the name God[dard] signals a synthesis between the psychological violence of the tide of white world supremacy and the white religious discourse used to validate it. Accordingly, Tom's stoic diatribe not only portrays him as a pretentious individual; Fitzgerald also foreshadows Tom's ardent anxiety about miscegenation. Of course, the primary objective of miscegenation laws and lynch laws was to prevent sexual relations between black men and white women. Last, Tom's racial discourse of domination and dismissal serves two narrative functions. First, Tom's arrogant hyperbole characterizes him as a white supremacist patriarch. Second, Fitzgerald ingeniously foreshadows a pale-skinned crossover, Jay Gatsby ("those other races"), as representing the narrative's critical racial tension and the racial threat to Tom Buchanan's fabulously wealthy white kingdom, personified by his seemingly Nordic wife, Daisy Buchanan. Thus, this early scene constructs the binary of whiteness and blackness.

In order to emphasize racial constructions and racial epistemology, F. Scott Fitzgerald plays with the rhythms, tones, and colors associated with time, place, and characterizations. Fitzgerald aptly marks his characters through what Meyer Shapiro identifies as "the intrinsic powers of colors and lines rather than through the imaging of facial expressions."[23] In a scene involving Tom Buchanan, Nick Carraway, and Myrtle Wilson, we discover Fitzgerald foreshadowing racial ambiguity with class and gender ambiguity. Here, Myrtle asks Tom to stop the automobile in order to buy a "police dog" from a street peddler. The old man selling the dogs, who "bore an absurd resemblance to John D. Rockefeller," suggests that the brown and white dog of an "indeterminate breed" that he gives to Myrtle is "more of an airdale" (32). An Airedale is actually a large terrier that has a wiry, black-and-tan coat. When Myrtle asks what the gender of the dog is, the old man responds that the dog is a "boy," but Tom with his taxonomic gaze (an obsession with categorizing and classifying human types and assigning a moral/intellectual hierarchy) inspects the hybrid dog and presumptuously and decisively declares: "It's a bitch." Realizing that he is being charged to excess and after giving him ten dollars, Tom tells the old man, "Go and buy ten more dogs with it" (32). The suggestion here is that that the old man misrepresents himself and the source of his income. This scene foreshadows Jay Gatsby's misrepresenting his genealogy and his wealth as a fraudulent John D. Rockefeller. With Tom Buchanan's lawyerlike investigation, the mongrel dog becomes defined as a "bitch," as Jay Gatsby will become defined as a "black" individual of an "indeterminate breed."

Fitzgerald describes Daisy Buchanan, unlike Jay Gatsby, in relationship to sophistication and wealth, but most especially in relation to representations of whiteness. Early in the novel, Jordan Baker (whose phallocentric name connotes gender ambiguity) and Daisy Buchanan "were both in white and their dresses were rippling and fluttering as if they had just been blown back in after a short flight around the house" (12). Later, they "lay upon an enormous couch, like silver idols, weighing down their own white dresses against the singing breeze of the fans" (122). Like a white Southern belle, Daisy Fay relates that, before her relationship with Tom Buchanan, her "white girlhood" was passed with Jordan Baker in Louisville, Kentucky; while dating Jay Gatsby in Louisville, Daisy Fay, who "dressed in white and had a white roadster," was quite popular with young officers. Here, Fitzgerald's numerous descriptions of Daisy's whiteness give her an agency of innocence and virginal purity that are wonderfully expansive and seductive. However, except for her "dark shining hair" and her "white face" (117), Daisy is amorphous, indistinct; she is representative and desired. Whereas Gatsby is never characterized by anything white, Daisy, an absurdly vacuous character, becomes the enduring but problematical metaphor and mimetic representation of whiteness.

Although Daisy represents whiteness, Tom's tendentious and taxonomic discourse raises uncertainty about Daisy's racial purity and insinuates her racial ambiguity when he includes Nick Carraway and Jordan Baker in his Nordic world of white superiority but only after "an infinitesimal hesitation" includes Daisy. This "infinitesimal hesitation" guilefully suggests that Daisy may be tainted with non-Nordic Otherness; her racial ambiguity and the "pale magic of her face" (160) foreshadow Gatsby's blackness. Daisy, with her Southern heritage, also slyly suggests miscegenation possibilities when she tells Nick that "I've been everywhere and seen everything and done everything" (22). In a period exemplified by a free-wheeling approach to sex, we wonder if there is a racially sexual connotation to this statement, especially when Daisy, describing her daughter, Pammy, states, "She doesn't look like her father" (123). Daisy's statement reinforces Tom's horror of miscegenation between blacks and whites. In America, miscegenation conveys that individuals are too often caught between two races that sometimes combine and sometimes clash. Despite his numerous adulterous relationships and his explosive sexual tryst with Myrtle Wilson, who lives desperately and dies in "the valley of ashes," Tom is arrogantly committed to maintaining domination over his presumably pristine household where white supremacy and depraved moral values reside.

Daisy's names hold an interesting racial possibility, because daisies are flowers that have mixed colors. In terms of Fitzgerald's naming of Daisy Buchanan, according to *Webster's International Dictionary* a "nigger daisy" is yellow outside and brown inside. The suggestion here is Daisy may also be a product of miscegenation or possibly a light-skinned black woman passing as white. Fitzgerald delicately whispers at this possibility through naming and characterizations. Recalling Fitzgerald's description of Daisy's voice, there is the suggestion that like jazz music her voice has an improvisational character. These textual hints of Daisy's blackness are intensified by her juxtaposition to Gatsby, another passing figure. Although Daisy's maiden name, "Fay" (ofay), from the old French, means "fidelity," the eminent racial and sexual (miscegenation) threat to Tom Buchanan's immense kingdom of whiteness is the nefarious Other, Jay Gatsby. Gatsby will become Tom's hellish Nordic nightmare.

If the performance of racial passing delineates criminality, Fitzgerald's characterizations of Jay Gatsby's illegal activities reinforce this theme. Fitzgerald uses rumors of criminality, bootlegging, and selling of illegal bonds as a mask to explore representations of Gatsby's blackness. Before encountering the racially threatening Jay Gatsby, there are numerous "wild rumors" that suggest that he has been involved in criminal activities, that he has committed murder and even that he is possibly a "nephew or a cousin of Kaiser Wilhelm's" (37) or "a German spy" (48). Gatsby's obsessive-compulsive desire for Daisy reinforces these rumors of criminality. As Amos N. Wilson explains:

> Criminality may heuristically be perceived as a sociological symptom of a society, not unlike as obsessive-compulsive may be considered a psychological symptom of an individual. It may furthermore be perceived, in the classical Freudian sense, as a maladjustive compromise between two or more conflicting forces within a social or societal personality which have not yet been completely integrated.[24]

Despite his wealth, Gatsby lives a fragmented life and can become completely integrated or whole and white only through his marriage to Daisy. Equally important, Wilson's analysis connects Gatsby's criminality to the psychodynamics of passing, where the pale black individual is constantly negotiating between repression and acceptance of two separate racial identities. Moreover, Fitzgerald's characterizations of Gatsby elucidate W. E. B. Du Bois's theory of double consciousness, where a black individual struggles with two masks. Extending Du Bois's analysis, Patricia J. Williams notes: "In its most literal sense the ability to be one person rather than two refers to some resolution of the ethically dangerous position of finding oneself split between the one one is and the one one feels one *has* to be. The sheltered self and the masquerade."[25] For Gatsby, more so than the class tensions exemplified by the characterizations of criminality as an aspect of upward mobility, the conflicting forces within the "societal personality" may involve his racial personality.

Class tensions between East Egg and West Egg reinforce the novel's racial tension. At one of Gatsby's lavish parties or "succession of carnivals"[26] in less fashionable West Egg, we hear: " 'He's a bootlegger,' said the young ladies, moving somewhere between his cocktails and his flowers. 'One time he killed a man who had found out that he was nephew to von Hindenburg, and second cousin to the devil. Reach me a rose, honey, and pour me a last drop into that there crystal glass' " (65). The ambiguity around Gatsby's past behavior mirrors the ambiguity around his racial identity; like a magician, Gatsby creates and projects an illusion. Even better, like an actor with costume and makeup, studied language, accent, and of course, an appropriate stage name, Gatsby attempts a performance of upper-class whiteness. As Stanley Crouch points out, "Jimmy Gatz thought that upper-class identity could easily be achieved through name changes, claims to social pedigrees, expensive accoutrements, and big parties."[27] Also, there is the scuttlebutt that Gatsby is a bootlegger with an "underground pipeline to Canada" (103). Recalling the heroic journey of the former slaves William and Ellen Craft, we hear in this last statement of hearsay an echo of black people's movement from slavery to freedom, an idea in accord with the notion that during Prohibition alcohol was being piped into the United States from Canada. This was an era where gangsters posed as businessmen and ordinary businessmen posed as savvy gangsters. As one historian argues, this was the period of "the bootleggers and the speakeasies, the corruption of police and judiciary, the highjackers and their machine guns, the gang wars, the multimillionaire booze barons, the murders and assassinations, the national breakdown of morals and manners."[28] In a period of intense racial unrest, the national breakdown of morals and manners suggests, among other possibilities, both the horrific taboo of miscegenation (especially black men and white women) and the challenge posed by black people as constitutional aliens seeking socioeconomic agency in a racist white society. Gatsby's luxuriant parties attempt to mask his desire for Daisy and his subsequent threat to the dominant law-abiding white society represented by Tom.

Nick's speculations about Gatsby's genealogy also indicate that he is the nonwhite Other. Although not as arrogant as Tom, Nick contemptuously states: "I would have accepted without question the information that Gatsby sprang from the swamps of Louisiana or from the lower East Side of New York" (54). The site of Louisiana is reinforced when we learn that before she married Tom, Daisy "was presumably engaged to a man from New Orleans" (80). Whereas the lower East

Side of New York suggests mainly poor immigrant whites such as the Irish, Italians, and Jews, Nick's reference to "the swamps of Louisiana" deftly insinuates Gatsby's association with blackness and the jazz music at Gatsby's parties. In fact, here jazz music is the music of the outsider, and who is more outside the American Dream than the black man? Likewise, Fitzgerald's repeated mention of Louisiana reinforces the novel's theme of intraracial breeding as the catalysis to racial passing. In fact, "pasabone" is a Creole word for quadroon, a fair-skinned black individual who in other places could pass for white. As Williard B. Gatewood argues:

> The concept of the three-caste society was perhaps more fully developed in Louisiana and Gulf port cities such as New Orleans than anywhere else in antebellum America. Extramarital unions between European males and black females, in addition to liberal manumission policies under the French and Spanish, resulted in a large population of *gens de couleur libre*. . . . In New Orleans the so-called Creoles of color, who were usually fair complexioned and often identified with French culture, thought of themselves as a caste apart from other blacks.[29]

Despite the racial connotations and the unflattering rumors of Gatsby's involvement in criminal activities, Fitzgerald paints a resplendent picture of individuals who enjoy the splendor and extravagance of Gatsby's parties. But, as Matthew J. Bruccoli notes, "Despite his prodigious faith in money, Gatsby does not know how it works in society and cannot comprehend the arrogance of the rich who have been rich for generations."[30] Accordingly, these exorbitant parties and Jay Gatsby's ostentatious displays of wealth and power mask his immutable desire for Daisy Buchanan as he fails to understand the difference between his new money and Tom Buchanan's old family money. Despite the notable status differences, for both Gatsby and Tom, whiteness is represented by wealth, power, property, and white women.

Gatsby's extravagant parties at West Egg, designed to attract Daisy, reveal the comical aspect of Gatsby's desire for her, all a symbol of his desire for whiteness. Describing the party's atmosphere, Nick concludes that the partygoers at Gatsby's house "conducted themselves according to the rules of behavior associated with amusement parks" (45). It is interesting to note that Nick describes Gatsby's profligate mansion as having "forty acres of lawn and garden" (9). With Gatsby as a passing figure and an extravagant impostor moving from blackness to whiteness, these "forty acres" and a mansion recall the Freedmen's Bureau's tacit promise that the black former slaves would receive "forty acres and a mule." Along with Gatsby's enormous acred mansion, his yellow car, which Tom contemptuously names a "circus wagon," and Gatsby's "pink suit," gold ties, and colorful shirts, Fitzgerald overtly conveys not only the comical characterizations of Gatsby but also depicts him as the shadowy master of ceremonies of the circus-like atmosphere. Like a black actor in whiteface, these descriptions create a minstrel image of Gatsby. It is here that Tom speculates to Nick about the source of Gatsby's enormous wealth: "A lot of these newly rich people are just big bootleggers, you know" (114). Beyond Tom's lawyerlike reference to the unlawful and clandestine production, sale, and transportation of liquor, "bootleg" also connotes a racial imitation, an aberrant and inferior (miscegenation) mix. Accordingly, by definition, Gatsby's illegal activities suggest his racial masquerade. Despite Gatsby's vast wealth, Tom's dissecting master gaze views him as an inferior Other because for Tom, class difference (wealth without pedigree) equals a subordinate status. As the masquerading and bootlegging Gatsby moves closer to whiteness (Daisy), the law-minded and self-righteous Tom will soon turn his speculations into making "a small investigation" into Gatsby's genealogical (racial), class, and sexual background.[31] Obviously, for Tom, with his taxonomic perspective, Gatsby is not who or what he appears to be; Tom rightly senses the absolute danger of Gatsby's desire.

Because racial passing always necessitates prevarication, the orchestration of Gatsby's five-year-long masquerade of attaining boundless wealth to impress Daisy is reinforced by the numerous glaring fabrications that he shares with Nick Carraway. During an automobile ride, Gatsby tells Nick, "I am the son of some wealthy people in the middle-west—all dead now. I was brought up in America but educated at Oxford because all my ancestors have been educated there for many years. It is a family tradition" (69). The word "dead" is significant in that those light-skinned black individuals who pass for white become symbolically "natally dead," with no obligations to their families, their traditions, and their friends. Compounding his psychological projections and pathological prevarications about his family with ignorance, Gatsby answers, "San Francisco," when Nick asks him where in the Midwest his family lived. Gatsby's constant mendaciousness and denials about his family, his education, and his past announce critical stratagems in the performance of passing. At the very least, the performance of passing for white requires a perfected denial and death to one's former black life.

Gatsby cunningly realizes the limits of his performance as symbolized by his impressive, yet unread library. At one of Gatsby's parties, an individual with "owl-eyed spectacles" points out to Nick the realism within Gatsby's masquerade the library represents: "Absolutely real—have pages and everything. I thought they'd be a nice durable cardboard. . . . It's a triumph. What thoroughness! What realism! Knew when to stop too—didn't cut the pages" (50). Paradoxically, the book that this quaint individual picks out echoes Tom's diatribe on Nordic superiority. Nick relates: "Taking our skepticism for granted he rushed to the book cases and returned with Volume One of the 'Stoddard Lectures.'" Of course, the irony of the reference to Lothrop Stoddard is that, out of necessity, many black individuals who pass for white often support and advocate white supremacy. Like the hordes of obscure and famous individuals who come to the parties without invitations, Gatsby's unread library serves only to give him the illusion of formal education, literacy, and white upper-class sophistication. Likewise, the uncut books in the library metaphorically represent Gatsby's concealed ancestry and mask his present illegal activities in bootlegging and bonds. Despite this charade, Gatsby has two important mentors. The pioneer-businessman Dan Cody and the Jewish gambler-criminal Meyer Wolfshiem[32] serve as the counselors and catalysts that propel the chameleon, Gatsby, toward the extraordinary world of upper-echelon whiteness.

Another literary aspect consistent with the racial masquerade is the changing of one's name; like a crude Platonist, Gatsby changes his name from James Gatz to Jay Gatsby at the age of seventeen in preparation for a future with enhanced socioeconomic possibilities. Reflecting the rumors that Gatsby is a murderer, the name change conveys the death of James Gatz. Hence, self-naming creates new possibilities. As Nick narrates, "So he invented just the sort of Jay Gatsby that a seventeen year old boy would be likely to invent, and to this conception he was faithful to the end" (104). Fitzgerald reinforces this concept of self-invention when we discover that the young Jimmy Gatz's daily schedule in the back cover of the book *Hopalong Cassidy* relates: "Practice elocution, poise and how to attain it" and "Study needed inventions" between the hours of 5:00 and 9:00 P.M. (181). Except for the "Work" entry, these two categories represent the longest entries in Gatz's schedule. This youthful desire to invent himself, combined with the present illegal activities, suggests that Gatsby's name change defines his as being fundamentally a risk taker. Moreover, it indicates Gatsby's criminal impersonation in being a "young man without a past" (156). In narratives of passing, black individuals reinvent and rename themselves before they embrace their respective futures, escaping the spirit-crushing environments and abject poverty of their families and name associations. As Ralph Ellison explains: "A people must define itself, and minorities have the responsibility of having their ideals and images recognized as part of the composite image which is that of the still forming American people."[33] Ellison's analysis conveys Gatsby's attempt to transform himself into a composite image of elite whiteness. Soon after the young Gatz attains his "brand new name," he meets the wealthy father figure Dan Cody. Gatsby is transformed into steward, mate, secretary, and skipper on Cody's yacht, the *Tuolomee*. More important, it is on his first voyage with Cody that Gatsby goes to the "West Indies and the Barbary Coast" (106). At this point in the narrative, Fitzgerald guilefully juxtaposes Gatsby with two geographic locations generally associated with blackness.[34] The connotative implication is that although a black individual may clandestinely attempt to transcend his or her racial identity by denial, displacement, and equivocation, racial identity remains. Although a name alone can never solely define a person's racial identity, the naming process operates as the place of empowerment, a place where light-skinned black individuals can repudiate a family prescribed or a socially defined definition and advance themselves to positions of socioeconomic power in a society where whiteness reigns.

Fitzgerald's signifying synthesis of race, color, and diction strongly implies that Gatsby is coming from an impecunious background; Gatsby's insecurities and genealogical denials commence in Louisville, Kentucky, where, as a young soldier he becomes mesmerized by Daisy's untarnished world of wealth and whiteness:

> There [Daisy's home] was a ripe mystery about it, a hint of bedrooms upstairs more beautiful and cool than other bedrooms, of gay and radiant activities taking place through its corridors and of romances that were not musty and laid away already in lavender but fresh and breathing and redolent of this year's shining motor cars and of dances whose flowers were scarcely withered. (155–156)

In this Eden of wonderment, Gatsby's desire for Daisy is an escape from his parents who "were shiftless and unsuccessful farm people," and Gatsby's "imagination never really accepted them as his parents at all" (104). To engage in this absolute denial of one's parents is to deny implicitly who and what one is; by extension, Gatsby denies his identity. Here, Gatsby essentially denies and divorces his "shiftless" parents. This issue of divorce works in a dual manner. Gatsby moves away from his parents and moves toward his desire for whiteness, and, since Daisy is married to Tom, a divorce is necessary for Gatsby to realize his romantic desire. Yet, the tension between divorce and desire foreshadows Gatsby's death. Equally important, within racial discourse the term "shiftless" has often been a pejorative signifier directed at black people. Gatsby's father's first name, "Henry," denotes a "ruler of the home" or "mighty lord." Paradoxically, Gatsby attempts to become what his father's name symbolizes, but his self-inventive aspirations mean rejecting his father because of his slothful behavior and perhaps demeaning class status.

Interestingly, we never learn anything about the race or ethnicity of Jay Gatsby's mother. In a novel with a plethora of uncertainties, this narrative absence enhances the possibility that Gatsby's mother may be black, a nonwhite Other. The absent or deceased parent is a common paradigm found in the novels of racial passing written by Chesnutt, Johnson, Larsen, and Faulkner. Notwithstanding his insecurities concerning his genealogy and his inferior class status, like a desperate criminal, Jay Gatsby, under false pretenses, "took what he could get, ravenously and unscrupulously—eventually he took Daisy Fay one still October night, took her because he had no real right to touch her hand" (156). Here, Fitzgerald's language conveys a sexual assault on the virginal and virtuous Daisy by the nonwhite Other. Gatsby steals Daisy's virginity. Within white supremacist discourse, black men as "bucks" are viewed as ravenous, unscrupulous, and sexually out of control. Like the racial criminal Joe Christmas in William Faulkner's *Light in August*, who masquerades in blackness and whiteness and who is suspected of raping and beheading a white woman, Joanna Burden, this suggestion of criminality, along with the synthesis of genealogy and class differences, inscribes Gatsby as the culturally apprehensive, inferior Other with an added element of parental hatred.

Along with the criminality, Fitzgerald aptly employs music and dance to convey the miscegenation connection between whites and blacks. Jazz music, like ragtime music, is a synthesis of European and African American musical art forms. Nick relates that, when the extravagant parties occur, music constantly comes from Gatsby's house, played by "no thin five piece affair but a whole pit full of oboes and trombones and saxophones and violas and cornets and piccolos and low and high drums" (44). This racial and musical synthesis is made more resounding by Fitzgerald's diction when Nick relates that Gatsby's orchestra plays the jazz-based music named "yellow cocktail music" (44). The author's unique miscegenation musical reference suggests the appropriation of black music as a means of expression that whites themselves might utilize. In fact, the description of Gatsby's wild parties resembles that of goings-on at a sophisticated jook house. As Katrina Hazzard-Gordon describes: "Jooks, honky-tonks, and after-hours joints are secular institutions of social interaction and entertainment, usually associated with some quasi-legal activity such as liquor sales [bootlegging] or gambling."[35] Hence, the color yellow suggests the general theme of something nonwhite, impure, and someone not sanctioned; even more specifically, yellow connotes jazz music, miscegenation, and the novel's subversive theme of the tragic mulatto or high-yellow individual passing for white.

Jay Gatsby's dancing further implies his blackness. Nick's gaze reveals: "Daisy and Gatsby danced. I remember being surprised by his graceful conservative fox-trot—I had never seen him dance before" (112). The fox-trot, as Fitzgerald's suggestive racial analogy of Daisy and Gatsby, is literal and figurative. As Jacqui Malone makes clear: "Urban whites began dancing in new ways in new rhythms, borrowing steps from black Americans and adapting them to their own cultural style. Such European-American dances as the schottische and the waltz were rapidly eclipsed by a series of black vernacular dances including the shimmy, Texas tommy, turkey trot, and fox-trot."[36] Nick's surprised expression, along with his speculations about Gatsby's genealogy, can be read as evidence of Jay Gatsby's racial ambiguity and racial passing. Fitzgerald also mentions "Frisco dances." This directly refers to Joe Frisco, a comedian who invented the dance called the "black bottom." Avoiding any pejorative racial signification, here again, Fitzgerald connects Gatsby's racial identity to blackness through America's mulatto popular culture. The point here is that Fitzgerald signifies on Gatsby through black cultural productions.

Fitzgerald's most telling evidence of Gatsby as a passing figure is the juxtaposition of Gatsby with representations of blackness and upper-crust black individuals. In the first incident with blacks, Gatsby and Nick are riding in Gatsby's ostentatious yellow automobile on their way to meet Meyer Wolfshiem, an American Jew. The fancy automobile "was a rich cream color, bright with nickel, swollen here and there in its monstrous length with triumphant hatboxes and supper-boxes and tool-boxes, and terraced with a labyrinth of windshields that mirrored a dozen suns"(68). During the ride from West Egg to Manhattan, over the Queensboro Bridge, Nick, revealing his own xenophobia and white supremacist views, relates that:

> A dead man passed us in a hearse heaped with blooms, followed by two carriages with drawn blinds and by more cheerful carriages for friends. The friends looked out at us with tragic eyes and short upper lips of south-eastern Europe and I was glad that the sight of Gatsby's splendid car was included in the somber holiday. *As we crossed Blackwells Island a limousine passed us, driven by a white chauffeur, in which sat three modish Negroes, two bucks and a girl. I laughed aloud as the yolks of their eyeballs rolled toward us in haughty rivalry.* (73; emphasis added)

In a time of escalating immigration from southeastern Europe and black people's notable migration from the South to the North, both immigrants and black "bucks" represent the threat to Nordic whiteness. Structurally and symbolically, Gatsby, as represented by his "splendid car," is in the middle of a southeastern European identity and a black identity. But, since Fitzgerald's exaggerated emphasis here resides on the three "modish" black individuals, the issue of Gatsby's connection to blackness becomes much more emphatic. In fact, Gatsby's cream-colored yellow automobile connects to the yellowed "yolks" of the black "bucks" and the girl. Of course, like Tom's use of the word "bitch," Nick's use of the word "girl" represents a pejorative signifier for black woman. As Ann Douglas rightly argues, these blacks are "Gatsby's rivals, perhaps his superiors, if only in audacious pretense; after all, their chauffeur is white."[37] Here, I partially concur with Douglas's analysis because, like the upper class of Harlem society, these three black individuals with their "reckless eyeballing" have obviously achieved financial success, symbolized by the white chauffeur, without having to deny their blackness; in fact, they seem to celebrate their blackness while challenging whiteness.[38]

On the other hand, Gatsby, with "audacious pretense," represents their inferior because he lives and dreams in a constant state of denial and apprehension. Accordingly, this scene conveys a Lacanian mirror stage for Gatsby; symbolically, Fitzgerald has Gatsby looking into the mirror, and the image he sees is that of blackness looking back with a haughty challenge. Quite simply, these black individuals challenge Nick's master gaze. Although the moment is articulated through Nick's discourse, Gatsby's illusion of coherent selfhood forms the basis of social selfhood, which is marked by his yellow (miscegenation) automobile. Unlike Gatsby, these well-to-do black "bucks" and the "girl" have literally bypassed whiteness as represented by the Nordic, Nick, and by the seemingly white Gatsby. Likewise, when Nick arrogantly uses the racist terms "bucks" and "girl" in direct contradiction to his father's advice to "remember that all the people in this world haven't had the advantages that you've had" (5), the terms conveys the horrific enslavement and sexual exploitation (buck breeding) of black people that produced tremendous white wealth.[39]

This scene of rivalry between the three blacks with their rolling eyeballs and Gatsby and Nick suggests the unifying self-pride and self-actualization indigenous to the Harlem Renaissance, when black people challenged white hegemony. More so, these three "modish" blacks probably wanted to become wealthy, but they did not want to become white; they seem to have realized their dreams without racial repudiation. In this regard, Fitzgerald's harrowing use of the word "bucks" conveys a double entendre, with black men representing a sexual and an economic threat. Simply put, bodacious black "bucks" with "bucks" are dangerous. On the other hand, Nick's rather grotesque description of these blacks, with their rolling, yolk-colored eyeballs, recalls how black individuals were caricatured in D. W. Griffith's film *The Birth of a Nation* (1915). This film was critical in portraying many white people's horror of miscegenation and the myth of black men as sexually out of control. In the film, a black soldier proposes marriage to a virginal and virtuous white girl; she shies away and runs off, with the soldier, who does not intend to harm her, in pursuit. Ultimately, the hysterical white girl throws herself off a cliff—a tragic incident that is used as the excuse for forming the Ku Klux Klan.[40] Coincidentally, like the black soldier in the film, Gatsby is a former soldier who desires to marry the "virginal white girl," in this case Daisy Buchanan.[41]

Another way to view Nick's statement about the racial rivalry is that blackness and whiteness really exist between Gatsby and Nick. Both Nick and Gatsby come to New York City to fulfill their desires. Nick works in the legal bond (white) business, whereas Gatsby schemes in the bootlegging and counterfeit bonds (black market) business. Whereas Nick has his genealogy traced through a "clan" of white males and desires wealth, Gatsby, despite his new wealth, becomes characterized as the black body that is incomplete, fragmented, never fulfilled; he is left to desire whiteness. Although Fitzgerald's characterizations of Gatsby's criminality and shameless duplicity are raceless, these aspects, combined with the signifiers of blackness, aptly signal the act of racial passing. Besides, like the bootlegging business, the counterfeit bonds suggest that in terms of his presumed whiteness, Gatsby is racially counterfeit. During this particular car ride, Gatsby consistently tries to impress Nick. While Nick comes from a stable and well-established Nordic family in St. Paul, Minnesota, Gatsby, despite his wealth, is unconnected in terms of his pedigree and is insecure about his past. Relating an experience from his past, Gatsby tells Nick about being promoted to the rank of major during the war and receiving decorations from "every Allied government." More important, Gatsby complacently tells Nick about receiving a decoration from Montenegro, a small country in southeastern Europe near the Adriatic Sea. Nick states that Gatsby's golden "smile comprehended Montenegro's troubled history and sympathized with the brave struggles of the Montenegrin people" (71). Fitzgerald's eight references to Montenegro are significant. First, this country is associated with the funeral procession of the individuals with the "tragic eyes and short upper lips of south-eastern Europe." Furthermore, recalling the three black individuals in the white chauffeured limousine, who are mountainous in terms of their wealth, there is a connotative connection between these "three modish Negroes" and the modishly clad Jay Gatsby in his monstrously long automobile.

Taken together, the numerous references to the Slavic people of Montenegro reverberate on the troubled history and the brave, protracted struggles of black people who resist the plagues of white supremacy and Jim Crow segregation. Hence, with the denotative definition of Montenegro as a "black mountain" connected to Gatsby's wealth and blackness in America, Gatsby, with his towering mansion, poignantly symbolizes a black mountain. Accordingly, the grand "joke" of racial passing may be on the loud, laughing Nick, who, with his racial comments, unknowingly rides with the black trickster figure, Gatsby, who, during the war, was symbolically validated and venerated by "blackness." As a trickster figure, Gatsby lives at the crossroad of blackness and whiteness. As in the aforementioned Lacanian scene, Fitzgerald's repetitious references to Montenegro surreptitiously reinforce the xenophobic notion that southeastern Europeans and black people, particularly black "bucks," with their "haughty rivalry," pose a threat to the notion of Nordic superiority. Fitzgerald dramatically emphasizes this when Nick describes some parvenu individuals who come to Gatsby's party as "a whole clan named Blackbuck who always gathered in a corner and flipped up their noses like goats at whosoever came near" (66). Accordingly, the haughtiness of black bucks reinforces the racial challenge posed by Gatsby's desire for Daisy; of course, Jay Gatsby with his origins among shiftless and unsuccessful farmers, has to buck his way through Tom Buchanan to fulfill his five-year-long desire.

The contradictions between the enigmatic Gatsby and the guileless Nick emphasize that they are doubles. However, whereas Gatsby, a dangerous dreamer who acts out his desire and a vulgarian who forces his fabrications to become true, is constantly aware of his doubleness, Nick appears oblivious to his double vision. In the literature of passing, doubling is a consistent paradigm. Despite his whiteness, Nick struggles in the bond business, and Gatsby, with his invisible blackness, thrives with his bootlegging and counterfeit-bonds activities. As exemplified by this scene of rivalry, the Jazz Age was a period of racial reversal: many white people were eating chitterlings and many black people were drinking champagne. Interestingly, Gatsby does not have a black chauffeur or any black household staff. It is possible that he fears his secret blackness could somehow be exposed. Last, Fitzgerald's rather phallocentric description of Gatsby's swollen, cream-colored car, with its "monstrous length," has a sexualized connotation that insinuates the stereotypical and racist discourse associated with the black man's genitalia. In sum, Jay Gatsby tragically represents a dangerous outsider and a licentious black "buck" who has his covetous gaze centered on Nick Carraway's cousin, Daisy Buchanan. However, reversing the paradigm of "playing in the dark," Fitzgerald, playing in the light, explicitly characterizes the cruel adulterer and modern-day buccaneer Tom Buc[k]anan as a Nordic "buck." Daisy accuses her husband of having hurt her little finger: "You did it, Tom. . . . I know you didn't mean to but you did do it. That's what I get for marrying a brute [buck] of a man, a great, big hulking physical specimen of a—" (16). Of course, Daisy's diction ironically echoes the sexually ravenous and piratical white males (buccaneers) who during American slavery created pale individuals through the miscegenation molestation of black women; accordingly, within white supremacist discourse, the naming of black males as "bucks" represents a psychological projection by those white males who themselves engaged in the buck breeding of black people. The rivalry between Tom and Gatsby represents "two bucks" seeking the attention of the yellow and brown doe, Daisy. Thus racial doubling and racial splitting exists between both Gatsby and Nick and Gatsby and Tom. Accenting Gatsby's duality, R. W. Stallman examines Fitzgerald's use of this doubling and splitting technique:

> Fitzgerald shows a marked predilection for doubling identities of persons, places and things fashioning them by twos or pairs. Gatsby has two fathers . . . his life is divided into two [racial] parts; he is tricked by two women. Nick has two girls [one in the east and one in the West] . . . There are two timetables, two eggs, two necklaces, and so on. . . . Nothing is complete and whole as a thing in itself; nothing therefore is without imperfection.[42]

This seemingly simple juxtaposition of black and white foreshadows Gatsby's tragic death and funeral; Fitzgerald employs the three "modish" blacks to mirror the equally modish and pretentious Gatsby. Fitzgerald makes use of the "dead man" in the "hearse heaped with blooms [daisies?]" to symbolically represent Gatsby's "dead" past, as exemplified by his fraudulent statements to Nick that his ancestors studied at Oxford University and that his parents were deceased.

By naming Roosevelt Island or Welfare Island, "Blackwells Island," Fitzgerald signifies on the upper-middle-class black people who do "well" socioeconomically. Before this critical scene occurs, New York is described as a city with "wild promise of all the mystery and the beauty in the world," and immediately afterward, Nick theorizes that "Anything can happen now . . . anything at all." The novel relates that "[E]ven Gatsby could happen, without any particular wonder" (73). In this time of vast possibilities and "wild promise," "anything" includes the three wealthy blacks (along with Gatsby) and the not-so-remote possibility that Jay Gatsby "could happen" and somehow be a pale-black individual masquerading as white. Still, implicit in Nick's statement is the possibility of exposure that always lies beneath the performance of blacks who pass for white. Indeed, this represents the greatest irony of the novel, because, in terms of wealth and property, Jay Gatsby as a black man or black "buck" does do exceedingly well. Likewise, as Nick relates the disturbing presence of blacks, his analysis suggests that many white nationalists speculate on the possibility of a blackless country. As Ralph Ellison points out, "despite its absurdity, the fantasy of a blackless America continues to turn up. It is a fantasy born not merely of racism but of petulance, of exasperation, of moral fatigue. It is like a boil bursting forth from impurities in the bloodstream of democracy."[43] Ellison's analysis reveals the ludicrous notion of the "one-drop-of-black-blood" theory and the racial paradox of America's democracy, symbolized by Nick's speculations on the Dutch sailors' eyes as they beheld the

> fresh green breast of the new world. Its vanished trees, the trees that had made way for Gatsby's house, had once pandered in whispers to the last and greatest of all human dreams; for a transitory enchanted moment man must have held his breath in the presence of this continent, compelled into an aesthetic contemplation he neither understood nor desired, face to face for the last time in history with something commensurate to his capacity for wonder. (189)

With the "single green light, minute and far away" (26) that burns all night at the end of Daisy Buchanan's dock, Gatsby's desire for Daisy imbues this passage. Here, Gatsby's house and his incredible dream become analogous; yet, like the Dutch sailors who brought twenty black Africans to Jamestown, Virginia, Gatsby does not understand the complexity of his grand desire. Like Gatsby, black people face a relentless white supremacist culture, yet he and they continually dream of constitutional and cultural inclusion. Equally important, this passage brilliantly conveys the birth of a "new" nation, suggesting the birth of whiteness symbolized by the erasure of nature and the erasure of the Other. However, as Ralph Ellison reminds us, despite the notion that America is a country that resists ambiguity of any sort, to be an American is to be both black and white. In fact, American culture is blackness.

The second of three scenes involving Gatsby's juxtaposition to blackness occurs in New York at the Plaza Hotel (where black people, unless they were passing for white, were not allowed entrance as guests) with Tom, Daisy, Nick, Jordan, and Gatsby. Gatsby's use of the term "old sport" is dramatically revealed when Gatsby openly declares his love for Daisy and challenges her to renounce any love for her husband. Repeatedly, Gatsby uses the term "old sport"[44] in reference to Nick Carraway; yet Nick states that the "familiar expression held no more familiarity than the hand which reassuringly brushed my shoulder" (57). At the Plaza Hotel, Tom challenges Gatsby about the same expression. Tom asks, "All this 'old sport' business. Where'd you pick that up?" Representing the law, Tom realizes that the word "sport" and the sporting life signify on the camaraderie of drinking establishments, the actions of betting in gambling houses, and the cynical use of prostitutes.

Having done an investigation on Gatsby and his activities, like a statue in search of a pedestal, Tom triumphantly reveals to the gathered throng that Gatsby "and this [Meyer] Wolfshiem bought up a lot of side-street drug stores here and in Chicago and sold grain alcohol over the counter. . . . I picked him for a bootlegger the first time I saw him and I wasn't far wrong" (141). Finally, all the "wild rumors" result in Gatsby's being characterized as a "sport" and a "bootlegger." Gatsby's constant use of the term "old sport" is a psychological projection of his attempt to pass beyond his sordid and sinister past. Equally significant, as "the last barrier of [white or Nordic] civilization" (137), Tom's taxonomic gaze and explosive discourse straightforwardly connects the unsophisticated Gatsby and his seemingly Nordic wife Daisy, to America's greatest taboo: illicit miscegenation between blacks and whites: "I suppose the latest thing is to sit back and let Mr. Nobody from Nowhere make love to your wife. Well, if that's the idea you can count me out. . . . *Nowadays people begin by sneering at family life and family institutions and next they'll throw everything overboard and have intermarriage between black and white*" (137; emphasis added).[45] Here, the rootless Gatsby, as an "invisible man," becomes raced with blackness; in fact, by racializing class status and sexuality, Tom exposes Gatsby's phallus as black. The implication is that one cannot escape the racial body simply because one has a white or pale phenotype. Like that of Ralph Ellison's invisible man, Gatsby's invisibility defines him as "Mr. Nobody from Nowhere." As this compelling passage reveals, there is no mistaking that Tom's discourse on Nordic hopes and dreams, juxtaposed against his horror of illicit miscegenation, has moved from the general ("those other races") to those of the specific "black" race. This statement of fear echoes Tom's earlier warning that other races may gain control of things (Daisy) and that "if we [Nordics] don't look out the white race will be—will be utterly submerged" (17). His controversial racial analogy positions Gatsby as an unsophisticated and unconnected black buck who sexually threatens Tom's white "family life," especially his white wife, Daisy.[46] Equally important is Gatsby's reticence in the face of Tom's incendiary racial indictment; at no point in the novel does the prevaricating protagonist acknowledge his whiteness or deny his invisible blackness. It is at the Plaza Hotel that Daisy tacitly informs Gatsby that he lacks the education, taste, and class, despite his enormous wealth, to be a sophisticated white man. To put it another way, coupled with

Tom's racial emphasis, Daisy now understands that Gatsby is impure, nouveau riche, and that his new money is "black money." By definition, "black money" is income earned illegally, usually in cash, and not reported to the government so as to avoid paying taxes. Gatsby's income from bootlegging and counterfeit bonds can thusly be considered "black money." Heavily intoxicated by white supremacy and apprehension, Tom, racializing Gatsby's class status, cunningly implies that, although Gatsby could become fabulously wealthy, he could neither transform his blackness (otherness) into whiteness nor transform his new money into old money. Hence, as a "black" bootlegger, Jay Gatsby attains a money-based status that rests on black market achievements and deception, whereas Tom Buchanan's upper-class status rests on a foundation of Nordic birth and breeding, a pedigree.

Seemingly, like the "Jazz Cleopatra" Josephine Baker, who served as a focal point for decades of contemplation about race, Jordan Baker singularly understands Tom Buchanan's provocatively racial insinuation, especially directed at Jay Gatsby, and defends him by murmuring: "We're all white here" (137).[47] At this point in the novel, we know Gatsby is not white, and we know he is not because only a fabricator says so. Here, Fitzgerald's white solipsism does not reject the racial discourse that labels the privileged members of American society as white. Within America's racial culture, laying claim to whiteness positions one with privilege and power. Unlike being black, to be white is to have an irrefutable claim of existence. Jordan's racial discourse establishes the power and primacy of whiteness. However, with her allegiance to Daisy and with no knowledge of Gatsby's racial genealogy, Jordan is not creditable because she is an opportunist whom Nick describes as "incurably dishonest," one who will do whatever she must to be successful. Paradoxically, it is the equivocator, Gatsby, who describes Jordan as august and truthful: "Miss Baker's a great sportswoman, you know, and she'd never do anything that wasn't all right" (76). Two liars validate each other. As a congenital liar, Jordan displays a self-centeredness and a corruptibility exemplified by her cheating at her first major golf tournament and her lying about an automobile that gets wet because she left the top down. Further, nothing in the novel suggests Jordan's intimate knowledge of Gatsby's genealogy other than his white appearance. Simply stated, Fitzgerald has a compulsive prevaricator defining and defending Gatsby's whiteness, and this literary stratagem all the more suggests Gatsby's blackness. Consequently, whiteness becomes defined with regard to blackness, and the seemingly pure and innocent Daisy becomes defined with regard to the impure and dangerous Gatsby. Socialized to embrace only the white phallus, Daisy must reject Gatsby's black phallus masquerading as a white phallus. Nevertheless, Daisy, as a metonymic representation of whiteness, signifies death and destruction, and her own moral vacuity foreshadows Gatsby's physical death. The implication here is that a black Jay Gatsby would somehow foul Daisy Buchanan. Moreover, Tom's tendentious perspective has been foreshadowed when Nick contemplates that both Tom Buchanan and the gas station owner George Wilson simultaneously realize that their wives are having adulterous affairs and observes that "there was no difference between men, intelligence or race, so profound as the difference between the sick and the well" (131). Again, the language of the novel reveals the notion of individuals who pass and who thereby challenge racial and class boundaries; in other words, by definition, a pale passing individual who in a sophisticated manner disguises his or her blackness can break boundaries.

Disrupting Gatsby's attempt to embrace whiteness, Tom symbolically castrates him by ripping the mask of whiteness off Gatsby's face and exposing his blackness and bootlegging. Like glass shattering, Tom breaks Gatsby's phallus. Then Tom dictates, "You two start on home, Daisy. . . . In Mr. Gatsby's car" (142). In this third of three scenes in which Fitzgerald juxtaposes Gatsby to blackness, Gatsby's yellow car, driven by Daisy with Gatsby in the passenger seat, strikes and kills Tom's lover, Myrtle. Fitzgerald describes this desolate wasteland of death and desire between West Egg and New York City as "a fantastic farm where ashes grow like wheat into ridges and hills and grotesque gardens, where ashes take the forms of houses and chimneys and rising smoke and finally, with transcendent effort, of men who move dimly and already crumbling through the powdery air" (27). It is ironic that Myrtle, who is so vivacious, greets death in this land of ashes. Further, with Gatsby's automobile or phallus bloody and mutilated as a result of having virtually torn off Myrtle's breast—which represents her depleted vitality ("her left breast was swinging loose like a flap")—undoubtedly another death is imminent. Ironically, Myrtle Wilson's mantra has been "You can't live forever, you can't live forever" (40). This mantra represents a synthesis of Gatsby's and Myrtle's desires for the American Dream, represented by the seemingly upper-class, racially pure Nordic society, and a veiled foreshadowing of the tragic deaths of Gatsby and Myrtle. Fitzgerald's physical descriptions of Gatsby reinforce the theme of racial passing. Although Gatsby leaves the bloody death scene without stopping, Gatsby's automobile is identified by a "pale well dressed Negro" who is passing by George Wilson's garage. This light-skinned black individual informs the police officer at the scene that "It was a yellow car," and he adds, "Big yellow car. New" (147). Like the black spotters used to detect light-skinned individuals who attempt to pass in segregated hotels, movie theaters, and clubs, a "pale" black man unknowingly identifies the "pale" Jay Gatsby through his yellow automobile. This "well dressed Negro" recalls the two well-to-do black bucks in the white chauffeured limousine. By linguistic and semiotic reversal, Gatsby's presence is confirmed by his absence, and by Fitzgerald's imaginative reconfiguration of doubling, Jay Gatsby becomes a wealthy "pale well dressed Negro" who becomes connected to miscegenation and to the murder of Myrtle Wilson.

Fitzgerald's earlier references to Jay Gatsby as "pale" and as always well dressed ingeniously imply a synthesis of Gatsby and blackness. Before Gatsby sees Daisy again, Nick observes, "An hour later the front door opened nervously and Gatsby in a white flannel suit, silver shirt and gold colored tie hurried in. He was pale and there were dark signs of sleeplessness beneath his eyes" (89) and later "Gatsby, pale as death, with his hands plunged like weights in his coat pockets, was standing in a puddle of water glaring tragically into my eyes" (91). "Pale as death" foreshadows the chain of events that will lead to Gatsby's death. Fitzgerald's use of the word "pale" is not insignificant because those black individuals who were light skinned and straight haired too often subscribed to the belief that they could actually attain whiteness by passing. Hence, the "yellow" color of Gatsby's "monstrous" automobile and the yellow at Gatsby's house signify on the pejorative discourse in which pale blacks are often referred to as "high yella," "white honky," "white nigger," "nigger white," and "mongrel"; the color yellow reinforces the novel's theme of miscegenation. Symbolically, Gatsby is "big" and "new" in terms of his enormous wealth from bootlegging, and he represents the tragic mulatto as characterized by his pale-colored complexion and the "monstrous length" of his automobile. Fitzgerald's subversive racial encoding forces us to see blackness.

Along with phenotype, Fitzgerald uses hair texture and language to illuminate racial and class passing. Light-skinned black individuals who pass are very conscious about their hair texture and their language; they realize that blackness can be associated with both. In the novel, Nick relates that Gatsby's "tanned skin was drawn attractively tight on his face and his short hair looked as though it was trimmed every day" (54); about Gatsby's elocution, Nick says "I was looking at an elegant young rough-neck, a year or two over thirty, whose elaborate formality of speech just missed being absurd. Some time before he introduced himself I'd got a strong impression that he was picking his words with care" (53). In a society where difference is "treated as controlled substance: to be enjoyed in small doses, always under conditions of moderation and restraint,"[48] Jay Gatsby represents danger because of his new wealth and his apparent whiteness. These characterizations are significant because they suggest that Tom Buchanan fearfully understands that too often miscegenation between blacks and whites promotes assimilation and racial passing despite the prejudices and the barriers constructed by white wealth, Jim Crow law, and systematic white supremacy. However, the question of America's being fundamentally a country of assimilation and miscegenation is spelled out by Arthur M. Schlesinger Jr.:

> Those intrepid Europeans who had torn up their roots to brave the wild Atlantic wanted to forget a horrid past and to embrace a hopeful future. They expected to become American. Their goals were escape, deliverance, assimilation. They saw America as a transforming nation, banishing dismal memories and developing a unique national character based on common political ideals and shared experiences. *The point of America was not to preserve old cultures, but to forge a new American culture.* (emphasis added)[49]

Implicit in Gatsby's desire is his attempt to create a "new" American family with Daisy and perhaps her daughter, Pammy. At the same time, Tom wonders how Gatsby, while in Louisville, Kentucky, "got within a mile" of Daisy unless he "brought the groceries to the back door" (138). Certainly, racial etiquette in the South required black people to use the back door when coming to a white person's house. On this account, Tom essentially views Gatsby as an impertinent black buck aping the ways of sophisticated white folks. Also, Tom's reference to "the back door" insinuates Gatsby as a sexual threat to the pristine Daisy. Tom's hegemonic perspective of

98 | THE TRAGIC BLACK BUCK

Gatsby highlights what Nathaniel Mackey argues: "Social othering has to do with power, exclusion, and privilege, the centralizing of a norm against which otherness is measured, meted out, marginalized."[50] Besides, the word "groceries" slyly implies Gatsby's involvement in bootlegging activities. As Irving Lewis Allen points out, the term "groceries" may have been "influenced by "liquor groceries," a common name for a place that dispensed liquor by the bottle and often by the drink. Years later, during Prohibition, words such as "grocery," "greengrocery," and even "delicatessen" and "confectionery" were recalled from the good old days and used as humorous synonyms for "speakeasy."[51] Through Tom's discourse, Fitzgerald's rhetoric of dread and sexual desire indicates the dangerous yet erotically appealing black body masquerading in whiteness. Hence, through Fitzgerald's discourse, Gatsby represents the racial illusion of racial inclusion.

Like many other narratives of racial passing, *The Great Gatsby* concludes with tragedy. Myrtle Wilson's husband, George, as the apocalyptic assassin, overcomes the grief of his wife's death and begins to track down the owner of the deadly "yellow car." Since George Wilson has previously seen Tom Buchanan drive Jay Gatsby's car, like a hag-ridden paddyroller tracking down a runaway slave, George eventually finds Tom. Although it is never clear exactly what Tom tells George, when discussing Tom and Daisy as paragons of corruption, Nick relates that immediately after the accident, "There was an unmistakable air of natural intimacy . . . and anybody would have said that they were conspiring together" (152–153). Likewise, when Nick runs into Tom several months after Gatsby's solemn funeral, Tom arrogantly states, "I told him [George Wilson] the truth . . . That fellow [Gatsby] had it coming to him. He threw dust [blackness?] into your eyes just like he did in Daisy's but he was a tough one. He ran over Myrtle like you'd run over a dog and never even stopped his car" (187). Through Myrtle's tragic death, Daisy's degradation is exposed.

Although it is hypocritical, Tom's demagoguery constructs the racial binary in which blackness represents dirt, death, and disaster and whiteness represents law— truth, responsibility, and morality. Indeed, with Fitzgerald firmly establishing the racist and elitist judgments of Tom and with Tom's discovery that Daisy and Gatsby were having an ongoing affair, we can only speculate about what Tom tells the emotionally distraught and armed George, whom Fitzgerald describes characteristically as a Nordic blond with blue eyes. It is possible that because the deranged George has a revolver, Tom, despite the tremendous class differences between them, bonds with George because of their Nordic whiteness and insinuates that Gatsby is the dangerous racial Other. Earlier, Fitzgerald establishes that Tom is Gatsby's enemy when Meyer Wolfshiem states: "Yeah Gatsby's very careful about women. He would never so much as look at a friend's wife" (77). If we hypothesize that Tom, with his fears of miscegenation, informs George that Gatsby is black, he would be evoking white America's greatest sexual-racial taboo, because white women regardless of class bear the enduring burden of keeping the white race pure. Following Lonthop Stoddard's ideology, white men must come together to eliminate blackness.

Like Joe Christmas, Jay Gatsby must die because of his threat to whiteness. Believing that Gatsby, not Tom, is Myrtle's lover, George finds, shoots, and kills Gatsby. It is possible that George believes that Gatsby, the light-skinned black man, has committed miscegenation and murder. In the role of a white avenging angel, George, upholding Nordic supremacy, must kill the nonwhite sexual transgressor. In this symbolic lynching, not only does Tom benefit from Daisy's lover being killed, but also he receives an added benefit when the self-sacrificing George kills himself; as Nick observes, "the holocaust was complete" (170). Fitzgerald's use of "holocaust" denotes that the fires of Gatsby's desire have been extinguished and connects the protagonist to the holocaust of black people's grim enslavement and the all too common lynch-burning of black men in America during this race-charged period.

The twisted irony of Jay Gatsby's tragic misadventure is the rubric of misrecognition with rumors of miscegenation. Earlier, Myrtle Wilson believes that Jay Gatsby's yellow car belongs to Tom Buchanan, and later, when she attempts to stop the car, believing that Tom is with Daisy, it is Daisy who kills Tom's lover. When Gatsby drives Tom's blue coupe and the blue-blooded Tom, with his desire to experience Otherness, drives Gatsby's yellow automobile, Fitzgerald emphasizes the racial reversal of passing. Later, Tom informs George: "I bought it last week" (130). When Gatsby drives Tom's blue coupe with Daisy by his side, he temporarily has the key to the magical door of the American Dream. On the other hand, Tom's equivocation about owning Gatsby's automobile highlights his desire to control Gatsby's black phallus; historically, this control suggests the fact that when black "bucks" were lynched-burned, mutilated, and castrated, the black man's genitalia were the prized possession. With the reversal of the automobiles, blackness takes the place of whiteness and whiteness takes the place of blackness; nonetheless, whiteness remains supreme. Ironically, it is Daisy who starts the tragic chain of events that leads to Gatsby's "pushing up daisies." In other words, Daisy Buchanan symbolizes the phallic woman who, with a phallus of gold (Gatsby's yellow automobile), ultimately destroys Jay Gatsby. Of course, Daisy's hardhearted actions reverse the "rape" scene in which Gatsby took her ravenously. Symbolically, Daisy as a femme fatale emasculates and "castrates" the black Gatsby when she rips open Myrtle and kills her. Signifying on Tom's white supremacist discourse, Daisy kills Gatsby; whiteness destroys blackness. Fitzgerald deftly foreshadows Myrtle's and Gatsby's deaths when Daisy "[s]uddenly . . . threw the cigarette and the burning match on the carpet" (139) and tells Gatsby that he wants too much from her and that she "can't help what's past." Essentially, Daisy has moved from a philosophy that "rich girls don't marry poor boys" to one that insists that white women do not marry black men regardless of their status. With racial and gender reversals, Myrtle's and Gatsby's zealous desires for upper-echelon whiteness as pointedly represented by Tom and Daisy are violently extinguished.

As a pale black man, Gatsby is given a funeral that completes the irony of his greatness, especially when the man with the owl eyes, commenting on the few people in attendance, states: "The poor son-of-a-bitch" (183). Here, Fitzgerald's ingenious synthesis of race and class suggests the themes of miscegenation, hybridity, and breeding, because Gatsby becomes connected to the mongrel dog that Tom buys for Myrtle. The tragedy of Gatsby's attempting to pass racial and class boundaries is dramatized by the sparsely attended funeral. Except for Gatsby's father, no one knows the real Jay Gatsby. Thus, Gatsby's tragic death personifies and prefigures a holocaust designed to eliminate miscegenation individuals of "inferior" or indeterminate breeding. Accordingly, Gatsby becomes defined as illegitimate, rootless, and mongrelized. As Leslie A. Fiedler asserts: "Not only were dwarfs and other 'useless people' sent to Nazi extermination camps . . . but other unfortunate human beings regarded—at that time and in that society—as undesirable deviations from the Norms [Nordics] were also destroyed: Jews and Gypsies first of all, with Blacks, Slavs and southern Europeans presumably next in line."[52]

The bitter irony of Fitzgerald's ridiculous title is that, despite his great wealth, his grand desire, and his failed attempts at savior-faire, Gatsby, like black people who have "some heightened sensitivity to the promises of life," is excluded from the American Dream. For Gatsby to be a black man would be the greatest irony; accordingly, as a black individual, he is excluded from Tom and Daisy Buchanan's world of whiteness. Even with his attempt to escape from the fear of poverty and despite his tremendous wealth, Gatsby of West Egg can never be a part of the elite white world of East Egg, where the Buchanans reside.

With Fitzgerald's ingeniously signifying use of race, color, and diction, and by playing the miscegenation blues, Jay Gatsby, a dandy of desire, becomes characterized as the tragic mulatto passing. The tragedy of Gatsby's death is compounded by his self-deceptive illusion that he could somehow reconstruct the past. He vehemently questions Nick: "'Can't repeat the past?' he cried incredulously. 'Why of course you can!'" Then Gatsby declares, "I'm going to fix everything just the way it was before" (116–117). Although Gatsby understands that whiteness means wealth and privilege, his comprehension of white privilege is superficial. With his immense wealth and his immense desire, Gatsby attempts to buy his way back into the favorable aspects of his past and possibly to buy his way out of blackness. However, it is his majestically romantic desire for Daisy that, from Nick's glorious perspective, gives Gatsby a "romantic readiness such as I have never found in any other person and which it is not likely I shall ever find again. No—Gatsby turned out all right at the end; it is what preyed on Gatsby, what foul dust floated in the wake of his dreams that temporarily closed out my interest in the abortive sorrows and short-winded elations of men" (6–7). Here, Nick vindicates Gatsby. Following the intensity of Nick's self-reflective argument and connecting it to the issue of race, as Morrison explicates it, often the "images of blackness can be evil and protective, rebellious and forgiving, fearful and desirable—all of the self-contradictory features of the self. Whiteness alone is mute, meaningless, unfathomable, pointless, frozen, veiled, curtained, dreaded, senseless, implacable" (6–7). In a narrative in which racial differences overlap and conflate, we also discover the elusive ambiguity and synthesis of different classes, ethnicities, and religions. For example, Tom and George are reduced to the same psychological state because of their wives' desires; the provincial Gatsby and Myrtle represent similar tragic desires with regard to the Buchanans (Gatsby desires Daisy and Myrtle desires Tom). Also, Daisy, with her stained white radiance, becomes falsely defined as Catholic. Nick and Jordan aptly perform their roles as enablers. In fact, most of the characters in this novel desperately want to escape the shallowness and vacuity of their lives. The possibility that identities can be submerged or altered represents the fallacy of hegemonic constructs, especially that of white superiority.

For any black person to achieve financial and social success in America's white supremacist culture represents a genuine mark of greatness. Like those of the robber barons, Gatsby's sojourn to American wealth and power is made through bootlegging and selling counterfeit bonds. Instead of realizing the American Dream, symbolized by wealth, a large mansion, a beautiful seemingly white woman, and a luxurious automobile, he has unwittingly entered Daisy's heart of darkness. In other words, Gatsby tragically attempts to buy his way into a tradition of upper-class whiteness that will never accept him. Though Daisy is an attractive nonentity, as Leslie A. Fiedler makes clear, "white and gold make a dirty color [mulatto]; for wealth is no longer innocent, America no longer innocent, the Girl who is the soul of both turned destructive and corrupt" (313). Like Gatsby, most black people assiduously believe in the "orgiastic future" of America, but often blacks meet white America's consistent contempt and moral mendaciousness.

Before Gatsby attains his wealth, Fitzgerald, rooted in American cultural mythology, describes his exotic and primitive nature along with his darkness: "For over a year he had been beating his way along the south shore of Lake Superior as a clam digger and a salmon fisher. . . . His brown, hardening body lived naturally through the half fierce [half-savage], half lazy work of the bracing days" (104). Fitzgerald's description of Gatsby, with his more "brown" than white complexion, suggests his racialization by the author in two ways. First, Gatsby's "brown" body reinforces the novel's theme of miscegenation in that he represents a synthesis of blackness and whiteness. In other words, Gatsby's "brown" body becomes a signifier of blackness and a signifier of racial mixture. This is evident in the pale descriptions of Gatsby that we get from Nick. In narratives of passing, skin color and hair texture are the characteristics used to detect an individual's blackness. Hence, along with Gatsby's skin color, his short hair, trimmed every day, suggests an attempt to hide his blackness. Second, Fitzgerald's characterizations of how Gatsby lived reinforce the idea of the exotic primitive, and the duality of his work latently suggests Gatsby's racial duality. For example, too often in "race talk" the faulty binary of black/white often equates to that of bad/good and shiftless/ hard-working. Fitzgerald's description of Gatsby doing "half fierce, half lazy work" conveys this faulty binary. This black and white binary is reinforced when Nick recounts: "On the *white steps* [of Gatsby's house] an obscene word, scrawled by some boy with a piece of brick, stood out clearly in the moonlight [moonshine] and I erased it, drawing my shoe raspingly along the stone" (188; my emphasis). Recalling Tom's taxonomic gaze regarding the exposure of the mongrel dog as a "bitch" and the unrefined and sexually menacing Gatsby as "black," perhaps this "obscene word" directed at Jay Gatsby is "bastard," "nigger," or especially Nick's racial and sexual pejorative signifier, "buck." Regardless of the specific "obscene word," Nick's actions declare a desire to erase the impure stain of blackness and the "black money" crime of bootlegging so that Gatsby's dream of whiteness and racial inclusion can radiate. Nick's erasure conveys another stratagem in narratives of passing: the desire of sympathetic others to assist a pale black individual in inventing and maintaining his or her whiteness. Better still, Nick raspingly attempts to preserve the mythology of Gatsby's whiteness and reinforces the preeminence of white supremacist culture because Gatsby has literally and figuratively stepped into whiteness. Commenting on the importance of Nick's vision of Gatsby, Richard Lehan argues: "He saw that in the death of Gatsby not only a certain kind of romantic individual was passing but also a whole way of life and state of mind. . . . Nick Carraway realizes that the passing of Gatsby is sad, but he further realizes that the passing of what Gatsby stood for is even sadder" (34). Hence, this description of Gatsby's dark body and Nick's attention to preserve his "white steps" indicate the racial essentialism where nature and black individuals exist as inferior elements to be controlled or erased by whiteness. This reification of whiteness illustrates the weight that representation has in the specious process of racial construction.

In Jay Gatsby's racial construction we see the devastating power of the white supremacist culture terminating the performance of the nonwhite Other. It is within this culture that, regardless of wealth and power, the dangerous black body becomes an icon of deficiency. In breaking with the past, Gatsby tragically fails to realize that the past is always present, or, better, that the past is forever. In a journal entry, Fitzgerald confirms the possibilities rooted in the past: "I look out at it [American history] — and I think it is the most beautiful history in the world. It is the history of me and my people. And if I came here yesterday . . . I should still think so. It is the history of all aspiration — not just the American Dream but the human dream and if I came at the end of it that too is a place in the line of pioneers."[53] This analysis conveys the comprehensive phenomenon of American life and literature in which dauntless black individuals attempt to reinvent themselves in a society structured on the pervasive dogma of worldwide white supremacy.

Whether Gatsby is black or non-Nordic, the critical point is that Fitzgerald's characterizations and constructions of Gatsby consistently figure him as the nonwhite Other and that blackness is the author's constant racial signifier of otherness. This contemplation of Gatsby's black presence may open up further space for discovery, intellectual adventure, and close exploration. Hence, *The Great Gatsby* as national literature in a wholly racial society is perhaps more perplexing than we have ever known. Along with the theme of the attempts of desperate and desiring individuals to pass in terms of class subjectivity, the novel's subversive subject is the paradoxical phenomenon of racial passing, the racial masquerade implicit to many black people's desire for enduring inclusion in the American Dream. By appropriating the symbolism, diction, and associations of racial passing, Fitzgerald illuminates the miscegenation core of the American Dream. In this process, he exposes and reinscribes white supremacist perspectives about blackness. Accordingly,

American literature during the Jazz Age reveals that America's black national identity and whiteness are inextricably related. Jay Gatsby's masquerade and consummate rags-to-riches story illustrates how imperceptible the performance of being an American truly is. Within America's institutionalized white supremacist culture, race and class cannot be separated in terms of the American Dream. Simply put, race constructs class. Light-skinned or pale black individuals who pass for white live off center between two racial and cultural systems as they attempt to embrace the often elusive American Dream. However, Jay Gatsby is "faithful to the end" to his vacuous dream, Daisy Buchanan; he searches for the golden flower of his dream, but he is consumed by the blazing fires of his own quixotic desire. Daisy never dreams of Gatsby's desire. By engaging in the self-negating Faustian phenomenon of passing for white, Jay Gatsby has tragically sold his birthright for Daisy Buchanan, an extravagant desire for the American Dream paid for in the human stain of "black" blood.

5

JOE CHRISTMAS, A BLACK BUCK WITH ATTITUDE

The Virulent Nexus of Race and Color in William Faulkner's Light in August

In the core of the heart of the American race problem the sex factor is rooted, rooted so deeply that it is not always recognized when it shows at the surface. Other factors are obvious and are the ones we dare to deal with; but regardless of how we deal with these, the race situation will continue to be acute as long as the sex factor persists.
—JAMES WELDON JOHNSON, *Along This Way*

With William Faulkner's brutally tragic passing novel[1] *Light in August* (1932), we come full circle to the Jim Crow South. Here we are confronted with a white Southern perspective on the issue of passing, a perspective that is deadly in its racism. The social and geographic aspects reveal a characterization that is decidedly less sympathetic to our "passing" character, Joe Christmas, whose racial identity is inherently unknowable. The key point is that what can only be termed William Faulkner's own grotesque racism results in a decidedly horrific characterization of the phenomenon of passing and an exhaustive case study of a sex-crazed and violent psychopath. In other words, Faulkner's presentation in *Light in August* mirrors representation.

In terms of representation, it is interesting to note that Faulkner was also an individual who "passed" or who fraudulently misrepresented himself. As C. Vann Woodward relates, while in the Royal Air Force, William Faulkner passed himself off as a British subject and, back home in Oxford, Mississippi, with unearned insignias on his uniform, related stories of being shot down over France. Faulkner never served in France, "had never left the ground." Also, Woodward relates that Faulkner assumed the role of a Virginia aristocrat, a hunter, and a horseman. On this point, Woodward corrects the record by stating that Faulkner "was described by a friend as a 'terrible' rider, and the smashed vertebra and shattered bones that he sustained from many frightful falls were not imaginary." Before his vast literary achievements, Faulkner seemed to be struggling with his own sense of individuality and struggling with a "human heart in conflict with itself."[2]

Born in 1897, one year after *Plessy v. Ferguson,* Faulkner grew up in semirural Mississippi during the violent resurgence of Jim Crow law.[3] Like Fitzgerald's romantic tragedy, his narrative of passing and masquerading[4] inevitably casts an enduring and virulent shadow over Faulkner's fictional community of Jefferson, Mississippi. Mississippi appears a "closed society still fierce in its isolation within the often closed society of the South itself . . . a nation socially and psychologically outside the nation that enclosed it legally and physically."[5] More important, all of the protagonists we have discussed thus far who pass and masquerade as white have direct and intimate knowledge of both their black and white ancestry. To have this intimate knowledge in America's pervasively racist society and culture gives our "tragic mulatto" characters the opportunity to create a mask that often "grins and lies" in order to confront the seemingly immutable boundary of race.

Yet, to have no concrete knowledge of one's racial ancestry in this "closed society" is a dangerous and tragic flaw; for the protagonist, Joe Christmas, this lack of genealogical knowledge is part of what kills him. Unlike Lucas Beauchamp, who, in *Go Down Moses* (1942) and *Intruder in the Dust* (1948), overcomes the psychological conflict of his mixed blood, Christmas experiences constant alienation, confusion, and social pandemonium. Christmas is both black and white, which could not be tolerated in the Mississippi of that era; his two-way passing performance increases the novel's overall sense of complexity. Equally important, Christmas experiences other identity confusions, also related to "race." With Christmas, we have a psychologically tormented character in a society structured on strict racial distinctions and racial fragmentation. Discussing Christmas's tragedy, Faulkner states that "he didn't know what he was, and so he was nothing. He deliberately evicted himself from the human race because he didn't know what he was. *That was his tragedy, that to me was the tragic central idea of the story—that he didn't know what he was, and there was no way possible in life for him to find out*"[6] (emphasis added). Faulkner's language repeatedly suggests that the burden lies with Christmas. Whereas Chesnutt and Johnson are quite explicit about the racial identities of their characters, Faulkner is the first to present us with a "passing" character who literally does not know what his racial identity is. Not surprisingly, Christmas undergoes an intense psychological struggle and creates racial turmoil through his "miscegenated" identity, as symbolized by speculative notions of his dual white and black heritage. In this regard, *Light in August* represents the ultimate paradoxical paradox of passing for both white and black. Hence, the tragic buck, and protagonist, Joe Christmas, represents a racial and religious oxymoron.[7] Critical to the construction of Christmas's identity is the spurious theory that one's "blood" determines one's character (conduct) and, more important, that it determines one's racial identity.[8]

When death casts a grim and spiteful shadow over the "murderous" Christmas and when he makes a half-spirited attempt to escape his captors, *Light in August* presents the notion that one's "blood" and one's behavior are somehow analogous concepts. As Eva Saks points out, the autonomy of miscegenation discourse as a nationwide phenomenon was inherently criminalized. This discourse, Saks acutely argues:

> frequently lacked external physical referents: the crime that it defined and punished was a crime of "blood," a metaphor that miscegenation law itself helped to invent and promote. The central criminal element of miscegenation was a difference in blood which existed only as a figure of speech: "white blood" and "black blood," which were mutually constitutive and equally fictitious.[9]

Like the eccentric lawyer Pudd'nhead Wilson in Mark Twain's *The Tragedy of Pudd'nhead Wilson* (1894),[10] District Attorney Gavin Stevens has an absurd theory concerning Christmas's mixed blood that denotes criminality, desire, and death:

> But his blood would not be quiet, let him save it. It would not be either one or the other and let his body save itself. Because the black blood drove him first to the negro [*sic*] cabin. And then the white blood drove him out of there, as it was the black blood which snatched up the pistol and the white blood which would not let him fire it. . . . It was the black blood which swept him by his own desire beyond the aid of any man, swept him up into the ecstasy out of a black jungle where life has already ceased before the heart stops and death is desire and fulfillment.[11]

Although blackness becomes equated with trepidation and evil, whereas whiteness becomes associated with tranquility and virtue, Faulkner's characterization of whiteness is nearly as negative as blackness. Here Faulkner conveys the spurious and sinister notion that "blood" determines behavior and racial identity to illustrate that Christmas, who masquerades as black and masquerades as white, becomes victimized by the many linguistic, cultural, and historical dictates of white supremacy. Unlike Chesnutt and Johnson, Faulkner does not cite a legal decision, but as a lawyer, Stevens produces a discourse that suggests how law is critical to the social construction of race. Also, Stevens's reductive discourse, with its echoes of Faulkner's prose, is an offensively spittoon-racist analysis of a complex situation and represents just one of many examples of Christmas's being acted upon and constructed by racist discourse. As Lee Jenkins judiciously observes: "Stevens' discourse is a substitution for narrative description, and seems to be Faulkner's presentation of a final summation of Joe's situation. I think that Faulkner shares a personal complicity in its creation, no matter how many disclaimers he makes of Stevens's being his mouthpiece."[12] Like our three other passing narratives in which there is a connection between passing and legal discourse, Stevens's reductive analysis provides the legal context for the phenomenon of passing and illustrates why a society committed to constructing rights on the basis of race has always legally frowned on miscegenation. As Eva Saks observes, miscegenation law represents "the gap between social and legal definitions of race and property; the power of legal language to construct, criminalize and appropriate the human body itself."[13] In this regard, Stevens's miscegenation discourse places emphasis on the hegemonic "one-drop" rule and on the hypo descent rules under Jim Crow, along with the duality of Christmas's socially inscribed racial identity. As F. James Davis points out, "the animus against miscegenation and mulattoes in the South became very strong, reaching a peak by 1907. As in the 1850s this hostility was expressed in heightened concern about the number of mulattoes, about who was and was not a Negro, and about passing as white."[14] The theory of the "one-drop" rule became accepted as cultural law by both black and white people. By examining the novel's critical concern with race as a linguistic and social construct, rather than a biological construct, the literary and historical tropes of miscegenation, mimicry, and masquerade reveal that specifically, in the South, blackness and whiteness are paradoxically represented as speculative, yet ironclad racial and cultural categories. Faulkner's linguistic concerns can be summed up in the words of Roland Barthes: "how meaning is possible, at what costs and by what means . . . not man endowed with meanings, but man fabricating meanings."[15]

Published in the year of Charles Waddell Chesnutt's death, *Light in August* was originally titled *Dark House*.[16] Like the other passing narratives examined here, *Light in August* illustrates the anxiety of racial masquerading with manifestations of psychological violence and physical violence.[17] In this regard, Faulkner's enduring anxiety about race provides an interesting context for any analysis of his literary canon and especially of this novel about numerous outcasts and rootless individuals seeking wholeness. For example, in "A Word to Virginians," a speech given at the University of Virginia, Faulkner asserted that perhaps "the Negro is not yet capable of more than second-class citizenship. His tragedy may be that so far he is competent for equality only in the ratio of his white blood."[18] Whiteness becomes Faulkner's measuring stick for black people's humanity and subjectivity. Hence, Faulkner's "Go slow now" benighted racist discourse and hegemonic notion of "blood" (miscegenation) represent and suggest a theory that goes beyond his fictional works.[19]

In another statement, Faulkner expresses his prowhite zealotry and antiblack hysteria in a racial analogy. Faulkner asserts that "Negroes" must learn

> self-restraint, honesty, dependability, purity; to act not even as well as just any white man, but to act as well as the best of white men. If we don't, we will spend the rest of our lives dodging among the five hundred unbridled horses; we will look forward each year to another Clinton or Little Rock not only further and further to wreck what we have so far created of peaceful relations between the two "races, but to be international monuments and milestones to our ridicule and shame."[20]

In terms of the often violent historical relationship between whites and blacks in the South during slavery and beyond, the words "self-restraint," "honesty," "dependability," and "purity" are particularly grotesque. It should be noted that

Faulkner's racist vision of black people as wild animals is present throughout his oeuvre, especially in *Absalom, Absalom!* (1936). Despite this pejorative, demeaning, and contemptuous view of black people, Faulkner struggles with his repression and guilt and attempts to characterize the complex nature of the black psyche. Through his fascination with the social issues of race and democracy, Faulkner criticizes the trenchant cultural and psychological currents in Southern society, as well as the Southern response to its history of defeat and disillusionment.

As *Light in August* illustrates, the fearful response of many white Southerners to their history of defeat and disillusionment has been the grim restoration and expansion of white nationalism. Frantz Fanon aptly views white nationalism or the "white collective unconsciousness" as culturally transmitted from generation to generation. Fanon defines white unconsciousness as "purely and simply the sum of prejudices, myths, and collective attitudes of a given group."[21] Faulkner signifies on Thomas Jefferson's miscegenation (Jefferson is the name of the county where Joe Christmas meets Joanna Burden and settles after years of roaming) and his legacy of masquerade (Jefferson's reputed illicit involvement with Sally Hemmings) and uses the Southern prejudices, myths, and attitudes to highlight America cultural conversation concerning the problematic binary of blackness and whiteness. In fact, Jefferson's racial discourse mirrors Faulkner's offensive language about black people as inferior beings. In *Notes on the State of Virginia* (1787), Jefferson tentatively asserts, "I advance it therefore as a suspicion, only, that blacks, whether originally a distinct race, or made distinct by time and circumstances, are inferior to the whites in the endowments both of body and mind. It is not against experience to suppose, that different species of the same genus, or varieties of the same species, may possess different qualifications."[22] With Jefferson as America's leading intellectual and ideological spokesman on race and white supremacy, it is not surprising that Faulkner's miscegenation novel of passing for white straightforwardly concludes in the mythical town of Jefferson, a society that purports to define itself by inclusion but that in fact defines itself by violent racist exclusion.

Jefferson's and Faulkner's racist discourses reveal how language and semiotics influence culture and law. White (Jeffersonian and Faulknerian) discourse has often been a major instrument that many white people use to full value in America's democratic society.[23] In *Light in August,* the connotations and denotations of blackness are the psychological factors that entangle our protagonist, Joe Christmas. Connecting blackness to society, the legal scholar Patricia J. Williams astutely expounds: "The blackness of black people in this society has always represented the blemish, the uncleanliness, the barrier separating individual and society. *Castration from blackness becomes the initiatory tunnel, the portal through which black people must pass if they are not to fall on their faces in the presence of society, paternity, and hierarchy*"[24] (emphasis added).

Language depends to a large degree upon the power of the nation or community that controls and advocates that language; black people in America are often the targets of linguistic and psychological violence. For example, "Negro," the white man's creation, and the pejoratively racist signifier "nigger" are very common in Faulkner's novels and continue to exist as the linguistic nexus of white thought. As Jacques Lacan suggests, "the world of words creates the world of things," and the individual becomes the "slave of language."[25] Although Lacanian analysis can lead us to conclude that all persons are slaves of language, *Light in August* reinforces the critical importance of the racial hegemony of language and the enduring symbolic master-slave dialectical power relationship between many white and black people. Spiritually and symbolically, Joe Christmas's passing-flight experiences within the greater paradigm of the tragic mulatto are akin to those of the escaped black slave running toward freedom and identity.

Structurally, *Light in August* is framed by the comic-tragic adventure of Lena Grove's sanguine attempt and failure to be reunited with the father of her child, Lucas Burch (Joe Brown), as well as Gail Hightower's[26] ineffectual search for an irretrievable past. Faulkner's interweaving of the lives of Lena Grove, Joe Christmas, and Gail Hightower and their search for wholeness (one in terms of marriage and family, one in terms of racial identity, and one in terms of the past) creates a narrative balance. As John T. Irwin makes clear, Faulkner's literary style has distinct psychological patterns in conveying the abstractions in the lives of these individuals:

> Spatial and temporal doubling, spatial and temporal incest, narcissism, the Oedipus Complex, the castration complex, repetition, sameness and difference, recollection, repression, revenge, substitution, reversal, sacrifice and mediation. And it is not simply that every element is simultaneously present to and interacting with every other element, it is that every element, considered in its relationship to every other element in the structure, is simultaneously present to and interacting with every other element.[27]

In *Light in August,* the tropes of doubling, repetition, revenge, repression, reversal, and the castration complex will be especially germane to my discussion. As the schizophrenic "white nigger" and a caricature of white racial hysteria, Christmas's matrix of desire is conceived through miscegenation. Consequently, whether Christmas's sexual relationship involves a black woman or a white woman, the portentous shadow of miscegenation hangs over him like a dark cloud.

Like Douglass's *Narrative* of 1845, *Light in August* is a narrative of desire. Trying to make sense of his racial identity, Christmas is never able to break through problematic perceptions and the mythology of racial and sexualized discourse. Christmas is always passing because he does not know who he is. My central focus will be on Joe Christmas (especially with regard to his "miscegenation" relationships with women), his early life at the orphanage, his life with the tyrannical McEacherns, and his tempestuous life in Jefferson. These episodes reveal the interconnecting and overlapping themes of miscegenation, mimicry, and masquerade. As I explore these episodes in the following sections, I also argue that Christmas becomes tragically characterized as a racial monster, as an anti-Christ, and as a tragic black buck who must be destroyed.

On a Christmas evening, Joe Christmas's grandfather, Eupheus Hines (Doc Hines), deposits his grandson, wrapped in a blanket, on the doorstep of a white, prisonlike orphanage in Memphis, Tennessee. For the next five years, Christmas comes under the dissecting gaze of his grandfather, who is convinced that he is a "nigger." Hines's knowledge of Christmas's father's racial identity is uncertain, yet after Joanna Burden is murdered and Christmas is captured, Hines's wife describes to Gail Hightower and Byron Bunch what happened "when the trial was over and the circus owner come back and said how the man [Christmas's father] really was a part nigger instead of Mexican, like Eupheus said all the time he was, like the devil had told Eupheus he was a nigger" (377). The "trial" concerned Hines's hysterical chase, shooting, and killing of the "nigger" who, he later finds out, impregnated his daughter, Milly. Faulkner reverses the common paradigm of miscegenation (a white man and a black woman) to place emphasis on the greatest miscegenation taboo—that of a black man and a white woman.

Historically, this paradigm of the American family romance is critical in two regards. First, because of the legacy of slavery, the status of the child was legally determined by the status of the mother. Second, the notion of the purity of white womanhood was an enduring aspect of Southern culture. For a Southern white woman to give herself to a black man (and potentially to bear his child) was perhaps the ultimate violation of Southern racial etiquette. By naming Milly's lover a "nigger," Hines transforms a commonplace seduction into the horror of miscegenation. When Doc Hines facilitates the death of his daughter, Milly, by not allowing her to receive medical attention during the birth of Christmas, Hines's religious fanaticism and racial intolerance transcend ties of blood and kin. Having abducted his grandson and taken the janitor's job at the orphanage in Memphis, Hines lies in wait for Christmas's nigger blood to be exposed as a "sign and a damnation for bitchery" (127). In this regard, Hines's religious fanaticism and foreboding concerning miscegenation create a contagious racist legacy.

Faulkner's passing narrative suggests that Hines's constant discriminating and dissecting gaze at Christmas somehow confirms for the white children at the orphanage that Christmas is a "nigger." For the twenty-seven-year-old dietician, Miss Atkins, Christmas's racial identity is acknowledged during a primal scene. The doctor, Charley, who finds Christmas on the doorstep of the orphanage, and Miss Atkins, his source of nourishment (food), briefly symbolize his father and mother. Consequently, when Christmas, while eating toothpaste[28] from behind a curtain, hears Miss Atkins and Charley having a sexual tryst and is discovered, his racial identity and genealogy become critically connected. Violently snatching the curtain aside, the dietician furiously hisses: "Spying on me! You little nigger bastard!" (122). Symbolically, the curtain represents a veil that shields Christmas's racial identity and the dietician's racist and demeaning convictions. Once Christmas is exposed, the punishing dietician's discourse combines two of the nation's most explosive signifiers. Christmas represents the absence of white purity (miscegenation) and natal alienation. The signifiers "nigger" and "bastard" are among the lowest rungs on the ladder of racial and genealogical designation. To be a "nigger" is to be an enduring victim of white supremacy, and to be a "bastard" is to be without patriarchal validation, love, and support. In essence, the dietician's verbal stoning discourse conveys that Christmas is not only racially and genealogically inferior but also dangerous.[29] By making the punishing figure a dietician, Faulkner places emphasis on Christmas as one who is unnurtured and one who is unknowing of his racial and genealogical identity. This is one of the few places that Faulkner expresses sympathy for Christmas, the victimized child. Also, it is here that Faulkner constructs the cross-combinations of food and sex and the cross-combination of food and race. Through the disturbing discourse of Hines and the dietician, Christmas becomes completely subject to the dominant culture's definitions.

Like the Ex-Coloured Man, Christmas gradually understands his racial, social, and genealogical "inferior" place in white society. As in Johnson's passing narrative, Christmas encounters a double estrangement. As Anatole Broyard states:

> The inauthentic Negro is not only estranged from whites—he is also estranged from his own group and from himself. Since his companions are a mirror in which he sees himself as ugly, he must reject them; and since his own self is mainly a tension between an accusation and a denial, he can hardly find it, much less live it. . . . He is adrift without a role in a world predicated on roles.[30]

Yet, unlike the Ex-Coloured Man, Christmas has no mirror or mother to turn to in order to ascertain his racial identity. With the other children consistently calling him "nigger" and Hines asking him, "Do you think you are a nigger because God has marked your face?" (383), Christmas innocently asks a black man working at the orphanage, "How come you are a nigger?" (383). The black man's indignant and prophetic response mirrors Faulkner's aforementioned discourse concerning the Christmas tragedy:

> "Who told you I am a nigger, you little white trash bastard?" and he says "I aint a nigger" and the nigger says "You are worse than that. *You dont know what you are. And more than that, you wont never know.* You'll live and you'll die and you wont never know" and he says "God aint no nigger" and the nigger says "I reckon you ought to know what God is, because dont nobody but God know what you is." (384; emphasis added)

Although this black man's discourse reverses the dietician's racist discourse, the spirit of rejection remains the same. The tragedy of Christmas's genealogy remains a constant, propelling him to an uncertain and problematic future. In essence, the black man tells Christmas that his "whiteness" has been bastardized. The black man's caustic statement represents a paradox. He (un)names Christmas as "white," whereas the whites (un)name him "nigger." Christmas realizes that he cannot be both "white" and a "nigger." It is here that Christmas's double consciousness and racial schizophrenia, like those of the Ex-Coloured Man, begins. In terms of racial identity, Christmas does not know what he is, and Faulkner then brings that lack of knowledge to the level of cosmic significance.

Further, it is the primal scene that leads the dietician to attempt to bribe the illegitimate "nigger," to confront Hines about the fatherless "nigger," and to reveal to the matron that a misbegotten "nigger" has been in the midst of the white orphan-age. These three incidents become critical in determining Joe Christmas's future of mimicking and masquerading, positioning him as a perpetual outsider.

Faulkner's theme of knowledge and ignorance is revealed in the dietician's hys-terical assumption that the five-year-old Christmas realized that she and Charley were having sex and that he would tell someone. Yet, her repetitive discourse sug-gests that she has no doubt about Christmas's racial identity. In *The House Behind the Cedars,* John Walden gives his sister, Rena, a dime with a hole in it, and in Johnson's *The Autobiography of an Ex-Coloured Man,* the protagonist's white father gives him a ten-dollar gold piece with a hole in it, but here the dietician offers Christmas an unflawed silver dollar for the silence of her secret witness. The irony of this bribe is that it hardens Christmas in the Calvinist tradition of expecting to be beaten for evil, rather than being rewarded for goodness. For Christmas, the dollar is transformed into the toothpaste that caused him to vomit. He rejects the bribe. For refusing the bribe that connects sex and race, Christmas hears: "Tell, then! You little nigger bastard! You nigger bastard!" Copulation brings this white woman and this little "nigger" together. In fact, the dietician wonders whom she hates more, Charley or the "nigger" in the closet, spying on her. Milly's "miscegen-ation" act of copulation and the symbolic miscegenation framed by this primal scene become the catalyst for *Light in August*. This primal scene becomes the defin-itive moment for Christmas's future relationships with women. All of his female relationships are encased in the shadow of miscegenation and the ambiguous na-ture of his racial identity. Thus, Faulkner's statement that "Memory believes before knowing remembers. Believes longer than recollects, longer than knowing even wonders" (119) becomes critical. Doc Hines's memory believes Christmas is a "nig-ger" before knowing remembers, and his critically dissecting gaze has the effect of convincing the dietician that Christmas is black.

The language of this primal scene and its aftermath represent Christmas's mir-ror stage wherein he doesn't recognize himself in a fantasy of his future bodily wholeness and assumes, as "the armour of an alienating identity," the template or "rigid structure" that determines his subjectivity.[31] Lacan suggests that the identifi-cation of the self with an outside image provides a basis for identity by substitut-ing the coherent image of the other for a complex, unstable identity. Christmas be-comes stigmatized with the identity of "nigger," as opposed to an identity that comprises both black and white.

Putting the pieces of the enigmatic puzzle together concerning Hines's insis-tent gaze and Christmas's appearance, and seeking validation of her racial hatred, the dietician confronts Hines: "You knew before the other children started calling him Nigger. You came out here at the same time. You weren't working here a month before that Christmas night when Charley found him on the doorstep yon-der. Tell me" (127). Apprehensive that Christmas might disclose her sexual indis-cretion with Charley, she reveals to Hines that she fears being fired. For Hines, the dietician's revelation is prophetic: "I knowed he would be there to catch you when God's time came. I knowed. I know who set him there, a sign and a damnation for bitchery" (127). Christmas becomes a vile semiotic representation for women's fornication. On the other hand, Hines's religious discourse mirrors the deadly fanaticism directed at his daughter, Milly, and his fears of miscegenation. Faulkner's juxtaposition of the dietician and Hines's daughter, Milly, suggests a synthesis of Hines's misogyny and his hatred of miscegenation. The conflict between the dietician and Hines concludes with the dietician's threat to expose the "nigger" to the orphanage authorities.

When Hines abducts Christmas, the dietician reveals to the matron that Christmas is a "nigger." Again we have the theme of knowledge and ignorance. The shocked matron acknowledges that she had no idea that Christmas is black. Yet the dietician vaguely responds to the matron's inquiry about how she knows Christmas's racial identity: "They [the children] have been calling him Nigger for years. Sometimes I think that children have a way of knowing things that grown people of your age and my age dont see. Children, and old people like him [Hines] that old man" (133). This recalls Johnson's novel, in which the black children acknowledge that they knew the protagonist was black even while the white children assumed that he was white. Hence, the racial identity of the "parchment-colored" Christmas is socially constructed by the children who call him "nigger" and by the critical gaze of Hines.

Faulkner's discourse suggests that either Hines's behavior influenced the children or the children's behavior somehow confirmed and validated Hines's specious theory about Christmas's racial identity. This double trope highlights the paradoxical nature of racial passing. It is possible to pass for white and it is possible to pass for black, but you can never rest in between. In America's white supremacist culture, where blackness is too often associated with inferiority and pathology, passing for black except in terms of minstrelsy is a rare social performance.[32] Also, it is here that the physical characteristics of Christmas are discussed. The matron states: "I dont see how we failed to see it [Christmas's blackness] as long as we did. You can look at his face now, his eyes and hair. Of course its terrible. But that's [a black orphanage] where he will have to go I suppose" (134). The matron's discourse seems more of a rationalization or an excuse for her inability to detect Christmas's racial identity. In essence, a "nigger" got past her racial scrutiny. Of course, the matron's cogitative discourse confirms Irene Redfield's sagacious statement in *Passing* that many white people believe in the "silly rot" that an individual's hair, eyes, ears, or fingernails can be used to detect the ontology of racial identity. Second only to skin color, hair texture and language are critically linked to racial classification.[33] Further, the matron's vague discussion of Christmas's physical characteristics reveals that, in Faulkner's work, unlike Johnson's, the lack of a detailed physical description furthers the theme of Christmas's racial ambiguity.

Faulkner further complicates the paradox of passing when we consider that, although Himes fervently believes that Christmas is black, he brings him to a white orphanage. Is Doc Hines trying to pass Christmas off as white? And, after the dietician threatens to expose the "racially impure" Christmas to the matron, Hines, like a thief in the night, takes him to another white orphanage where the place

"was no different from the one which they had left in the night—the same children, with different names; the same grown people, with different smells: he
[Christmas] could see no more reason why he should not have stayed there than
why he should ever have left the first one" (140). Hines's behavior appears antithetical to his raving belief in white supremacy and his Jim Crow philosophy that
black people and white people should be segregated. Paradoxically, Hines and his
wife are dependent on black women who bring "dishes of food"; yet he was sanc-
timoniously "going single handed into remote negro churches and interrupting
the service . . . and in his harsh, dead voice and at times with violent obscenity,
preach to them humility before all skins lighter than theirs, preaching the superiority of the white race, himself his own exhibit A, in fanatic and unconscious paradox" (343–344). Here we have a synthesis of Doc Hines's religious and racial fanaticism. Intrinsic to the religious-based theory of white supremacy is the
spurious notion that a light-skinned individual is superior to a dark-skinned individual. This theory might help to explain why Hines, with his firebrand racism,
places Christmas in the white orphanage. Hines reveres whiteness. Faulkner's narrative technique suggests that, because Christmas's racial identity is generally acknowledged and accepted as white (he can pass for white), Hines believes he
should be in a white institution despite his being a "nigger."

Hines is not alone in passing Christmas off as white and not alone in believing
that his presumably tainted grandson should be raised in an all-white environment.
Despite finding out that Christmas is black, the matron of the orphanage states
that a white "place" should be found "at once," and she acts quickly and clandestinely in order to remove him and to pass him into a white family. When Simone
McEachern, the adoptive parent, asks about Christmas's family background, the
matron states: "As I told you before, he was left on the doorstep here on Christmas
Eve will be five years this two weeks. If the child's parentage is important to you,
you had better not adopt one at all" (142). Simone McEachern's concern about
family background foreshadows Gavin Stevens's analysis of the unpredictability
associated with "blood." In addition, it is here that we discover that Miss Atkins,
the dietician, has been corresponding with the McEacherns to place Christmas,
but, of course, she has not revealed his racial heritage. Thus, like the teacher and
the protagonist mother in *The Autobiography of an Ex-Coloured Man,* like Judge
Straight and Molly Walden in *The House Behind the Cedars,* all of whom acquiesce
in the philosophy of white supremacy, Doc Hines, Miss Atkins, and the matron
are three-party conspirators who facilitate the process of assisting Joe Christmas to
cross over and establish a white identity. By prevaricating and passing Christmas
off as white, they contradict their deep-seated racist beliefs and expose the fallacy
of racial fragmentation. Yet, the psychological damage done to Christmas is irreversible. Consequently, Christmas becomes immersed in the tangled weeds of the
paradox of racial passing.

Like the Ex-Coloured Man, Christmas has largely been socialized to be white,
and, when the traumatic episode with the dietician occurs, he must somehow
mimic or negotiate whiteness and blackness. Joe's memory believes in his innate

whiteness and blackness before his knowing remembers. Like our other passing characters, Christmas represents a racial oxymoron living on the fringes of Southern society.

Christmas experiences a spartan, brutal life with the McEacherns. Simone McEachern doubles for Hines, the religious fanatic. Creating echoes of Frederick Douglass's account of being equated with the "horses and men, cattle and women, pigs and children"[34] McEachern views Christmas with "the same stare with which he might have examined a horse or a second hand plow, convinced before hand that he would see flaws, convinced before-hand that he would buy" (142). Subsequently, when Christmas refuses to learn the Presbyterian catechism, McEachern beats him until he becomes unconscious. Like the young girl Alice at the orphanage (the only character who shows Christmas unconditional concern), Mrs. McEachern attempts to mother Christmas by providing him with "secret dishes" of food. Her attempts fail. Yet, in payment for the dishes, Christmas contemplates telling this "patient, beaten creature without sex demarcation"[35] (165) that Simone McEachern "has nursed a blasphemer and an ingrate. I dare you to tell him what he has nursed. That he has nursed a nigger beneath his own roof, with his own food at his own table" (168). Although he lives in this world of firebrand religious whiteness, Christmas has accepted Hines's speculation that he is a "nigger." In reaction to this religious fanaticism and this austere life, Christmas has two relationships with women—one black and one white—that place emphasis on his attempt to mimic whiteness within the shadow of miscegenation.

As an adolescent, ten years after the events previously described, the white-black Christmas, along with four white boys, has an "arranged" sexual encounter with a black girl. While the other boys are sexually satisfied, Christmas enters the barn, and soon the smell of the "womanshenegro" aggravates and enrages him as he recalls the primal scene with the dietician:

> There was something in him trying to get out, like when he had used to think of toothpaste. But he could not move at once, standing there, smelling the woman smelling the negro all at once; enclosed by the womanshenegro and the haste, driven, having to wait until she spoke: a guiding sound that was no particular word and completely unaware. . . . He kicked her hard, kicking into and through a choked wail of surprise and fear. She began to scream, he jerking her up, clutching her by the arm, hitting at her with wide, wild blows, striking at the voice perhaps, feeling her flesh anyway, enclosed by the womanshenegro and the haste. (156–157)

No longer the auditory voyeur and no longer the "nigger" hiding in the closet, as if in a trance, Christmas confronts a black girl who unknowingly forces him to face his black self-hatred, his racially torn identity, and his desire to be like the four other boys—white. In addition, Christmas senses his own "womanness" along with his blackness—both embodied in the pathetic black girl. Faulkner's description of the "womanshenegro," a synthesis of signifiers, moves from the concrete to the abstract and from the common to the pejorative: "Then it seemed to him that he could see her—something, prone, abject; her eyes perhaps. Leaning, he seemed to look down into a black well and at the bottom saw two glints like reflections of dead stars" (156). Images of despair, desolation, and death abound with this description. This scene reverses Lacan's mirror scene. Christmas sees himself in the black girl's eyes, not merely in the reflection but in his recognition of racial ancestry. The image is not one that allows him to project his ego; Christmas violently reacts to the shame and degradation to which the boys have subjected the girl. The metaphor of "dead stars" aptly represents the linguistic tension between the signifiers of black and white. Faulkner's unnamed black girl becomes an object on which these white boys satisfy their lust and enact their roles as powerful white males. More important, this miscegenation spectacle suggests Christmas's dismal future with his black and white identity in a white-dominated society; accordingly, he becomes hysterical with rage. This brutal miscegenation incident foreshadows Christmas's future violence toward white women and his growing restlessness with his black identity.

Faulkner reverses yet repeats the "womanshenegro" paradigm with Christmas's relationship with the childlike waitress Bobbie Allen. Her name refers to the Anglo-American folk ballad of love cruelly ended.[36] Unlike the nameless black girl, Bobbie has a name and a complex identity. In fact, when Christmas returns to the diner, he hears the name "Bobbie" and assumes that the waitress has been fired and replaced by a man. "She gone. They [Mame and Max Confrey, the restaurant owners] have got a man in her place. I have wasted the dime, like he [Mr. McEachern] said" (179). This gender ambiguity, along with Mrs. McEachern's description, mirrors Christmas's growing racial ambiguity and foreshadows the dual ambiguity of both Christmas and Joanna Burden. Faulkner complicates the gender ambiguity: Bobbie is both a waitress and a prostitute; the diner is masquerading as a brothel, with Max and Mame as Bobbie's pimps. What is significant about Christmas's relationship with Bobbie is that Christmas for the first time verbally acknowledges his blackness. Twice Christmas (seeing a naked woman for the first time and bringing attention to his skin and his hair) informs Bobbie: "I think I got some nigger blood in me" and then adds, "I don't know. I believe I have" (196–197). This racial doubt is a psychological plague. Bobbie, who thought he was a "foreigner," responds with disbelief. It is also here that Christmas tells her of the "womanshenegro" in the mill shed. These revelations bring emphasis to Christmas's racial confusion, yet represent an honest attempt to face the tragedy of miscegenation.

Like the incidents with the dietician and with the "womanshenegro," Christmas's relationship with the prostitute Bobbie accentuates the nexus of sex, money, and race. In addition to these three critical factors, the religious fanaticism of Doc Hines and Simone McEachern positions Christmas as a despotic pariah. About Christmas, Hines's apprehensions center on race, whereas McEachern's apprehensions center on "lying and lechery." Through the juxtaposition of these two fanatics, the theme of miscegenation endures and escalates as Christmas's sexual identity matures.

Although unsure that he is "paying with money for pleasure" (191), Christmas gives Bobbie money stolen from Mrs. McEachern. And, like Bobbie's other men,

Christmas discovers that she sells herself for money: "He could see now what he discovered that he had known all the time: the idle men in the restaurant, with their cigarettes bobbing as they spoke to her in passing, and she going back and forth, constant, downlooking, and abject" (199). Christmas's ignorance and knowledge of Bobbie's sexuality will be later echoed as Christmas defends her honor when the frantic McEachern follows him to a dance and, upon seeing her, orders Bobbie: "Away, Jezebel . . . Away, harlot" (204). When Christmas crashes a chair on McEachern's head and believes that Bobbie will now run away with him, Bobbie's ignorance and her knowledge of Christmas's conflicting racial identity smack him in the face. True to her name, Bobbie Allen cruelly terminates her brief encounter with Christmas. Echoing the dietician's racist and demeaning discourse, Bobbie screams: "Bastard! Son of a bitch! Getting me into a jam that always treated you like you were a white man. A white man!" (217) and then, to Max and Mame: "He told me himself he was a nigger! The son of a bitch! Me f.ing for nothing a nigger son of a bitch that would get me in a jam with clodhopper police. At a clodhopper dance!" (218). Bobbie's previous disbelief about Christmas's racial true identity ("black blood") is transformed into a conviction when she needs to distance herself from him. For Bobbie, who once doubted his blackness, Christmas is now a nigger bastard. Yet, when a shattering blow sends Christmas to the now bloodstained floor, a voice inquires: "Is he really a nigger? He don't look like one" (219). Again, Faulkner, foreshadowing Christmas's tragic death, juxtaposes racial certainty with racial skepticism.

Christmas's obstreperous life with the McEacherns (Faulkner leaves unresolved the question of whether Simone McEachern survives Christmas's assault, as he does other ambiguities) concludes when an unnamed person attempts to ascertain his racial identity by drawing blood. "We'll find out. We'll see if his blood is black" (219). Mame stops the bloodletting. When Christmas regains consciousness, he refigures the biblical story of Jesus going into the wilderness; Christmas goes into a racial wilderness. Before Christmas permanently settles in Jefferson, he spends years mimicking blackness and whiteness. Like a racial bohemian or a chameleon, he alternates between living with black people and living with white people. Mimicking solidifies Christmas's racial confusion and alienation.

Despite the difference in the number of years invoked in the biblical paradigm of Jesus Christ's spiritual journey into the wilderness, Faulkner creates an analogy with Christmas and the fifteen years he spends on the street.[37] Faulkner's remark that the "thousand streets ran as one street" (223) connects geographical mobility to the phenomenon of passing. Gypsylike, Christmas roams the "imperceptible corners and changes of scene, broken by intervals of begged and stolen rides on trains on trucks, and on country wagons he at twenty and twenty-five and thirty sitting on the seat with his still, hard face and the clothes (even when soiled and worn) of a city man and the driver of the wagon not knowing who or what the passenger was and not daring to ask" (223–224). Indeed, like the former slaves William and Ellen Craft, Christmas is "running a thousand miles for freedom." Faulkner's rubric of the roaming and rootless individual recalls the geographically transforming experience of John Warwick in *The House Behind the Cedars* and the national and international travels of Johnson's Ex-Coloured Man. A critical difference here is that there is no rest for Christmas anywhere—not even for a moment—and, in consequence, there can be few thrills in the masquerade to equal the thrills that John Warwick, Rowena Warwick, and the Ex-Coloured Man experience.

Christmas travels to Chicago and Detroit, joins the army for four months, becomes a deserter, and makes money as a laborer, a miner, a prospector, and a gambler. Recalling the racially pragmatic John (Walden) Warwick, Christmas understands that a change in geography has seductive possibilities that will allow him to assume either a white identity or a black identity. Attempting to pass from whiteness to blackness in Detroit, Christmas

> lived with Negroes, shunning white people. . . . He now lived as man and wife with a woman who resembled an ebony carving. At night he would lie in bed beside her . . . trying to breathe into himself the dark odor, the dark and inscrutable thinking and being of Negroes, with each suspiration trying to expel from himself the white blood and the white thinking and being. And all the while his nostrils at the odor which he was trying to make his own would whiten and tauten, his whole being writhe and strain with physical outrage and spiritual denial. (225–226)

With his multiple color-coded identities intact, Christmas uses his relationships with women as a testing ground to play out and play on America's inherently stereotypical racial divisions. For his socioeconomic and sexual advantage, Christmas mimics whiteness and mimics blackness. On the "street" (a metaphor for miscegenation, mimicry, and masquerade), where individuals' names become like whiffs of smoke, Christmas "bedded with the women and paid them when he had the money, and when he did not have it he bedded them anyway and then told them that he was a negro" (224). With the notion of white being superior, Christmas masquerades as white; when in an inferior state (without money), he masquerades as black. As Fanon maintains, this inferiority complex is the outcome of a double process: part economic and part the result of the internalization of this inferiority.[38] Consequently, assuming his without money black identity, Christmas expects to be cursed out, beaten, and thrown in the street or in jail. Here, Faulkner reinforces the theme of Christmas's refusal to accept a single racial identity. Accordingly, he continues this bizarre behavior until he beds a white woman who has no compunction about sleeping with a black man. Christmas, who has now internalized the theory of white superiority, becomes enraged, and, as in the miscegenation scene at the mill in which the four white boys pull him off the "womanshenegro," it "took two policemen to subdue him. At first they thought that the woman was dead" (225). Despite the dominance of white supremacy, Christmas, nauseous, discovers that some white women "would take a man with a black skin." By bringing attention to himself, Christmas behaves in a way that represents a paradox in that he beats the white woman because she does not adhere to the Southern notion of white female purity. Here again, Fanon argues: "We know historically that the Negro guilty of lying with a white woman is castrated. The Negro who has had a white woman makes himself taboo to his fellows."³⁹ This racial revelation causes Christmas to be sick for two years. In addition, this miscegenation scene recalls the Ex-Coloured Man's miscegenation discomfort (regarding a black man and a white woman) at the club where the black man, in an enraged paroxysm of jealousy, shoots his white lover in the throat. Both the Ex-Coloured Man and Christmas are rootless roamers who embrace whiteness in their ineffectual endeavors to escape the pain and tragedy of their childhoods. For Christmas and for Faulkner, race matters, and whiteness is essentially superior to blackness.

The final path on this "street" leads Christmas to the town of Jefferson, Mississippi, where Faulkner's racial and gender ambiguities reach a cataclysmic crescendo. With Christmas's tragic relationship with Joanna Burden and in its aftermath, the intricate issues of miscegenation, mimicry, and masquerading become woven together.

With pangs of hunger, Christmas climbs catlike through the window of Joanna Burden's colonial plantation house. Like John Warwick and his mansion, with its shadows of slavery, there is irony in the Burden family's living in such a home, since the family had been opponents of slavery. Faulkner correlates the past and the present by relating the dietician's color-coded statement. The dietician realizes that if Christmas is sent to the black orphanage, he "will look just like a pea in a pan full of coffee beans" (130). Later, Christmas makes a discovery: "'Its peas,' he said aloud. 'For sweet Jesus. Field peas cooked with molasses'" (230). Like a field nigger granted entrance to the master's white house, Christmas is greeted by an emotionally cold Joanna. "'If it is food you want, you will find that,' she said in a voice calm, a little deep, quite cold" (231).

Faulkner innovatively uses food to emphasize racial passing and miscegenation. When Joe Christmas goes to the diner alone to see the waitress-prostitute Bobbie, the symbolically miscegenation dessert he orders is "Lemon coconut chocolate" pie (179). This multicolored food/sex metaphor suggests the black and white racial mixture that produces the passing high-yellow tragic mulatto. Also, like Clare Kendry's two white aunts in *Passing*,⁴⁰ who use the biblical parable of the descendants of Ham as the hewers of wood and drawers of water to rationalize the inferiority of black people, the exasperated Christmas makes this (food throwing) connection when Joanna serves him "Ham" that is *"Set out for the nigger. For the nigger"* (238; author's emphasis). Christmas's infuriated and rancorous behavior aptly suggests that "Ham" is for the nigger, the descendants of "Ham" are niggers, and a nigger with his "tainted black blood" is cursed at birth.⁴¹ Faulkner's juxtaposition of Joe and Joanna suggests the Southern miscegenation legacy of the white-master-black-slave dialectic. This dialectic is borne out by Christmas's being only a perpetual visitor to the house (mainly for food and sex); his permanent residence is in the dilapidated "nigger" cabin (where enslaved black people once lived) below Joanna's house.

From the start, Christmas, who struggles with his racial duality, encounters gender trouble. Joanna, Christmas discovers, has a "dual personality: the one the woman at first sight of whom in the lifted candle . . . there had opened before him, instantaneous as a landscape in a lightning flash, a horizon of physical security and adultery if not pleasure; the other the man-trained muscles and the man-trained habit of thinking born of heritage and environment with which he had to fight up to the final instant" (235). This duality of demeanor leads Christmas to question not only his manhood and masculinity but also Joanna's femininity.[42] When he beds her, "'My God,' he thought, 'it was like I was the woman and she was the man.' But that was not right either. Because she had resisted to the very last. But it was not woman resistance, that resistance which, if really meant, cannot be overcome by any man for the reason that the woman observes no rules of physical combat" (235).

Indeed, *Light in August* characterizes Joanna as the master of the house and as the master of this obstreperous black-and-white psychosexual relationship. Whereas there exist narrative rumor and speculation concerning Joe Christmas's genealogy, there exists no narrative skepticism concerning the legacy of miscegenation in Joanna Burden's family. Faulkner complicates the racial dynamics by intertwining dynamics of gender. The name Joanna suggests a synthesis of Joe and Anna (Miss Ann) and a synthesis of male and female. Faulkner repeatedly conveys that Joe and Joanna do not adhere to simplistic racial or gender constructs. Joanna's last name, "Burden," suggests the painful linguistic marginality characterized by painful racial and gendered marginality.

In the most tranquil scene in *Light in August,* Joanna, sitting in the dark cabin, solemnly relates to Christmas the enduring burden of her family history. Joanna's father, Calvin Burden, a tall Nordic man, married "the daughter of a family of Huguenot stock" (241) and produced a son who "inherited his mother's build and coloring" (242). Together, father and son looked "like people of two different races" (242). The son, Nathaniel, following his father's example, chose a Spanish woman as his mate. Years later, scrutinizing Nathaniel's son for the first time, Calvin states, "he got a man build anyway, for all his black look. By God, he going to be a man as big as his grandpappy; not a runt like his pa. For all his black dam and his black look, he will" (248). This legacy of miscegenation reinforces the dogma of white supremacy and the pejorative nature of blackness. It recalls the speculations about Christmas's father being a "Mexican" and Doc Hines's hatred for blackness. Both Joanna Burden and Joe Christmas are trapped by their histories. Whether factual or speculative, Joanna and Christmas have fanatical family legacies of miscegenation that are inescapable.

Continuing to discuss her family history, Joanna relates that she was taught by her fanatically religious and abolitionist father to despise two things: "hell and slaveholders." More important, Joanna is charged with enacting redemption for the murder of her grandfather (killed by Colonel Sartoris) and of her brother, murdered for fighting for black people's voting rights. Faulkner connects this personal charge with the Hametic legacy. Joanna's father mandates: "You must struggle, rise. But in order to rise, you must rise the shadow with you. But you can never lift it to your level . . . But escape it you cannot. The curse of the black race is God's curse. But the curse of the white race is the black man who will be forever

God's chosen own because He once cursed him" (253). This patriarchal charge has led to Joanna's becoming a consultant and adviser to a "dozen negro schools and colleges through the south" (233). In this intimate genealogical sharing session, Christmas repeats that he does not know who his parents are "[E]xcept that one of them was part nigger" (254). Yet, when confronted by Joanna's sincere attempt to ascertain the certainty of his black racial heritage, Christmas candidly acknowledges that "I dont know it" and "If I'm not, damned if I haven't wasted a lot of time" (254). Later, Christmas, who believes he has been Hametically and historically cursed with "black blood," comes under Joanna's patriarchal charge.

This patriarchal charge leads Joanna to attempt to transform Christmas from a dual-passing (passing for black and passing for white) individual into a permanent black individual. Joanna suggests to Christmas that he elevate black people out of the "darkness" by going to a black school and becoming a black lawyer:

> "But a nigger college, a nigger lawyer," his voice said, quiet, not even argumentative; just promptive.
> "Tell them," she said.
> "Tell niggers that I am a nigger too?" She now looked at him. Her face was quite calm. It was the face of an old woman now.
> "Yes. You'll have to do that. So they wont charge you anything. On my account."
> (276–277)

Joanna, believing Christmas to be a "nigger," relates his racial identity to economic subjectivity.[43] Like Christmas, Joanna views blackness as being related to a wretched and inferior economic status. Blackness means poverty. Poverty means blackness. Equally pejorative, Joanna has sexualized blackness. Christmas often finds her naked or with clothes half-torn "in the wild throes of nymphomania" (259). Panting and with her hands flaying like a wild octopus, Joanna beckons: "Negro! Negro! Negro!" (260). Despite her altruistic behavior, Joanna imagines herself the white virgin raped and despoiled by a crazed "Negro." Joanna clearly aligns herself with white supremacy. Just as important, Joanna's internalization of problematic notions of blackness and her racial charge push Christmas to make a definitive choice. Joanna's deadly mistake is that she attempts to dictate what is in the best interest of Christmas without being herself in a position to make such a critical judgment. Consequently, when Joanna, revolver in hand, asks Christmas to kneel and pray, race and religion combine to cause the razor-bearing and enraged Christmas to decapitate and burn her.[44] Like the white woman shot in the throat in *The Autobiography of an Ex-Coloured Man,* Joanna and her decapitation are especially important in furthering the abhorrence of miscegenation. The female head as a sexualized symbol with its voice disrupts the gender distinctions that privilege men's link to discourse. As Howard Eilberg-Schwartz contends:

> Decapitation is one way of solving the dilemma. Removing the female head relieves woman of both identity and voice and reduces her to a mere sexual and reproductive body. But there are other, less obvious, forms of beheading. The eroticization of the

female head extends the body, turning the head into an alluring and sexually provocative organ. In this way, the female head becomes part of a woman's genitalia.[45]

With sex as the troubled center of the theme of miscegenation, Faulkner's treatment of women (misogyny) is different from Chesnutt's and Johnson's. Christmas's "castration" of Joanna eliminates her challenging racial and religious discourse. And this blood drama is an ironic comment on Thomas Jefferson's apprehension and jeremiad warning that black people would seek revenge for years of enslavement. Jefferson states: "Indeed I tremble for my country when I reflect that God is just: that his justice cannot sleep for ever: that . . . a revolution of the wheel of fortune, an exchange of situation, is among possible events: that it may become probable by supernatural interference! The Almighty has no attribute which can take side with us in such a contest."[46] Yet, as a sexual symbol, Joanna's decapitated head highlights whites' abhorrence of miscegenation.

As Richard Wright does in the second chapter ("Flight") of his *Native Son* (1940),[47] Faulkner illustrates a dramatic chase-and-capture episode. Race becomes the rallying point for racist white individuals who "believed aloud that it was an anonymous negro crime committed not by a negro but a Negro and who knew, believed, and hoped that she [Joanna] had been ravished too: at least once before her throat was cut and at least once afterward" (288). For these whites, the belief that a "nigger" has ravished a white woman and engaged in necrophilia becomes the motivation for murder. This speculation points out how immensely sexualized Southern ideology is and how sexualized racial encounters are. Having confided in his partner and cabin mate in the illegal whiskey business,[48] Lucas Burch (Joe Brown), about his black identity, Christmas becomes exposed to the authorities as a "nigger" who has had a long-term sexual relationship with Joanna. Judas-like, Lucas hopes to receive not the "thirty pieces of silver" but the "thousand-dollars reward" for giving up the "nigger." With Joe Brown passing as Lucas Burch, Faulkner reinforces the theme of masquerade and suggests that the "dark-complexioned" Joe Brown is a double for Joe Christmas. In fact, *Light in August* characterizes Lucas (Joe) as a mirror image of Christmas: "I reckon he must have looked more like a murderer than even Christmas. And he was cussing Christmas now, like Christmas had done hid out just for meanness, to spite him and keep him from getting that thousand dollars" (303). Like Bigger Thomas, Joe Christmas becomes characterized as the nigger-rapist, the decapitator, and the murderer.

While in "flight" and carrying his "life like it was a basket of eggs" (337), Christmas behaves and appears physically in a manner that Faulkner describes as oscillating (masquerading) between that of a white man and that of a black man. It is here in the novel that Christmas epitomizes both the trickster figure and the "bad nigger."[49] In terms of race, most of the black and white people in and around Jefferson do not know what to make of Christmas. In a riotous "battle royal" scene, which recalls Doc Hines's preaching white supremacy to black people, Christmas, like a maniac, invades a black church. Reversing the religious paradigm, Faulkner conveys Christmas as a black-hating anti-Christ:

Then they [the black church folks] saw that the man was white. In the thick cavelike gloom which the two oil lamps but served to increase, they could not tell at once what he was until he was halfway up the aisle. Then they saw that his face was not black . . . and another woman on the mourners bench, already in a semihysterical state, sprang up and whirled and glared at him for an instant with white-rolling eyes and screamed "It the devil! It Satan himself. (322)

Like his grandfather, Doc Hines, Christmas has no veneration for black people at worship. After beating the preacher, Brother Bedenberry, and seventy-year-old Pappy Thompson, Christmas curses "God louder than the woman screeching" (323). Christmas's boisterous and rambunctious behavior suggests his belief in white supremacy and his hatred for blackness. Yet, paradoxically, Christmas accepts his blackness when he trades shoes with a black woman. This black woman tells the sheriff "about the white man on the road . . . and how he had swapped shoes with her, taking in exchange a pair of her husband's brogans which she was wearing at the time" (329). Cleverly mixing race (black for "white") and gender (male for female and back to male), Faulkner highlights the passing phenomenon. With his "black shoes smelling of negro" (331), Christmas, hunted by a gang of white men, moves toward "the black abyss which had been waiting, trying, for thirty years to drown him and into which now and at last he had actually entered, bearing now upon his ankles the definite and ineradicable gauge of its upward moving" (331). This "black abyss" reinforces the concept of miscegenation (Christmas's relationships with women) as the relentless force driving Christmas's tragic performances of mimicry and masquerading. We recall the "womanshenegro" in the barn as the first dark abyss that threatens to consume Christmas.

Black-hating white people do not know what to make of Christmas's enigmatic racial identity. These racist white individuals have preconceived notions concerning the social behavior of black and white people. Also, these white individuals believe they have a God-given right to be arrogant, whereas black people should be Hametically submissive. Christmas, in broad daylight, arrogantly walks into the town of Mottstown "like a white man, and because he looked like a white man they never suspected him" (349). Christmas is like an escaped slave coming into a new town and attempting to pass himself off as white. Christmas's everyday behavior irritates whites who use ocular analysis as the basis for racial validation: "He never acted like either a nigger or a white man. That was it. That was what made the folks so mad. For him to be a murderer and all dressed up and walking the town like he dared them to touch him, when he ought to have been skulking and hiding in the woods, muddy and dirty and running. It was like he never even knew he was a murderer, let alone a nigger too" (350). In the Jim Crow South, acceptable black behavior is associated with being submissive and knowing one's place. For any black individual to step outside white society's inscribed circle of black "inferiority" can be deadly. Faulkner conveys this racial duality and racial ambivalence in the clothes that Christmas wears. When Christmas first comes to the sawmill at Jefferson, his clothes reinforce his ambiguous racial identity:

He looked like a tramp, yet not like a tramp either. His shoes were dusty and his trousers were soiled too. But they were of decent serge, sharply creased, and his shirt was soiled but it was a white shirt, and he wore a tie and a stiffbrim straw hat . . . He did not look like a professional hobo in his professional rags, but there was something definitely rootless about him, as though no town nor city was his, no street, no walls, no square of earth his home. (31)

With Joanna's stolen money, Christmas as the quintessential "dirty white man"[50] gets a shave, gets his hair cut (the removal of hair suggests the removal of a dark mask), and recreates his "costume" (he buys a white shirt, a tie, and a straw hat) until Halliday confronts the "nigger." Halliday "hit the nigger a couple of times in the face, and the nigger acting like a nigger for the first time and taking it, not saying anything: just bleeding sullen and quiet" (350). For Halliday and the other whites, being sullen and submissive are proper behavior for niggers. Yet, many white people acknowledge the brazen Christmas as being the linguistically and racially contradictory "white nigger." Christmas becomes an "uppity" white nigger, and the subsequent "lynching" is the ultimate expression of a white supremacist desire to eroticize, control, and consume the black body. On the porch, whites engaging in race-talk in Mottstown speculate that "He dont look any more like a nigger than I do. But it must have been the nigger blood in him. It looked like he had set out to get himself caught like a man might set out to get married" (349). This statement suggests the connection between racial passing and marriage. The idea of a marriage to Joanna, along with the idea of fatherhood,[51] which Christmas seems to fear, appear restricting in comparison to the freedom Christmas associates with passing for white and passing for black. Furthermore, the most dangerous thing that Joanna attempts is to try to compel Christmas to accept his blackness, a fixed racial identity. As the accused murderer of a "Southern" white woman (when the racial frenzy reaches its peak, Joanna is transformed from a Northern, nigger-loving woman to a Southern white woman) and submitting to the Jim Crow "inferiority" of blackness, Christmas ensures his own violent death.

Ironically, Mottstown is the hometown of Christmas's grandparents, Doc Hines and Mrs. Hines. Upon hearing the news that Christmas has murdered a white woman, Doc Hines works himself into racial hysteria, calling for the death of his nigger-grandson: "Kill the bastard!" Doc Eupheus Hines, like a modern-day Pontius Pilate, hysterically cries, "Kill him, Kill him" (345). Of course, the irony here is that the crazed Doc Hines has created this "nigger bastard" by killing Christmas's father and by his rancorous neglect of Christmas's mother, which led to her death soon after Christmas's birth. Also, at the orphanage, Hines's relentless scrutiny and racial discourse have created his "nigger" grandson; Hines's rage may also lie in his inability to pass Christmas off as a white child. It is not literary hyperbole to contemplate a connection between *Light in August* and Mary Shelley's *Frankenstein* (1818). In fact, the monster's discourse concerning his physical and genealogical dilemma mirrors Christmas's racial and genealogical dilemma: "My person was hideous and my stature gigantic. What did this mean? *Who was I? Whence did I come? What was my destination?* These questions continually recurred, but I was unable to solve them"[52] (emphasis added). Like Doc Hines, Doctor Victor Frankenstein conveys a fanatical rage and a desire to kill his "hideous" creation.[53] This father-and-child relationship suggests an allusion to Hegel's concept of "lord and bondsman" in *The Phenomenology of Mind* (1977). While at the orphanage, Doc Hines is the "master" in the sense of "creator"; he neither depends on Christmas nor is a beneficiary of anything Christmas produces. Yet, Hegel's dialectic comes into play when Christmas becomes an adult and must face rumors that he has Joanna's blood on his hands. Christmas then becomes the "master" in the sense that Doc Hines is now forced to respond to his creation's murderous actions. As Eric J. Sundquist affirms, the oppressed/oppressor relationship involves masking that is first impenetrable and second hallucinatory: "The first is a masking that grows out of a responsibility for and confrontation with, the second; and it develops by the paradox that, the more strenuous and intricate the probing of oppressed by oppressor becomes, the more the black mask may become fixed until it seems a reflection of the white, distortion upon distortion in an endless recession of mirrored images."[54] Like the monster, Christmas's ambiguous appearance is the basis for his difference and becomes the rationalization for his marginalization, exclusion, and bloody ritualistic persecution. Doc Hines's abhorrence of racial mixing has been the critical agent in this tragic circle of miscegenation, mimicry, and masquerade. In fact, Christmas acknowledges the cataclysmic and inescapable circular ruins of his life: "I have never got outside that circle. I have never broken out of the ring of what I have already done and cannot ever undo" (339). This circle appropriately becomes an enduring metaphor for the ruinous circular vestiges of passing and masquerading. Further, as metonymy, the circle represents Christmas's movement outside fixed racial categories until he can no longer sustain his own isolation.

Violence has been a means for Christmas to break out of the circle; violence necessarily becomes Christmas's language of negotiation. We recall Christmas beating the "womanshenegro" in the barn, beating of the waitress, Bobbie, Christmas crashing the chair on McEachern's head, the savage beating of the white prostitute, the trouncing of Lucas Burch in the cabin, the killing of Joanna Burden, and, finally, Christmas thrashing black people at the church. Although these ruthless acts of violence allow Christmas a disturbing subjectivity, they also deepen his sense of alienation from white society. Also, these acts of violence reinforce the extent of Christmas's dehumanization. Yet, Christmas's violent acts are framed by the oppressive violence and victimization imposed by Doc Hines and by McEachern. Christmas's violent episodes suggest Fanon's analysis that the oppressed man uses violence in an attempt to free himself from despair, and "it makes him fearless and restores his self-respect.[55] Paradoxically, if Christmas ever attains any degree of self-respect, it is when he decides to end the mimicry and the masquerade.

Christmas strolls through the black section of town, named "Freedman Town" (which recalls Nella Larsen's use of the name "Freeland"[56] in *Passing*). It is here that, after years of mimicry and masquerade, Christmas psychologically passes from blackness to whiteness. Language becomes a critical aspect for Christmas in his consideration of whiteness as a permanent racial and national identity. He realizes the "summer smell and the summer voices of invisible negroes. *They seemed to enclose him like bodiless voices murmuring talking laughing in a language not his"* (114; emphasis added). Socialized as a white individual, Christmas does not speak a black dialect. Christmas can never be a part of the community that speaks it. Leaving behind the smell and the voices of blackness, Christmas, "passing again between the houses of white people," enters an attractive world of whiteness: "Now and then he could see them: heads in silhouette, a white blurred garmented shape; on a lighted veranda four people sat about a card table, the white faces intent and sharp in the low light, the bare arms of the woman glaring smooth and white above the trivial cards. *"'That's all I wanted,' he thought. 'That dont seem like a whole lot to ask'"* (115; emphasis added). This scene becomes a symbolic representation of the American Dream. Finally, Christmas makes a decision to accept the dream of whiteness, but this present world of whiteness is too far behind him. The past cannot be "undone." Joanna's death has bloodily fixed Christmas in time and blackness. Christmas's crime of murder, the rumors about his raping a white woman and the rumors of necrophilia, the pursuit by whites with dogs, and the black man's shoes—all criminalize Christmas and criminalize blackness. Like an escaped slave on the run, Christmas is forced to accept his blackness and his impending death. Christmas acknowledges the drastic change: "I have been further in these seven days than in all the thirty years . . . the black shoes smelling of negro: the mark on his ankles the gauge definite and ineradicable of the black tide creeping up his legs, moving from his feet upward as death moves" (339). Like a prophetic boomerang, the past continues to strike Christmas in the head. Percy Grimm, as the lynching judge of Southern racial etiquette, eliminates Christmas's desire to permanently embrace whiteness.

Like the archangel of death, Percy Grimm, squirting blood in God's face, brings a trenchant and bloody halt to the circular vestiges of passing and masquerading. When Christmas escapes his captors, Grimm becomes the vitriolic, self-sanctioning force that will restore social and racial order to the Southern community of Jefferson. Escaping to the former Reverend Gail Hightower's house (along with the gender ambiguity of "Gail," again Faulkner suggests a synthesis between race and religion),[57] Christmas, who is hiding behind an upturned table, acquiesces in Grimm's murderous and castrating malevolence. Throwing away the bloody butcher knife after castrating Christmas, Grimm salaciously proclaims: *"Now you'll let white women alone, even in hell"* (464; emphasis added).[58] Faulkner uses repetition, reversal, and revenge to place emphasis on Christmas's "castration" of Joanna Burden. Emphasis is also placed on white society's desire to control and consume the black body. Accordingly, this castration highlights the synthesis between sex and lynching. In *Rope and Faggot*, Walter White writes:

> Despite the evidence of the figures showing that only a small percentage of lynched Negroes were even accused of rape, the vast majority of whites in the states where

lynchings are most frequently staged really believe that most murders are the result of sex crimes. *Having created the Frankenstein monster (and it is no less terrifying because it is largely illusory), the lyncher lives in constant fear of his own creation and, at the same time has by means of his creation caused more crimes against the women of his race than there would have been in a more sane and normal environment.*[59] (emphasis added)

In line with Fanon's phallus-centered comment that the "Negro symbolizes the biological danger,"[60] Christmas's genitalia are sacrificed for the purity of Southern white womanhood.[61]

Grimm's bloody baptism transforms Christmas into an enduring raceless and genderless memory. Like McEachern's behavior, Grimm's behavior is quite predictable and is a cataclysmic comfort to Christmas, who believes "that it was the woman alone who was unpredictable" (159). Unknowingly, Grimm becomes an avenging angel in the Faustian paradigm[62] who furiously closes the metaphorical curtain on Joe Christmas's tragic, yet memorable performance. Recalling the African American spiritual that says, "Before I'll be a slave, I'll be buried in my grave and go home to my Lord and be free," it is only through a violent death that Christmas finds "freedom." Yet, this horrifying and macabre scene is important as a quasi-public execution that reactivates power.

In *Discipline and Punish* (1979), Michel Foucault makes it clear that "The public execution did not re-establish injustice, it reactivated power. . . . The ceremony of public torture and execution displayed for all to see the power relation that gives this force to the law."[63] If justice requires humanity, Faulkner's characterization of Christmas is that of a monstrous black buck. Like the Ex-Coloured Man's presence at the lynch-burning of the black man, white people's hated and fear are the cornerstones of lynching; the killing of black men restores the whip-scarring sovereignty of white supremacy by manifesting itself in its most spectacular ritual of consumption. Ironically, Lena's baby is born in the cabin behind Joanna's house as Grimm slays the "monstrous" Christmas.[64] Through a monstrous death and a bucolic birth, the circular movement of the novel is emphasized.

Equally ironic (in terms of Faulkner's racist discourse)[65] and like the three other passing narratives, *Light in August* reads as a convincing indictment of a racist society. Yet, it is critical to restate that here we have a white Southern racist who abhors miscegenation and passing. Unlike Chesnutt, Johnson, and Fitzgerald, Faulkner provides plenty of objectified sex, blood, and violence and conveys little sympathy for the black individual who passes for white and passes for black. Compared to Chesnutt and Johnson, Faulkner places more emphasis on miscegenation than on mimicry and on the masquerade of passing. Unlike our black writers, Faulkner as a white Southerner is enduringly caught up in notions of "blood." Hence, Faulkner's strength is that Christmas becomes consistently characterized as a complex metaphor of racial essentialism and as an individual who is doomed; his story has a chilling, lethal inevitability from the start.

Yet, the limitation of this characterization is that we do not receive a definitive sense of Christmas's ultimate desire until doom is approaching, as we do for our black protagonists who pass for white. Moreover, *Light in August* points both to the crass closed-mindedness of white Southern culture and to the unchangeable, tragic nature of some human relations. Faulkner dramatically illustrates that racial discourse has created Christmas and that this racial discourse, along with racist white people's abhorrence of miscegenation, is responsible for Christmas's bloody demise. Faulkner captures the full range of Joe Christmas's behavior: "It was as if the very initial outrage of the murder carried in its wake and made of all subsequent actions something monstrous and paradoxical and wrong, in themselves against both reason and nature" (296). Like *The Autobiography of an Ex-Coloured Man, Light in August* reinforces the concept that race, birth, nationality, and wealth determine one's access to power, self-determination, and subjectivity.

Through the bloody beatings to the bloody ritualistic castration, Christmas is "called into existence."[66] In this Christmas tragedy we particularly discover how racism is virulently embedded in some white males' obsession with the black man's genital superiority and the former's obsession with emasculating and castrating the latter. Concerning this literature of passing, Joe Christmas adversely becomes the most symbolic, yet enigmatic character, a poignant testimonial to an American society unalterably contaminated by the South Jim Crow segregation and the violently oppressive philosophy of worldwide white supremacy.

Combining the old belief, articulated by Thomas Jefferson, that the ultimate desire of the black man is to have intercourse with the white woman, and Faulkner's anxiety about identity and his description of blacks as "the people who only three hundred years ago were eating rotten elephant and hippo meat in Africa rain forests, who lived beside one of the biggest bodies of water without thinking of a sail,"[67] we have a narrative of passing laden with racial scorn, racial anxiety, and racial ambiguity. With his passionate concerns about racial identity ("blood"), with so much miscegenation, especially in the South, and with Faulkner being "mammy made," perhaps William Faulkner, despite his repulsive racism and his bitter anti-black diatribes, feared that somehow, in some way, he himself was a black man passing as white.

CONCLUSION

100 DOLLARS REWARD. Will be given for the apprehension of my negro Edmund Kenney. He has straight hair, and complexion so nearly white that it is believed a stranger would suppose there was no African blood in him. He was with my boy Dick a short time since in Norfolk, and offered for sale . . . , but escaped under the pretence of being a white man.
    —RICHMOND WHIG, *6 January 1836*

I will tell you that, without any question, the most bitter anti-white diatribes that I have ever heard have come from "passing" Negroes, living as white, among whites, exposed every day to what white people say among themselves regarding Negroes — things that a recognized Negro never would hear. Why, if there was a racial showdown, these Negroes "passing" within white circles would become the black side's most valuable "spy" and ally
    —MALCOLM X, *The Autobiography*

Many are the comedies and many are the tragedies which these artificial lines of demarcation have created.
    —WALTER WHITE, *"The Paradox of Color"*

This project argues that black male individuals who pass for white represent one of the most enigmatic and enthralling phenomena in American literature. These four narratives by Charles Waddell Chesnutt, James Weldon Johnson, F. Scott Fitzgerald, and William Faulkner dramatically reveal the complex nature of racial relationships in American life, culture, and literature. Because of these writers' unique literary experiences, each author captures the inherently paradoxical dynamics of this social and literary phenomenon. These four writers, perhaps more so than other writers during the first third of the twentieth-century who wrote about passing, reveal that the doctrine of white supremacy is quintessentially American. Certain of their black characters, clandestinely living as white among whites, give testimony to the fallacy of the social and political construction of race. Paradoxically, such black-white characters also reveal that becoming an American is "an almost infinitely multiple act of impersonation; the essence of the stable American identity was to have no stable identity at all."[1] In order to embrace the possibility of the American Dream, these colorless protagonists become self-exiled within whiteness. Passing fundamentally means accepting an unstable identity and often a quintessentially tragic performance but often a comic performance.

These narratives of passing also give testimony to the enormous sacrifices required by racial passing and masquerading. Dead and desolate black bodies are everywhere in these literary mazes, especially in the works' concluding pages. In Charles Waddell's *The House Behind the Cedars*, Rena (Rowena) Walden dies in a secluded house with her mother, Molly Walden, in emotional desolation. Also, John Walden becomes symbolically dead to his mother. In F. Scott Fitzgerald's *The Great Gatsby,* Jay Gatsby, a threat to whiteness, is eliminated by George Wilson; in William Faulkner's *Light in August*, after Joanna Burden's horrific decapitation, Joe Christmas, graphically castrated by the machinelike Percy Grimm, bleeds to death. Equally tragic, James Weldon Johnson's melancholy conclusion in *The Autobiography of an Ex-Coloured Man* relates the spiritual, ethical, and artistic death of the nameless Ex-Coloured Man. The Ex-Coloured Man's opportunistic decision to "forsake his race" and pass for white occurs shortly after he observes the barbaric lynch-burning of an equally nameless black man in the South. Johnson reinforces the miscegenation theme of racial violence by the equally horrific scene in which the white woman is fatally shot in the throat by a black man. Hence, the deadly Faustian paradigm is intrinsic to all of these narratives of prevarication.

Despite such tragedies, the literature of passing emphasizes the tricky shoals of race as a pervasive means of socioeconomic exclusion and psychological fragmentation. Although the sacrifices are many, these light-skinned protagonists offer a profound challenge to the philosophy of white supremacy, the essentialism of whiteness, and the maintenance of rigid identity boundaries. Presenting trickster-ism, masquerade, and disappearance as challenges to the essentialism of racial identity, these novels convey the positive potential of passing, of constructing innovative identities, and of transmutation. Further, the discourse of passing conveys that the more general goal of socioeconomic agency also has become the main goal. These white-looking black protagonists seek entry into the white "promised land" of social and economic equality. Of course, this entry means that these same protagonists must remove themselves from their black families, their black friends, and their black culture. And their disappearances into whiteness mean that these chameleons and these racial impostors must live in constant fear of being found out. Passing is essentially fragmentation, because racial identity is bound by rigid social and legal constructs related to the physical body. Too often, American ideology tries to suggest that individual well-being and communal well-being are analogous, but the individual who passes must desert his or her community in the name of individual well-being. Hence, we can surmise that the performance of passing is inherently a criminal performance; this performance highlights the reality of the multitude of black people bypassed by the American Dream. Passing represents a challenge to the dictate that black people must know and stay in their "place."

The need to come to terms with one's blackness in a society dominated by whiteness is not unique to those who pass for white, but their anguish seems particularly painful. The oppressive legacy of the national narratives of racial identity—the *Fugitive Slave Act, Dred Scott v. Sandford*, and *Plessy v. Ferguson* reveal that in America, law is made by white men and administered by white men in the interest of white men. This literature of passing highlights the critical connection between passing and legal discourse. Within the frame of legal discourse, Nathan Huggins argues that the phenomenon of passing exacts a "psychic penalty" from those blacks who pass and produces anxieties in many white people. Huggins writes:

> "Passing" has been a product of the single consensus in American race relations: the promise of American life and the American Dream actually applied to white men. Throughout American history to our own day, laws, customs, and brute force have compelled Afro-Americans to know that they are not citizens. To use political power, to hold office, to own property, to get ahead, to protect one's family, and to survive may have been presumptions of the white American existence, but they were often impossibilities for black Americans. At best these conditions of citizenship have been problematic. Since being white made all the difference in American life, who would not be white if he [or she] could? But such reasoning exacted a psychic penalty. The man who worked as white but kept alive relations with black family and friends knew the immediate fear of detection. On the other hand, he who tried to play it safe by moving to another place and "disappearing" into the white world doubtless nurtured guilt because of deception and the abandonment of race and family. And the fact that Afro-Americans did "pass" only served to deepen white anxieties about racial identification.[2]

Huggins's analysis correctly conveys that social and economic agency are the attractions that motivate some black people to assume a white identity. In America, where whiteness is venerated, blackness too often becomes an inconvenience, and many black individuals who could be accepted as white seize the opportunity to advance their social and economic well-being. The fundamental desire in these narratives of passing, from slavery to the present, is the central desire for socioeconomic subjectivity. Those black individuals who abandon their black communities and pass seek the social privileges and economic power (freedom) associated with whiteness. As we have seen, the Ex-Coloured Man as an arrogant slumlord defines whiteness and success as "money," and Joe Christmas uses his ambiguous racial identity for both sexual and economic gain. As Claude Anderson contends:

> The root in black communities across America is race and the unjust distribution of our nation's wealth, power and resources. One race the descendants of white Europeans, seemingly has checkmated blacks' efforts to improve themselves. Whites live in privileged conditions, with nearly 100 percent ownership and control of the nation's wealth, power, businesses and all levels of government support and resources. White society has a monopoly of ownership and control.[3]

Passing as a subversive performance and phenomenon designed to position individuals closer to wealth and power represents the surreptitious and shadowy side of the American Dream.

Although my focus in this project concerns African American individuals who pass for white, much of American literature, from the time of the slave narratives to the present, can be thought of in terms of passing or challenging hegemonic boundaries. Accordingly, the phenomenon of passing involves blacks who pass for white and whites who pass for black. As Susan Gubar explicates, her synthesizing term "racechange" suggests an extravagant aesthetic construction and "the traversing of racial boundaries, racial imitation or impersonation, cross-racial mimicry or mutability, white posing as black or black posing as white, pan-mutuality."[4] Hence, passing becomes an enduring aspect of America's racial, cultural, socioeconomic, and legal conversation. Denial of one's racial heritage, mimicking, naming, unnaming, using one name as a emblem of opportunity and another as a masquerade, losing one's native regional dialect, equivocating about one's class position, and buying into the mythologies of the American Dream and the plucky Horatio Alger story are just some aspects analogous to the construction of an American identity.

Theodore Dreiser's *An American Tragedy* (1925) and Edith Wharton's *The House of Mirth* (1905), especially in terms of class, are excellent examples of "passing" narratives. Despite the tragically high costs the protagonists of these novels must pay, they are determined to enhance their social and economic status. In these narratives the fear of exposure is not centered around race; the protagonists fear exposure of their lower-class status. Moreover, using passing as an African American strategy in life and art establishes it as a unique literary category. This category signifies on black people's ongoing desire to be woven into the "warp and woof" of the American Dream. Too often, black people's passionate desire for socioeconomic agency has been a failed conversation with democracy and a failed conversation with a country that will forever bear black people's cultural stamp. Black people's enduring demand of virulent white America racism has been: if you give us a fair chance, we will better help you understand the true meaning of democracy.

It would be reductive and ineffectual to contemplate the phenomenon of passing for white as positive or negative. As these novels elaborately explicate, passing represents an extremely complex phenomenon that involves a challenge to the essentialism of identity politics, a challenge to the fraudulent notion of white supremacy, and a challenge to the often obdurate boundaries of race, class, and gender. These writers, with their rich variations on the theme of passing, reveal that skin color, hair texture, language, and geography are critical in interracial as well as intraracial relationships. Skin color is especially critical because recent studies suggest that one's ability to advance economically depends on pigment.[5] America's obsession with skin color and white supremacy can be traced to Thomas Jefferson, who saw the black body as offensive; more specifically, Jefferson viewed skin color as a critical racial distinction:

> They [black people] secrete less by the kidneys, and more by the glands of the skin, which gives them a very strong and disagreeable odour. . . . They are more ardent after their females: but love seems with them to be more an eager desire, than a tender delicate mixture of sentiment and sensation . . . in memory they are equal to the whites; in reason much inferior . . . in imagination they are dull, tasteless, and anomalous.[6]

Jefferson's discourse remains a national narrative on race and skin color. We also understand that the experiences of denying family, culture, and history among those who pass for white reveal that the psychic penalties and physical losses are quite tragic and often quite comic. What we can say without any hesitation is that these masquerading black male individuals, as tragic black bucks, paradoxically represent the remote possibility of a racial showdown in American society where race ceases to matter.[7] Thus, these passing narratives, as narratives of ascension and narratives of descent, significantly convey the intersection between art and life, while indicting the enduring legacy of white supremacy.

Indeed, Charles Waddell Chesnutt, James Weldon Johnson, F. Scott Fitzgerald, and William Faulkner, with their wide-ranging indictments, use the phenomenon of passing as their theme to portray the black male body as being involved in passionate struggles that are inherently political, but the black male body is also inescapably an issue of representation. Through the literature of passing and through the films about cross-racial masquerading, we tragically and comically discover that in America's white supremacist culture, the black body signifying on the white body becomes an unreliable and problematic signifier of race. And for most black people, race steadfastly remains America's national narrative of exclusion and exploitation. These critical and irrefutable characteristics ultimately allow these black chameleons, these racial impostors, these trickster figures to clandestinely "steal away, steal away, steal away" and attempt to become as "white" as they wanna be.

NOTES

Chapter 1

1. The shaping of America has mainly involved the mixing of blacks and whites. This mixing has served to raise literary concerns of identity for both black and white writers. As Judith R. Berzon points out in *Neither White nor Black: The Mulatto Character in American Fiction* (New York: New York University Press, 1978): "The mixed blood, caught between two cultures, has had to exist in an indeterminate area between the boundaries of the American caste system. The widespread preoccupation by black writers with the question of identity, both individual and collective, is given significance in the case of the mixed-blood individual. White Americans are not exempt from this search for identity. In fact whites are virtually addicted to the quest for self-knowledge and for rootedness within a society that has worshiped mobility, change, growth, and 'progress.' But whatever folly is committed, whatever failures are suffered during the continuing process of self-definition, at least white Americans are working within a cultural matrix that is their own. They are white people living in a white society. The images of American culture reflect a white aesthetic" (4–5).

2. James Kinney, *Amalgamation!: Race, Sex, and Rhetoric in the Nineteenth-Century American Novel* (Westport, CT: Greenwood Press, 1985), xii.

3. Aldon L. Nielsen, *Writing Between the Lines: Race and Intertextuality* (Athens: University of Georgia Press, 1994), 16.

4. As Cheryl I. Harris argues in "Whiteness as Property," *Harvard Law Review* 106: 8 (1993), "whiteness became the basis of racial privilege—a type of status in which white racial identity provided the basis for allocating societal benefits both private and public in character" (1709).

5. In terms of "crossing over," the crossing sign represents a metonymy for the transgression of racial boundaries. As Houston A. Baker Jr. argues in *Blues, Ideology and Afro-American Literature* (Chicago: University of Chicago Press, 1984), "The crossing sign is the antithesis of a place marker. It signifies always, change, motion, transience, process. To adept adherents of wandering, a crossing sign is equivalent to a challenge thrown out in brash, sassy tones by a locomotive blowing by: 'Do what you can' it demands. 'Do what you can—right here—on this placeless place, this spotless spot—to capture manifold intonations and implications of fluid experience" (202). This sign becomes particularly significant in terms of use of the ship and Johnson's use of the train as vehicles of freedom and the "adherents of wandering" in Faulkner's novels.

6. Marjorie Garber, *Vested Interest: Cross-Dressing and Cultural Anxiety* (New York: Routledge, 1992), 16.

7. Houston A. Baker Jr., *Modernism and the Harlem Renaissance* (Chicago: University of Chicago Press, 1987), 17.

8. Richard Maxwell Brown, *Strain of Violence: Historical Studies of American Violence and Vigilantism* (New York: Oxford University Press, 1975), 186–87.

9. James E. Cutler, *Lynching-Law: An Investigation into the History of Lynching in the United States* (New York: International Publishers, 1905), 24–31.

10. For a fuller discussion see Scott Ellsworth, *Death in a Promised Land: The Tulsa Race Riot of 1921* (Baton Rouge: Louisiana State University Press, 1982), and Michael D'Orso, *Like Judgement Day: The Ruin and Redemption of a Town Called Rosewood* (New York: Boulevard Books, 1996).

11. Toni Morrison, *Sula* (New York: Knopf, 1987), 103.

12. Frantz Fanon, *Black Skin, White Masks* (New York: Grove Press, 1967), 165.

13. Walter Francis White, *A Man Called White: The Autobiography of Walter White* (New York: Viking Press, 1948), 3.

14. John H. Burma, "The Measurement of Negro Passing," *American Journal of Sociology* 52 (1946): 1822.

15. Horace Mann Bond, "The Racial Islands in America," *American Journal of Sociology* 52 (1931): 554.

16. Michel Foucault, "Space, Knowledge, and Power," in *The Foucault Reader*, ed. Paul Rabinow (New York: Pantheon Books, 1984), 245.

17. Kathy Russell, Midge Wilson, and Ronald Hall, *The Color Complex: The Politics of Skin Color Among African Americans* (New York: Harcourt Brace Jovanovich, 1992). These authors argue: "Several interrelated factors explain the 'light on top' phenomenon in Black America leadership. In a society that is politically and economically controlled by Whites, those members of minorities with the lightest skin and the most Caucasian-looking features have been allowed the greatest freedom. The unique privileges granted to mulattoes under slavery enabled them to advance further, educationally and occupationally, than Blacks who were dark skinned. The result was a leadership pool of light-skinned Blacks with both money and education. Within that pool, it was often those Blacks light enough to pass who became the Black community's most vocal and active leaders" (34–35).

18. William and Ellen Craft, *Running a Thousand Miles for Freedom, or the Escape of William and Ellen Craft*, in *Great Slave Narratives*, ed. Arna Bontemps (Boston: Beacon Press, 1969), 286.

19. Masquerading and role reversal were not limited to enslaved black people seeking freedom. Whites on both sides of the slavery system engaged in these performative acts to

achieve their objectives. For example, Calvin Fairfield posed as a slaveholder, a Negro trader, and a peddler of eggs and chickens in order to assist enslaved blacks. In Jim Haskins's *Get on Board: The Story of the Underground Railroad* (New York: Scholastic, 1993), Haskins relates that Fairfield would visit plantations and secretly let it be known that he was there to help blacks escape. Fairfield "would suddenly disappear, and so would several local slaves" (38). On the other hand, Haskins states: "One Kentucky slave owner disguised himself as a Quaker and went into Indiana to get information about the Underground Railroad" and "Another slaveholder traveled through Indiana and Ohio posing as an anti-slavery lecturer. Whenever he learned of a fugitive slave in hiding, he notified the master, who then tried to claim his property" (130–31).

20. Sander L. Gilman, *Difference and Pathology: Stereotypes of Sexuality, Race, and Madness* (Ithaca : Cornell University Press, 1985), argues that during the nineteenth century, the notion of enslaved black people seeking freedom was often stereotyped as two distinct psychopathologies called "'Drapetomania, or the diseases causing slaves to run away' and 'dysaesthesia aethiopis or hebetude of mind and obtuse sensibility of body'—a disease peculiar to negroes—called by overseers, 'rascality'" (138). These two medical definitions were used to describe the behavior of those blacks and to label them as insane. Consequently, I would argue that some whites might view the desire of black individuals to pass for white as some form of dementia.

21. Garber, *Vested Interest*, 285.

22. Henry "Box" Brown, "Narrative of Henry 'Box' Brown," in *The Underground Railroad: First-Person Narratives of Escape to Freedom in the North*, ed. L. Blockson (New York: Prentice Hall, 1987), 135–38. Additionally, as Jim Haskins states, in *Get on Board*: "Like Brown, Lear Green was shipped to Philadelphia in a box, a sailor chest. Yet she has remained an obscure figure in the annals of Underground Railroad history" (100).

23. Hazel V. Carby, *Reconstructing Womanhood: The Emergence of the American Woman Novelist* (New York: Oxford University Press, 1987), 171.

24. *Dred Scott v. Sandford*, 19 How. 393 (1857) at 409.

25. F. James Davis, *Who Is Black?: One Nation's Definition* (University Park: Pennsylvania State University Press, 1991), 5. See also Melvin Harris, *Patterns of Race in the Americas* (New York: W. W. Norton, 1964), 56.

26. Joseph R. Washington Jr., *Marriage in Black and White* (Boston: Beacon Press, 1970), 108.

27. W. E. B. Du Bois, *The Souls of Black Folk* (New York: New American Library, 1969), 45.

28. Fanon, *Black Skin, White Masks*, 11.

29. Ibid., 12.

30. Joseph Washington, *Marriage in Black and White* (Boston: Beacon Press, 1970), 122.

31. This notion is confirmed by David Goodman Croly in *Glimpses of the Future, Suggestions as to the Drift of Things* (New York and London: Putnam, 1988). Croly states, "We can absorb the Dominion . . . for the Canadians are of our own race . . . but Mexico, Central America, the Sandwich Islands, and the West India Islands will involve governments which cannot be democratic. We will never confer the right of suffrage upon the blacks, the mongrels of Mexico or Central America, or the Hawaiians. . . . The white race is dominant and will keep their position, no matter how numerous the negroes may become" (22–24).

32. There exists extensive and sophisticated literature on whites' views of black people in this period. See George Frederickson, *The Black Image in the White Mind: The Debate on Afro-American Character and Destiny 1817–1914* (Hanover, NH: Wesleyan University

Press, 1987). An excellent theoretical statement on this issue is Barbara J. Fields, "Race and Ideology in America History," in *Region, Race, and Reconstruction: Essays in Honor of C. Vann Woodward*, ed. J. Morgan Kousser and James M. McPherson (New York: Oxford University Press, 1982), 143–77.

33. Yet, as Ralph Ellison points out in *Shadow and Act* (1953; repr. ed., New York: Vintage Books, 1972), Mark Twain, Emerson, Thoreau, Whitman, and Melville were "men publicly involved in various forms of deeply personal rebellion." These writers, at odds with the dominant white society, represented whiteness as a symbol of evil (32). See also *The Power of Blackness: Hawthorne, Poe, Melville* (Athens: Ohio University Press, 1958). Concerning blackness, whiteness, and Melville, Levin argues: "It may be that blackness stands out more for our writers because of its continual interplay with a not less pervasive sense of whiteness: la feuille blanche, le roman noir. The running contrast between them set forth all our dilemmas as black print upon a white page. The iconography of whiteness, pondered by Melville, has furnished one of the farthest-ranging chapters in our literature. The theme of blackness, enunciated by Melville, surpasses the mighty scope of the whale itself; the soundings that exemplify it here, accordingly, must be references passim" (28). In *Moby Dick* (New York: Macmillan, 1962), Melville attempts to extirpate the racist notions that whiteness is virtuous and blackness is diabolical: "This elusive quality it is, which causes the thought of whiteness which, divorced from more kindly associations and coupled with any object terrible in itself, to heighten that terror to the furthest bounds. Witness the white bear of the poles, and the white shark (requin) of the tropics; what but their smooth, flaky whiteness makes them the transcendent horrors they are?. . . and though in other mortal sympathies and symbolizing, this same hue (whiteness) is made the emblem of many touching noble things—the innocence of brides, the benignity of age; though among the Red men of America the giving of the white belt of wampum was the deepest pledge of honor; though in many climes, whiteness typifies the majesty of justice in the ermine of the Judge, and contributes to the daily state of kings and queens drawn by milk-white steeds; though even in the higher mysteries of the most august religions it has been made the symbol of the divine spotlessness and power; by the Persian fire worshippers, the white forked flame being held by the holiest on the altar; and in the Greek mythologies, Great Jove himself being made incarnate in a snow-white bull . . . yet for all these accumulated associations, with whatever is sweet, honorable, and sublime, there yet lurks an elusive something in the innermost idea of this hue, which strikes more of panic to the soul than that redness which affright in blood" (198–99).

34. Toni Morrison, "On the Backs of Blacks," *Time* Special Issue, "The New Face of America" (Fall 1993), p. 57.

35. See Edward Byron Reuter, *The Mulatto in the United States: Including a Study of the Role of Mixed-Blood Races Throughout the World* (Boston: Richard G. Badger, 1918); E. Franklin Frazier, *The Negro in the United States* (Chicago: University of Chicago Press, 1966). For a discussion of racist ideology in the early twentieth century that includes analysis of white attitudes toward mulattoes, see I. A. Newby, *Jim Crow Defense: Anti-Negro Thought in America, 1900–1930* (Baton Rouge: Louisiana State University Press, 1965).

36. Toni Morrison, *Playing in the Dark: Whiteness and the Literary Imagination* (Cambridge, MA: Harvard University Press, 1992), 5.

37. Russell, Wilson, and Hall, *The Color Complex*. As a result of internalization of the gospel of white supremacy, some black people have engaged in pathological behavior

to attain a white aesthetic of beauty. Describing this skin-lightening processes, the authors reveal: "American Negro women of the nineteenth century sometimes rubbed lye directly on their skin, and others applied harsh acidic products made for removing dirt and grime from floors and walls. There were also homemade concoctions of lemon juice, bleach, or urine to smear on the skin and arsenic wafers to swallow, all designed to 'get the dark out.' None of these methods worked, and all of them smelled, burned, or worse. One nineteenth-century mother tried unsuccessfully to lighten her unacceptably dark daughter by dunking her every day in a tub of bleach" (48–50). Also, Jervis Anderson, *This Was Harlem* (New York: Farrar, Straus and Giroux, 1981), provides excerpts from advertising copy: "Black-No-More was a cream for 'bleaching and beautifying' the complexion. Fair-Plex Ointment made the skin of women and men . . . bright, soft, and smooth.' The makers of Cocotone Skin Whitener advised, 'Don't envy a clear complexion, use Cocotone . . . and have one'" (92).

38. Russell, Wilson, and Hall, *The Color Complex*, 44–45.
39. Albert Murray, *The Omni-Americans: New Perspectives on Black Experience and American Culture—Some Alternatives to the Folklore of White Supremacy* (New York: Outerbridge and Dienstfrey, 1970), 49–50.
40. Paul Laurence Dunbar, "We Wear the Mask," in *The Collected Poetry of Paul Laurence Dunbar,* John Braxton, ed. (Charlottesville: University Press of Virginia, 1993), 71.
41. Alain Locke, ed., *The New Negro* (New York: Atheneum, 1986), 3. Furthermore, as Joel Williamson states, in *New People: Miscegenation and Mulattoes in the United States* (New York: New York University Press, 1984), 3: "Negroes in America in the 1920s were indeed a new people. First they were a new people physically. Social scientists soon developed some thirty specific traits (varying from fitting height to thirty-three shades of skin coloring, each with an identifying number) that they laboriously measured and elaborately described to prove the existence of a new physical type. Second and much more important, Negroes were a new people culturally. Negro language and literature, Negro music and dance, and Negro achievement in the visual and performing arts were all rising to undeniable beauty in the 1920s. In each case the art was like that of white America, but different. Elements of Negro culture merged and found signal expression in what came to be called the Harlem Renaissance. Along with cultural awareness inevitably came self-awareness. Awareness included a sense of being different both from other contemporary Americans and from preceding Negro generations. The Negro elite encapsulated the mood in the phrase 'the new Negro.' The phrase carried the idea that the Negro was neither African nor European, but both—and something more."
42. Russell, Wilson, and Hall, *The Color Complex,* 27.
43. Ibid., 24–25.
44. K. Wolfe, ed., *Thomas W. Talley's Negro Folk Rhymes* (Knoxville: University of Tennessee Press, 1991), 8–9.
45. As Robert J. C. Young points out in *Colonial Desire: Hybridity in Theory, Culture and Race* (New York: Routledge, 1995), Croly and Wakeman's text, titled *Miscegenation: The Theory of the Blending of the Races Applied to the American White Man and the Negro,* created an intense intellectual debate. Young states: "It was with this book that the word 'miscegenation' was first introduced, and the impact of the book can be measured from the fact that it caught on immediately. The authors begin with a short definition of the term as well as a cluster of other mostly nonce-words: miscegen, miscegenate, miscegenetic, melaleukation, malaleukon, melaleuketic (the last three terms,

from the Greek melas (Black) and leukos (white) leading to a further term, melamigleukation, 'the union of the races.' The strategy involved the production of a new word that would have the specific meaning of actual racial mixture than the customary term 'amalgamation,' which doubled as the term for the restoration of the Union" (144).

46. Edward B. Reuter, *The Mulatto in the United States* (Boston: R. G. Badger, 1918), 112.

47. Gunnar Myrdal, *An American Dilemma* (New York: Harper, 1944), 56.

48. Davis, *Who Is Black?* 78.

49. Barbara Christian, *Black Feminist Criticism: Perspectives on Black Women Writers* (New York: Pergamon Press, 1985), 15–16.

50. Jacques Lacan, "The Line and the Light," in his *The Four Fundamental Concepts of Psychoanalysis*, trans. Alan Sheridan (London: Hogarth Press and the Institute of Psycho-Analysis, 1977), 99.

51. Homi K. Bhabha, *The Location of Culture* (New York: Routledge, 1994), 86.

52. Nathan Hare, *The Black Anglo-Saxons* (Chicago: Third World Press, 1991 [1964], 36.

53. Lawrence Levine, *Black Culture and Black Consciousness* (New York: Oxford University Press, 1977), 51.

54. If we examine the advertisements for black individuals who escaped slavery, we see the phenomenon of passing. For example, in *"Pretends to Be Free": Runaway Slave Advertisements from Colonial and Revolutionary New York and New Jersey,* edited by Graham Russell Hodges and Alan Edward Brown (New York and London: Garland Publishing Inc., 1994), we read, in an advertisement that appeared in *The New York Weekly Journal* on May 25, 1747, about "a Mulatto man named Storde a Bermudian Born, aged about 23 years, pretty tall and pock broken, but not very much, but pretty large pits in his face, pretty fair, with his Head commonly shaved in order to make himself pass for a white man, by trade a carpenter, the clothes he used to wear before he left the vessel was a check'd shirt, a striped Flannel Jacket, a pair of Oznabug trousers" (21–22).

55. The behavior of those black individuals who pass for white is analogous to that of enslaved blacks and is suggestive of trickster figures who attempt to escape oppression and obtain economic agency. See John W. Roberts, *From Trickster to Badman: The Black Folk Hero in Slavery and Freedom* (Philadelphia: University of Pennsylvania Press, 1989). Roberts argues, "Therefore, in their everyday lives, enslaved Africans turned to behaviors which allowed them to subvert the masters' authority and control in ways that did not disrupt the system. Subversive behaviors became both a part of the everyday strategies of the enslaved and a primary focus of many personal experience stories told by former enslaved Africans. . . . Not uncommonly, the trickster simply emerged as a thief and malicious liar who manipulated others to achieve his goals" (32, 37).

56. Theodore Allen, "Slavery, Racism, and Democracy," *Monthly Review* 29 (1978): 57–63.

57. Lerone Bennett Jr., *The Shaping of Black America* (Chicago: Johnson Publishing Co., 1975), 18.

58. Peter Brooks, *Reading for the Plot: Design and Intention in Narrative* (New York: Vintage Books, 1985), 41.

59. This destruction of the self manifests itself in anxiety, alienation, and narcissism. Here I draw on the analysis of F. C. Welsing in *The Isis Papers: The Keys to the Colors* (Chicago: Third World Press, 1991), 17–38. To engage in racism and accept the theories of white supremacy and hierarchies of skin color constitutes a rock-hard form of alienation from the self and from others. Welsing argues, "Alienation is a powerful centrifugal, psychological and societal dynamic that, over time, drives human beings further

and further away from all effective, meaningful, emotionally supportive and truthful communication amongst one another" (18). Anxiety, according to Freud, arose out of the experience of separation from the mother (birth trauma) and from fear of castration. Individuals who pass view whiteness as a phallic symbol of power. Thus, having to walk a racial tightrope produces the constant fear of discovery (castration). Narcissism can be defined as a character disorder in which the libidinal energy is fixated upon the self. In a white supremacist culture and pigmentocracy there exists a grandiose importance placed on whiteness. Yet beneath the stance of white supremacy and white grandiosity, the insecurity of inadequacy, inferiority, and vulnerability remains to be displaced alternately (37).

60. Brooks, *Reading for the Plot*, 51.

61. Etienne Balibar, "Is There a Neo-Racism?" in *Race, Nation, Class: Ambiguous Identities*, ed. Etienne Balibar and Immanuel Wallerstein (London: Verso, 19991), 17–18.

62. Although my focus here is on the question of racial construction in America with regard to black people, passing goes beyond this border. As Russell, Wilson, and Hall argue in *The Color Complex*, passing "is hardly limited to African Americans—in Nazi Germany, Jews passed as Protestants; in today's army, gay men and women pass as straight; on job applications, older people try to pass as younger. In each case, the reason is traceable to some form of discrimination, be it on the basis of race, sexual orientation, or age" (73). For a discussion of the role of gender in passing see Anne Herrmann, "'Passing' Women, Performing Men," in *The Female Body: Figures, Styles, Speculations*, ed. Laurence Goldstein (Ann Arbor: University of Michigan Press, 1991). Here Herrmann states: "'Passing' functions as one of several terms used to designate the instability of gender identities and the ability to change sexes, even as gender is considered the only characteristic which remains totally invariant from birth. 'Passing' relies on cross-dressing—dressing in clothes of the opposite sex—for the purpose of convincing an 'unknown audience' that one is a member of that sex" (178–79).

63. R. Larson, *An Intimation of Things Distant: The Collected Fiction of* Nella Larsen (New York: Doubleday, 1992), xv.

Chapter 2

1. The phrase "The Circular Ruins" comes from a short story by Jorge Luis Borge in *Ficciones* (New York: Grove Press, 1962).

2. Charles W. Chesnutt, *The Journal of Charles W. Chesnutt*, ed. Richard H. Brodhead (Durham: Duke University Press, 1993), 78.

3. A more complex commentary about Chesnutt's sense of self is contained in a journal entry not used in his daughter's biography yet quoted in an article describing the effects of Helen Chesnutt's biography and her editorial practices on the image of Chesnutt in the biography. Chesnutt remarks, "I am neither fish, flesh, nor fowl—neither 'nigger,' white, nor 'buckrah.' Too 'stuck' up for the colored folks, and of course, not recognized by the whites." Williams L. Andrews, "A Reconsideration of *Charles W. Chesnutt: Pioneer of the Color Line*," *CLA Journal* 19: 142. It is interesting to note that Adam Clayton Powell Jr., who was easily taken for white, was beaten up by both Irish and black boys and told his first wife: "I'm neither fish nor fowl." Jeff Kisseloff, *You Must Remember This: An Oral History of Manhattan from the 1890s to World War ll* (New York:

Schocken, 1989), 296. Additionally, according to Sylvia Lyons Render's "Introduction" to Charles W. Chesnutt, *The Short Fiction of Charles W. Chesnutt* (Washington, DC: Howard University Press, 1981), W. E. B. Du Bois once described Chesnutt as one of "that group of white folks who because of a more or less remote Negro ancestor identified himself voluntarily with the darker group" (30). For Chesnutt's biography, see William L. Andrews, *The Literary Career of Charles W. Chesnutt* (Baton Rouge: Louisiana State University Press, 1980); Frances Richardson Keller, *An American Crusade: The Life of Charles W. Chesnutt* (Provo: Brigham Young University Press, 1978); J. Noel Hermance, *Charles W. Chesnutt: America's First Great Black Novelist* (Hamden, CT: Archon Books, 1974); Helen M. Chesnutt, *Charles Waddell Chesnutt: Pioneer of the Color Line* (Chapel Hill: University of North Carolina Press, 1952).

4. Drawing from James Kinney's use of the term "amalgamation" in *Amalgamation! Race, Sex and Rhetoric in the Nineteenth-Century Novel* (Westport, CT: Greenwood Press, 1985), "amalgamation" suggests interracial mixing, to the point of erasure of difference over generations.

5. Charles W. Chesnutt, "The Future American: What the Race Is Likely to Become in the Process of Time," *Boston Evening Transcript*, 18 August 1900, 20.

6. Discussing a 1923 silent film version of *The House Behind the Cedars*, Chesnutt states, "My most popular novel was distorted and mangled by a colored moving picture producer to make it appeal to Negro race prejudice." See Chesnutt, "The Negro in Art, How Shall He Be Portrayed," *Crisis* 33 (1926): 28–29. The producer and director of the film was Oscar Micheaux. In 1932, the year of Chesnutt's death, Micheaux made *Veiled Aristocrats,* another version of Chesnutt's romantic tragedy. Also, in 1947 Micheaux published *The Masquerade: A Historical Novel,* which closely resembles Chesnutt's novel. In the Acknowledgement, Micheaux states: "I had merely to select and rewrite whatever one of the old stories I like best, which in fact, was not merely so arduous as creating a new theme entirely, and, due to the fact that the story had been worked out very carefully when it was filmed, I found that it made a better and more convincing novel after I worked it back to story form. Accordingly, after deciding to do an historical novel as my next publication, I went back to my old file of motion picture scenarios and found one that just fitted my purpose: a scenario from a novel by Charles W. Chesnutt, published almost fifty years ago." The title of Micheaux's novel contains a double entendre; it refers to both the "great masquerade" of John Warwick's attempt to help his sister, Rena Northcross, become Rowena Warwick and pass for white and to his rewritten novel, which masquerades as Chesnutt's *The House Behind the Cedars.* There are numerous parts in Micheaux's novel that are taken verbatim from Chesnutt's novel. Micheaux's ending is significant in that Rena Northcross and Frank Fowler decide to marry and go north, to Chicago, to escape white racism and the color discrimination and caste conflict among blacks. We can only speculate on how Chesnutt would have reacted to Micheaux's *The Masquerade* and to his second film.

7. Here it should be noted that Chesnutt read law for two years in the office of Judge Samuel E. Williamson, where he earned his living as a stenographer. He later went down to Columbus to take the bar exam. In the March 4, 1887, edition of the *Cleveland Leader,* the following notice appeared: "Following is a list of applicants admitted to practice law by the Supreme Court . . . Charles W. Chesnutt, Cleveland . . . Mr. Charles Chesnutt stood at the head of his class, having made the highest per cent in the thorough examination, which was one of the hardest to which a class of students was ever subjected." See Helen M. Chesnutt, *Charles Waddell Chesnutt,* 39–40.

8. In Thomas Jefferson, *Notes on the State of Virginia* (Chapel Hill: University of North Carolina Press, 1954), 143: Jefferson states: "I advance it therefore as a suspicion only, that the blacks, whether originally a distinct race, or made distinct by time and circumstances, are inferior to the whites in the endowments both of body and mind. It is not against experience to suppose, that different species of the same genus, or varieties of the same species, may possess different qualifications." Despite Jefferson's doubts, his views stood as the strongest suggestion of black people's inferiority. Consequently, whereas Edward Long claimed that blacks and whites are separate species and that mulattos are sterile, making him the father of English racism, Jefferson can be considered the father of American racism.

9. B. R. Burg, "The Rhetoric of Miscegenation: Thomas Jefferson, Sally Hemmings, and Their Historians," *Phylon* 47 (1986), describes Jefferson's illicit relationships. He states: "The last of the three was Sally Hemmings. Jefferson's biographers as well as leading historians of the early Republic, it appears, were quite comfortable dealing with his encounters involving white women. They were remarkably casual, in fact, with the prospect of the Sage of Monticello copulating out of wedlock. It was only the subject of race that agitated them" (129). Furthermore, as John Chester Miller states in *The Wolf by the Ears: Thomas Jefferson and Slavery* (Charlottesville: University Press of Virginia, 1991), 176: "To give credence to the Sally Hemmings story is, in effect, to question the authenticity of Jefferson's faith in freedom, the rights of man, and the innate controlling faculty of reason and the sense of right and wrong. It is to infer that there were no principles to which he was inviolably committed, that what he acclaimed as morality was no more than a rhetorical facade for self-indulgence, and that he was always prepared to make exceptions in his own case when it suited his purpose. In short, beneath his sanctimonious and sententious exterior lay a thoroughly adaptive and amoral public figure—like so many of those of the present day."

10. Helen M. Chesnutt, *Charles Waddell Chesnutt*, 21.

11. Charles W. Chesnutt, *Frederick Douglass* (Boston: Small, Maynard, 1899), ix.

12. George P. Cunningham, "'Called into Existence': Desire, Gender, and Voice in Frederick Douglass's *Narrative of 1845*," *Differences: A Journal of Feminist Cultural Studies* 1.3 (1989): 109. It should be noted that Booker T. Washington also wrote a biography, *Frederick Douglass* (Philadelphia: George W. Jacobs & Co., 1907). Writing about Douglass, Washington states: "In nothing else was the life of Mr. Douglass so important as in the uplifting influence he exerted, directly and indirectly, upon the young men of his time. There were many good leaders worthy of emulation, but none who exercised the authority that he did over the opinions of the other members of his race" (339). Additionally, Cunningham's configurations of the triangles of desire in Douglass's narrative were extremely useful my analysis of Chesnutt's novel.

13. Charles W. Chesnutt, *Frederick Douglass*, ix.

14. Charshee C. L. McIntyre, *Criminalizing a Race: Free Blacks During Slavery* (New York: Kayode Publications, Ltd., 1992), vi.

15. Frantz Fanon, *The Wretched of the Earth* (New York: Grove Press, 1966), 27.

16. The phenomenon of black individuals passing for white signifies on the cultural performance of blackface minstrelsy. Here white individuals or "white Negroes" blackened their faces in order to perform as blacks, and black individuals blackened their faces to give exaggerated performances. As Eric Lott argues in *Love and Theft: Blackface Minstrelsy and the American Working Class* (New York: Oxford University Press, 1993), the white performers "rejected the Protestant ethic and escaped into the latitudes of

the entertainment world. In the course of such escape they came into contact with the music and dance of slaves and free blacks, and first tasted theatrical success in blackface performances . . . they nevertheless shared with their families certain political ties to the elite of the Democratic party, the party of Andrew Jackson, antimonopoly, expansionism—and white supremacy" (50).

17. With the stately cedar tree being of African and Asian origin, Chesnutt's title also suggests the violent uprooting and involuntary migration of African people, which placed them in a compromising position. For many African American writers, the tree becomes a metaphor for the enduring strength and flexibility of black people who braved the despotism of white supremacy. Additionally, it signifies on the life of Frederick Douglass because, in 1878, Douglass (a product of miscegenation) moved to a twenty-room house located on nine acres in Anacostia Heights, in the District of Columbia; the site of the house, called "Cedar Hill," overlooked the Capitol.

18. Charles Waddell Chesnutt, *The House Behind the Cedars* (1900; repr., New York: Penguin Books, 1993), 105. All further references to this edition will be cited parenthetically.

19. Frantz Fanon, *Black Skin, White Masks* (New York: Grove Press, 1967), 11.

20. Jacques Lacan, *Ecrits: A Selection*, trans. Alan Sheridan (New York: W. W. Norton, 1977), 1.

21. Laura Mulvey, "Visual Pleasure and Narrative Cinema," in *Feminism and Film Theory*, ed. Constance Penley (New York: Routledge, 1988), 60.

22. Fanon, *Black Skin, White Masks*, 202.

23. Douglass, *Narrative of the Life of Frederick Douglas: An American Slave Written by Himself* (1845; repr. ed., New York: International, 1950), 114–15.

24. Ibid., 5. Ironically, literacy is a curse that leads to liberation.

25. Fanon, *Black Skin, White Masks*, 145–46.

26. Here John Walden's desire connects with the Horatio Alger myth of individual uplift against the odds.

27. Houston A. Baker Jr. *Blues, Ideology and Afro American Literature: A Vernacular Theory* (Chicago: University of Chicago Press, 1984). This notion of a matrix of desire is suggested by Houston A. Baker's "blues matrix." The matrix of desire, like the "blues matrix," is, in Baker's terms, a "point of ceaseless input and output, a web of intersecting, crisscrossing impulses always in productive transit" (3).

28. Chesnutt, "Race Prejudice; Its Causes and Its Cure," in *Alexander's Magazine*, July 1905, p. 25.

29. W. E. B. Du Bois, "Races," *Crisis* (August 1911): 158.

30. Charles W. Chesnutt, "What Is a White Man," in *The Minority Presence in American Literature 1600–1900*, Vol. 2, ed. Philip Butcher (Washington, DC: Howard University Press, 1977), 280.

31. In James Weldon Johnson's *The Autobiography of an Ex-Coloured Man,* we will encounter a similar incident in which the white father gives the black protagonist a ten-dollar gold coin with a hole in it. Coincidentally, in William Craft and Ellen Craft's passing-slave narrative, *Running a Thousand Miles for Freedom*, William ironically recalls that one man "gave me a ten cent piece, and requested me to be attentive to my good master. I promised that I would do so, and have ever since endeavored to keep my pledge" (303).

32. Michelle Cliff, in *Claiming an Identity They Taught Me to Despise* (Watertown, MA: Persephone Press, 1980), describes the rules for passing in ways that recall Chesnutt's

novel. Cliff states: "Passing demands a desire to become invisible. A ghost-life. An ignorance of connections" (5). Further, Cliff argues: "Passing demands quiet. And from that quiet—silence" and "Passing demands you keep that knowledge to yourself" (6). See also Lawrence Otis Graham's *Our Kind of People: Inside America's Black Upper Class* (New York: HarperCollins Publishers, 2000).

33. As noted earlier, Chesnutt's characterization of John Warwick as Ivanhoe and the unnaming and renaming of Rena as Rowena (Ivanhoe's wife) reinforces the paradigm of incest. Furthermore, in Mark Twain's "Those Extraordinary Twins," in *Pudd'nhead Wilson* (1894; repr., New York: Penguin Books, 1986), 231, Rowena is a character caught between the affections of a set of twins. Twain, discussing Rowena, states: "It was awkward all around; but more particularly in the case of Rowena, because there was a love match on, between her and one of the twins that constituted the freak, and I worked it up to a blistering heat and thrown in a quite dramatic love-quarrel, wherein Rowena scathingly denounced her betrothed for getting drunk. . . . Yes, here she was, stranded with that deep injustice of hers torturing her poor torn heart." In Chesnutt's novel, this aspect highlights both Rowena's relationship with George Tyron and her being caught between John Warwick and George Tyron and between George Tyron and Jeff Wain. Like Chesnutt, Twain kills off Rowena in his text.

34. Douglass, *Narrative of the Life of Frederick Douglass,* 115.

35. This "Middle Passage" scene conveys miscegenation, as well. The rape of enslaved African women occurred not only on the continent of Africa but on the slave ships. Numerous African women arrived in America sexually terrorized and impregnated by their white male captors.

36. Paula Giddings, *When and Where I Enter: The Impact of Black Woman on Race and Sex in American Culture* (New York: Morrow, 1984), 183.

37. Lacan's theory of hysteria suggests John as a master manipulator and connects "acting out" to the notion of a divided self. He states: "The hysterical subject captures this object [object of desire] in an elaborate intrigue and his [her] ego is in the third party by whose mediation the subject enjoys that object in which his [her] question is embodied. For the hysterical subject, for whom the technical term 'acting out' takes on its literal meaning since he [she] is acting outside himself [herself], you have to get him [her] to recognize when his [her] action is situated" (89–90). *The Four Fundamental Concepts of Psycho-Analysis* (New York: W. W. Norton, 1978).

38. Sander L. Gilman, *The Jew's Body* (New York: Routledge, 1991), 63, 199.

39. Fanon, *Black Skin, White Masks,* 162–63.

40. Quoted in Mary Helen Washington, *Invented Lives: Narratives of Black Women 1860–1960* (New York: Anchor Books, 1987), 8.

41. Aldon Lynn Nielsen, *Reading Race: White American Poets and the Racial Discourse in the Twentieth Century* (Athens: University of Georgia Press, 1988), 3.

42. As Russell, Wilson, and Hall point out, "Light-skinned beauties, called 'fancy girls,' were auctioned at 'quadroon balls' held regularly in New Orleans and Charleston. A respectable White gentleman might buy a concubine, and when he tired of her, six months or so later, he might get himself another one. If he found he liked her, he might keep her for life" (18–19). In this regard, Chesnutt suggests that Molly Walden's fate has been that of a "fancy girl" and that symbolically Rena is being "auctioned" off to Jeff Wain.

43. Heather Hathaway, "'Maybe Freedom Lies in Hating': Miscegenation and the Oedipal Conflict," *Refiguring the Father: New Readings of Patriarchy,* ed. Patricia Yaeger and Beth Kowaleski-Wallace (Carbondale: University of Illinois Press, 1989), 154.

44. SallyAnn H. Ferguson, "'Frank Fowler': A Chesnutt Racial Pun," *Southern Atlantic Review* 50 (1985): 47.

45. Patricia J. Williams, "And We Are Not Married: A Journal of Musings upon Legal Language and the Ideology of Style," in *Consequences of Theory*, ed. Jonathan Arac and Barbara Johnson (Baltimore: Johns Hopkins University Press, 1991), 186.

46. Chesnutt, Address to the Boston Literary and Historical Association, cited in Hermance, *Charles W. Chesnutt*, 71–72. Despite Chesnutt's indictment of white supremacy, his prose and fiction suggest his color complex and class consciousness. By killing off Rena, Chesnutt suggests that there is no future for light-skinned individuals in a black community and that a marriage to the dark-skinned Frank Fowler is not a viable option. Perhaps this is why Chesnutt was so outraged with Oscar Micheaux's film version of the novel. Micheaux would later conclude his novel *The Masquerade: A Historical Novel* with Rena and Frank getting married and going north. (See note 6.) Although Sandra Gunning examines Chesnutt's *The Marrow of Tradition* (1901) in *Race, Rape, and Lynching: The Red Record of American Literature 1890–1912* (New York: Oxford University Press, 1996), she points to Chesnutt's color complex and class consciousness. Gunning argues: "Though there is a clear racial solidarity among most of the novel's African American characters, modern readers have often been disturbed by the lines of separation based on color: educated black characters—specifically mulattos like Miller and Janet, who signify the mixing of races Chesnutt favored—move upward from their humble origins, while fully black lower-class characters like Sandy and the old Mammy Jane, the Carteret family retainer, do not" (70). In essence, Chesnutt characterizes dark-skinned individuals as being locked into an inferior social position, and the middle-class mulattos are viewed as the progress group. Thus, despite Chesnutt's indictment, he internalizes the hegemonic ideology of radical racists.

Chapter 3

1. James Weldon Johnson, *The Autobiography of an Ex-Coloured Man* (1912; repr., New York: Penguin Books, 1990), 99–100. All further citations will be given parenthetically within the text.

2. In Richard B. Sewall, *The Vision of Tragedy* (New Haven: Yale University Press, 1980), Sewall discusses the interconnection of tragic and comic tradition. He states: "the highest comedy gains its power from its sense of tragic possibility, and the profoundest tragedy presents a full fleeting vision, through the temporary disorder, of an ordered universe to which comedy is witness. Without a sense of the tragic, comedy loses heart; it becomes brittle, it has animation but no life. Without a recognition of the truths of comedy, tragedy becomes bleak and intolerable" (1).

3. For a full discussion of *The Autobiography of an Ex-Coloured Man* and passing as autobiography see Donald C. Goellnicht, "Passing as Autobiography: James Weldon Johnson's *The Autobiography*," *African American Review* 30.1 (1996): 17–33.

4. Rudi Blesh and Harriet Janis, *They All Played Ragtime: The True Story of an American Music* (London: Sidgwick and Jackson, 1958), 7–8.

5. As Rudi Blesh and Harriet Janis point out, Scott Joplin (who was black) and John Stark (who was white) were "pioneers under the skin." Joplin, with his tyrannical creative urge and vision, combined with the browbeating, cajoling, and business-minded Stark

to create and promote ragtime piano music. Blesh and Janis relate that "Stark met Scott Joplin at the Maple Leaf Club and heard the rag named after it. It was in their conference next day at the music store that Stark bought the number for fifty dollars and royalties to the composer—good terms for that time" (50).

6. James Weldon Johnson, *Along This Way* (1933; repr., New York: Penguin Books, 1990), 411–12. All subsequent references to this text will be given parenthetically.

7. In *Along This Way*, Johnson relates how his brother suggested *The Chameleon* as a title: "I also debated with myself the aptness of *The Autobiography of an Ex-Coloured Man* as a title. Brander Matthews had expressed a liking for the title, but my brother had thought it was clumsy and too long; he had suggested *The Chameleon*. In the end, I stuck to the original idea of issuing the book without the author name, and kept the title that had appealed to me first. But I have never been able to settle definitely for myself whether I was sagacious or not in these two decisions. When I chose the title, it was without the slightest doubt that its meaning would be perfectly clear to anyone; there were people, however, to whom it proved confusing" (238).

8. Arthur P. Davis, *From the Dark Tower: Afro-American Writers 1900 to 1960* (Washington, DC: Howard University Press, 1974), 30.

9. Eugene Levy, *James Weldon Johnson: Black Leader, Black Voice* (Chicago: University of Chicago Press, 1973), 16–17. Levy states that Johnson, acting as a co-conspirator, never publicly identified D—.

10. Richard Wright, *White Man Listen* (1957; repr., New York: Harper Perennial, 1995), makes a connection between his poem and Johnson's near fatal experience. A few lines from Wright's poem read: "And a thousand faces swirled around me, clamoring that my life be burned. . . . And then they had me, stripped me, battered my teeth into my throat till I swallowed my own blood" (98). Furthermore, Wright states, "The Negro could not take his eyes off the auction block: he never had a chance to; he could not stop thinking of lynching: he never had a chance to. The Negro writer had no choice in his subject matter; he could not select his experiences. Hence, the monotonous repetition of horror that rolls in verse from one generation to another" (83). And, like lynching, passing for white is necessary and indeed a preoccupation for black writers.

11. Katrin Schwenk, "Lynching and Rape: Border Cases in African American History and Fiction," in *The Black Columbiad: Defining Moments in African American Literature and Culture*, ed. Werner Sollors and Maria Diedrich (Cambridge, MA: Harvard University Press, 1994), 313.

12. See Valerie Smith, "Split Affinities: The Case of Inter-racial Rape," in *Conflicts in Feminism,* ed. Marianne Hirsch and Evelyn Fox Keller (New York: Routledge, 1990), and Hazel Carby, *Reconstructing Womanhood: The Emergence of the Afro-American Woman Novelist* (New York: Oxford University Press, 1987).

13. Walter White, whose skin was white, whose eyes were blue, and whose hair was blond, was a black man. In *A Man Called White: The Autobiography of Walter White* (1948; repr., Athens: University of Georgia Press, 1995), White discusses the phenomenon of passing. He states: "Many Negroes are judged as whites. Every year approximately twelve thousand white-skinned Negroes disappear—people whose absence cannot be explained by death or emigration. Nearly everyone of the fourteen million discernible Negroes in the United States knows at least one member of his race who is 'passing'—the magic word which means that some Negroes can get by as whites, men and women who have decided that they will be happier and more successful if they flee from the proscription and humiliation which the American color line imposes on

them" (3–4).While investigating racial violence in Phillips County, Arkansas, White passes for white. After finding out that his real identity has been revealed, he escapes on a train bound for Memphis. On the train, the conductor informs him he will miss all the "fun." He tells White: "There a damned yellow nigger down here passing for white and the boys are going to get him" (31). While in Memphis, White ironically hears the news that he was lynched in Arkansas that afternoon.

14. See James Elbert Cutler, *Lynching: An Investigation into the History of Lynching in the United States* (New York: Negro Universities Press, 1969).

15. James Weldon Johnson, *The Book of American Negro Poetry* (New York: Harcourt Brace Jovanovich, 1931), 130.

16. Ibid., 122.

17. For biographical information on James Weldon Johnson, see Levy, *James Weldon Johnson*; Robert E. Fleming, *James Weldon Johnson* (Boston: Twayne, 1987); Benjamin Brawley, "Protest and Vindication," in his *The Negro Genius* (New York: Dodd, Mead, & Co., 1937), 206–14, and Hugh M. Gloster, "James Weldon Johnson," in his *Negro Voices in American Fiction* (Chapel Hill: University of North Carolina Press, 1948), 79–83.

18. Lerone Bennett Jr., *Before the Mayflower: A History of the Blacks in America* (New York: Penguin Books, 1993), 512, 517.

19. Sterling A. Brown, *Negro Voices in American Fiction* (Port Washington, NY: Kennekat Press, 1968), 45.

20. Eugene Levy argues that "By 1906, as a friend of Washington, he [Johnson] was also thoroughly familiar with *Up from Slavery*. Both works are written in a simple, straightforward prose style generally free of rhetorical flourishes; in both, the narrator seems to detach himself from the experiences he describes; and both authors make frequent asides to comment directly on the significance of particular incidents to America racial situation. It seems clear that *Up from Slavery*, more than any other literacy influence, led Johnson to the use of the psuedoautobiography" (130).

21. Zora Neale Hurston, in her autobiography, *Dust Tracks on a Road* (New York: Harper Perennial, 1991), with tongue in cheek suggests that her friend James Weldon Johnson is a white man passing for black. Hurston states, "this passing business works both ways. All the passing is not passing for white. We have white folks among us passing for colored. They just happen to be born with a tinge of brown in the skin and took up being colored as a profession. Take James Weldon Johnson, for instance. There a man white enough to suit Hitler, and he been passing for colored for years. . . . He tried all he knew how to pass for colored, but he just hasn't made it. His own brother is scared in his presence. He bows and scrapes and calls him The Duke" (216). Richard Wright adds his own class analysis to this mix when he states, in *White Man Listen!* (New York: Anchor Books, 1964), that James Weldon Johnson is "as conservative a Negro as ever lived in America" (93).

22. Johnson, in *Along This Way*, discussing the writing of *The Autobiography*, relates the challenge of this genre as a creative medium, the surmounting of technical difficulties and a feeling of exhilaration like that which accompanies freedom of motion. In making the decision to be anonymous, Johnson states, "I did get a certain pleasure out of anonymity, that no acknowledged book could have given me. The authorship of the book excited the curiosity of literate colored people, and there was speculation among them as to who the writer might be—to every such group some colored man had married white, and so coincided with the main point of which the story turned, is known.

I had the experience of listening to some of these discussions. I had a rarer experience, that of being introduced to and talking with one man who tacitly admitted to those present that he was the author of the book. Only two or three people knew that I was the writer of the story—the publishers themselves never knew me personally; yet the fact gradually leaked out and spread" (239). Despite this, it would be fifteen years before Johnson's name would appear as the author.

23. Henry Louis Gates Jr., *The Signifying Monkey: A Theory of African-American Literary Criticism* (New York: Oxford University Press, 1988), xxvi. Gates defines the term "talking text" as a black form of intertextuality in which black texts talk to other black texts.

24. James Olney, "'I Was Born': Slave Narratives, Their Status as Autobiography and as Literature," in *The Slave Narrative*, ed. T. Davis and Henry Louis Gates Jr. (New York: Oxford University Press, 1985), 152–53.

25. Eric J. Sundquist, *The Hammers of Creation: Folk Culture in Modern African American Fiction* (Athens: University of Georgia Press, 1992), 4–5.

26. Goellnicht, "Passing as Autobiography: James Weldon Johnson's *The Autobiography*," 19.

27. Robert B. Stepto, *From Behind the Veil: A Study of Afro-American Narrative* (Chicago: University of Illinois Press, 1979), 97.

28. Ralph Ellison, *Shadow and Act* (1958; repr., New York: Vintage Books, 1972), 55.

29. Frederick Jameson, *The Prison-House of Language: A Critical Account of Structuralism and Russian Formalism* (Princeton: Princeton University Press, 1972), 133, 135. Jameson argues that the "binary opposition is . . . at the outset a heuristic principle, that instrument of analysis on which the mythological hermeneutic is founded. We would ourselves be tempted to describe it as a technique for stimulating perception, when faced with a mass of apparently homogeneous data to which the mind and the eyes are numb: a way of forcing ourselves to perceive difference and identity in a whole new language the very sounds of which we cannot yet distinguish from each other. It is a decoding or deciphering device, or alternately a technique of language learning." He continues to state that this linguistic juxtaposition embodies "a tension in which one of the two terms of the binary opposition is apprehended as positively having a certain feature while the other is apprehended as derived of the feature in question."

30. For a detailed discussion of the similarities between Johnson's novel and Ellison's novel see Houston A. Baker Jr., "A Forgotten Prototype: *The Autobiography of an Ex-Coloured Man* and *Invisible Man*," *Virginia Quarterly Review* 49 (1973): 413–29. Reprinted in Baker, *Singers of Daybreak: Studies in Black American Literature* (Washington, DC: Howard University Press, 1974). See also Howard Faulkner, "James Weldon Johnson: Portrait of the Artist as Invisible Man," *Black American Literature Forum* 19 (1985): 147–51.

31. Ellison, *Shadow and Act*, 25.

32. Stepto, *From Behind the Veil*, 100.

33. Robert E. Fleming, "Irony as a Key to Johnson's *The Autobiography of an Ex-Coloured Man*," *American Literature* 43 (1971): 87.

34. Fanon, *Black Skin, White Masks* 14.

35. Simone Vauthier, "Textualité et Stereotypes: Of African Queens and Afro-American Princes and Princesses: Miscegenation in *Old Hepsy*," *Publications du Conseil Scientifique de la Sorbonne Nouvelle* 3 (1980): 91.

36. Here I refer to Freud's definition of the Oedipus complex, in which the son desires to

kill his father and marry his mother, whereas the Electra complex reveals the daughter's desire to murder her mother and marry her father.

37. Henry Louis Gates Jr., *Figures in Black: Words, Signs, and the "Racial" Self* (New York: Oxford University Press, 1987), 89.

38. Frederick Douglass, *My Bondage and My Freedom* (1855 New York: Arno Press, 1968), 175.

39. The cakewalk, ragtime music, spirituals, and folklore, as James Weldon Johnson points out in his preface to *The Book of American Negro Poetry,* represent the "power of the Negro to suck up the national spirit from the soil and create something artistic and original, which, at the same time, possesses the note of universal appeal, is due to a remarkable racial gift of adaptability; it is more than adaptability, it is a transfusible quality. And the Negro has exercised this transfusible quality not only here in America, where the race lives in large numbers, but in European countries, where the number has been almost infinitesimal" (20).

40. Ann Douglas, *Terrible Honesty: Mongrel Manhattan in the 1920* (New York: Farrar, Straus and Giroux, 1995), 76.

41. Werner Sollors, "National Identity and Ethnic Diversity: 'Of Plymouth Rock and Jamestown and Ellis Island'; or Ethnic Literature and Some Redefinitions of 'America,'" in *History and Memory in African-American Culture,* ed. Genevieve Fabre and Robert G. O'Meally (New York: Oxford University Press, 1994), 94–98, discusses a 1917 poster design by Howard Chandler Christy that reveals the problematic iconography associated with the idea of America being open to all regardless of their ethnicity. He states: "the allegorical figure who meant to signal the incorporation of various ethnic groups into 'America' is not a mulatto Madonna with an Indian headdress but 'the American girl,' an English-looking white woman, not sturdy like the Statue of Liberty—for which the Alsatian sculptor Frederic-Auguste Bartholdi's mother posed—but with a glitzy Christy style look. The poster did not simply honor ethnic diversity: Christy image contains a double message as ethnics are asked to assimilate to an Anglo-Saxon norm (its origins in mixing forgotten) that is constituted precisely in opposition to them. They are told to be 'Mr. American' by conforming to something that not even many of the Europeans immigrants might ever become physically."

42. Eric Lott, *Love and Theft: Blackness, Minstrelsy and the American Working Class* (New York: Oxford University Press, 1993), 25.

43. The horrific murder of this white woman by this black man is a symbolic decapitation and a cutting off of female discourse. In William Faulkner's *Light in August,* which connects miscegenation to murder, we will experience an equally graphic and grotesque decapitation and an elimination of female discourse.

44. Joseph T. Skerrett Jr., "Irony and Symbolic Action in James Weldon Johnson's *The Autobiography of an Ex-Coloured Man,*" *American Quarterly* 32 (1980): 553–54.

45. This incestuous moment mirrors John Warwick's attraction to his sister, Rena Walden, when he returns home after a ten-year absence.

46. Davis, *From the Dark Tower,* 31.

47. Sigmund Freud, *Totem and Taboo: Some Points of Agreement Between the Mental Lives of Savages and Neurotics,* trans. James Strachey (New York: Norton, 1950), 19, 20.

48. Fanon, *The Wretched of the Earth,* 163.

49. Fleming, "Irony as Key to Johnson's *Autobiography of an Ex-Coloured Man,*" 89.

50. Fanon, *Black Skin, White Masks,* 228.

51. Sundquist, *The Hammers of Creation,* 10.

52. We recall that in *Along This Way*, Johnson states that the black woman, with "her rich coloring, her gaiety, her laughter and song, her alluring, undulating movements—a heritage from the African jungle—was a more beautiful creature that her sallow, songless, lipless, hipless, tried-looking, tired-moving white sister" (121).

53. Karla F. C. Holloway, *Codes of Conduct: Race, Ethics, and the Color of Our Character* (New Brunswick: Rutgers University Press, 1995), 66.

54. Citing Harriet Beecher Stowe's *Uncle Tom Cabin* (1952), William Wells Brown's *Clotel; or the President Daughter* (1853), and Charles W. Chesnutt's *The House Behind the Cedars* (1900), as examples, Fleming argues that "none of these books, whether by white or black authors, goes beyond the stereotype view of the tragic mulatto, whose appeal to the reader is made on the basis of a high percentage of white blood and whose difficulties are external and primarily physical." Additionally, Fleming notes that William Dean Howells's *An Imperative Duty* (1892) and Mark Twain's *Pudd'nhead Wilson* (1894) are the only texts published before *The Autobiography* that explore possibilities beyond the tragic mulatto stereotype (84).

55. Toni Morrison, "On the Backs of Blacks," *Time* Special Issue "The New Face of America" (fall 1993), p. 57.

56. It is interesting to note that in a "tattered and yellowed article," Kathryn Talalay, author of *Composition in Black and White: The Life of Philippa Schuyler* (New York: Oxford University Press, 1995), discovered an acknowledgment by Philippa Schuyler that "I'm not sure what I am" (vii). What is fascinating about the daughter, a classical music child prodigy, of George and Josephine Schuyler is that she passed for white in Europe and Africa. Talalay writes: "The idea of shedding her African-American ballast, or even perhaps 'passing' into the white world began to cross Phillippa's mind as early as 1959. A significant number of people in Europe had told her by then that she did not look Negro at all but rather southern European, Levantine, Indian, or Oriental. In sub-Saharan Africa she was generally perceived as a 'European artist'" (222). George Schuyler's satirical passing novel *Black No More* (1931), among others, parodies James Weldon Johnson, W. E. B. Du Bois, and the NAACP.

57. Johnson, *Book of American Negro Poetry*, 9.

Chapter 4

1. Toni Morrison, *Playing in the Dark: Whiteness in the Literary Imagination* (Cambridge, MA: Harvard University Press, 1992), 5.

2. The name "Gatz" literally means comrade or peace in German; the name suggests the possibility that Jay Gatsby may be German or Jewish, with the shift from Gatz to Gatsby suggesting a shift from Judaism to Protestantism. Peter Gregg Slater, "Ethnicity in *The Great Gatsby*," *Twentieth Century Literature* 19 (1973), 53–62, points out that "[t]he ethnicity of Gatsby is somewhat vague though he is clearly not a *landsman of Wolfsheim*. His true name, Gatz, and the Lutheran faith of his father indicate that he is probably of German descent, with very likely, at least one immigrant grandparent which would preclude his being considered of Old American lineage. In a curious way, however, Gatsby possesses no ethnicity of any sort, being a product of his own dreams and conceits" (56).

3. Fitzgerald's use of blackness is unique in this novel. In F. *Scott Fitzgerald: The Princeton*

Years, Selected Writings 1914–1920 (Fort Bragg, CA: Cypress House Press, 1996), Chipp Deffaa argues, "Black characters rarely played significant, well-rounded roles in Fitzgerald's fiction. They tended to be treated sentimentally. The only one of Fitzgerald's short stories to feature a black protagonist was the sympathetic and moving "Dearly Beloved," which was written in the last year of his life; however, he was unable to sell that story. "Dearly Beloved" would appear in print for the first time 29 years after Fitzgerald's death" (103). Although it can be argued that blackness can relate to other ethnic identities, here black is more often than not associated with African Americans and their cultural productions.

4. It is interesting to note that Ross Macdonald's *Black Money* (New York: Vintage, 1996) is a meditation on the themes and patterns of action in *The Great Gatsby*. Here, Pedro Domingo, the Panamanian-born character, dreams of remaking himself and focuses on marrying a wealthy American girl, Ginny Fablon. Like Jay Gatsby, Pedro Domingo changes his name, here to Francis Martel, and is murdered. In the novel, Peter Jamieson, who seeks to save Ginny from Francis, tells Mr. Archer: "This man is apparently wanted by the police. He claims to be a Frenchman, a French aristocrat no less, but nobody really knows who he is or where he comes from. He may not even be Caucasian. . . . He's so dark. And Ginny is so fair. It nauseates me to see her with him" (4). Like Tom Buchanan, Peter Jamieson announces his horror of miscegenation between black and whites; later, Peter Jamieson shoots and kills Francis Martel. Whereas Jay Gatsby's desire conveys a futile attempt to bring the past and the present together, in *Black Money* the "past and present were coming together" (142). Also see Jerry Tutunjian, "A Conversation with Ross Macdonald," *Tamarack Review* 62 (1974), 32–45, where Macdonald states: "*Gatsby* is in modern times the central artistic expression of the American experience. It's about American idealism destroyed by American greed. It's about the struggle for the soul of America by opposing forces—idealism on one hand and money power on the other—misplaced idealism" (76).

5. F. James Davis, *Who Is Black?: One Nation's Definition* (University Park: Pennsylvania State University Press, 1991), 56.

6. Alan Hyde, *Bodies of Law* (Princeton: Princeton University Press, 1997), 223.

7. Robert Westbrook, *Intimate Lives: F. Scott Fitzgerald and Shelia Graham, Her Son's Story* (New York: HarperCollins, 1995), 369.

8. Ibid., 332.

9. Andrew Turnbull, ed., *The Letters of F. Scott Fitzgerald* (New York: Scribner's, 1963), 326.

10. Quoted in Karen Brodkin Sacks, "How Did Jews Become White?" In *Race*, ed. Steven Gregory and Roger Sanjek (New Brunswick: Rutgers University Press, 1996), 80.

11. James Mellow, *Invented Lives: F. Scott and Zelda Fitzgerald* (Boston: Houghton Mifflin, 1984), 420.

12. Quoted in Sara Mayfield, *Exiles from Paradise: Zelda and Scott Fitzgerald* (New York: Delacorte Press, 1971), 26–27.

13. James R. Mellow, *Invented Lives,* relates a compelling scene in which Fitzgerald explosively illustrates his fears concerning white purity and the horror of being tainted with blackness. "Enraged by his [Fitzgerald's] argument with Burttia, he was abusive on the subject in front of Lottie, asserting that it was because Burttia had been sold a bill of goods by the Communist Party that he was championing the black cause. Lottie, so she told Burttia, listened carefully. 'He [Fitzgerald] talked like a dyed-in-the-wool Southerner, thinking I was on his side' Fitzgerald began harping about radicals

wanting to mix the races. It was then, she said, that she decided to spell it out for him; she told him that she was only three-quarters white herself. Fitzgerald went into a rage, slamming around the room, opening drawers, looking for a drink. Then he broke down and bawled. 'Oh, God what's happened to me? What's happened to me?' Lottie tried to console him by saying that in her years in the South, everyone knew that 'a white boy wasn't a man till he smoked, got stinko under the kitchen table, and had himself a nigger in the barn.' She told Fitzgerald that he had now made it in style" (438–39).

14. Vincent Cheng, *Joyce, Race, and Empire* (New York: Cambridge University Press, 1995), 27.

15. Morrison, *Playing in the Dark,* 66.

16. Quoted in Jeffrey Meyers, *Scott Fitzgerald: A Biography* (New York: HarperCollins, 1994), 124.

17. In *The Jazz Age* (New York: New Directions, 1996), F. Scott Fitzgerald describes this period: "A whole race going hedonistic, deciding on pleasure. The precocious intimacies of the younger generation would have come about with or without prohibition—they were implicit in the attempt to adapt English customs to American conditions. . . . The word jazz in its progress toward respectability has meant first sex, then dancing, then music. It is associated with a state of nervous stimulation, not unlike that of big cities behind the lines of a war" (6). Also, as Leroi Jones argues in *Black Music* (New York: Harper Trade, 1971): "Jazz, as a Negro music, existed, up until the time of the big bands, on the same socio-cultural level as the sub-culture from which it was issued. The music and its sources were *secret* as far as the rest of America was concerned, in much the same sense that the actual life of the black man in America was secret to the white American" (13).

18. Nathan Irvin Huggins, *Harlem Renaissance* (New York: Oxford University Press, 1971), 56.

19. Juda Bennett, *The Passing Figure: Racial Confusion in Modern American Literature* (New York: Peter Lang, 1996), 63.

20. Quoted in Magnus Hirschfeld's analysis of racist dogma in Nazi Germany, titled *Racism,* trans. and ed. Eden Paul and Paul Cedar (London: V. Gollancz Ltd., 1938), 298.

21. F. Scott Fitzgerald, *The Great Gatsby* (1925; repr., New York: Simon and Schuster, 1995), 127, 12–14. All further references to this text will be given parenthetically.

22. Henry H. Goddard, *Efficiency and Levels of Intelligence* (Princeton: Princeton University Press, 1920), 1.

23. Meyer Shapiro, "Recent Abstract Painting," in *Modern Art 19th & 20th Centuries* (New York: G. Braziller, 1982), 215.

24. Amos N. Wilson, *Black-on-Black Violence: The Psychodynamics of Black Self-Annihilation in Service of White Domination* (New York: Afrikan World Infosystems, 1990), 2.

25. Patricia Williams, *Seeing a Color-Blind Future: The Paradox of Race* (New York: Farrar, Straus and Giroux, 1997), 26.

26. E. Franklin Frazier, *The Black Bourgeoisie* (New York: Free Press, 1967), 201.

27. Stanley Crouch, *The All American Skin Game, or the Decoy of Race: The Long and the Short of It 1990–1994* (New York: Pantheon, 1994), 147.

28. Isabel Leighton, ed., *The Aspirin Age, 1919–1941* (New York: Simon and Schuster, 1949), 34. Furthermore, it is strongly possible that the story of George Remus, the German-born American who became the richest bootlegger, was used by Fitzgerald. In

Prohibition: Thirteen Years That Changed America (New York: Arcade, 1996), Edward Behr argues that the real-life Remus and the fictional Gatsby "were self-made men both who gave lavish parties, both despised their guests' venality, and both were low-key hosts, observing rather than dominating the party scene. There was, however, a major difference between them. Remus, in 1923 was happily married—an adoring husband and doting father who lavished every type of expensive gift on Imogene's daughter Ruth, including a gold-plated grand piano—whereas Gatsby was a loner, at heart an unrequited romantic" (99).

29. Willard B. Gatewood, *Aristocrats of Color: The Black Elite, 1880–1920* (Bloomington: Indiana University Press, 1990), 13.

30. Matthew J. Bruccoli, *Some Sort of Epic Grandeur: The Life of F. Scott Fitzgerald.* (New York: Harcourt Brace Jovanovitch, 1981), 222.

31. In the film version of *The Great Gatsby* (1974), directed by Jack Clayton, Tom Buchanan, played by Bruce Dern, instructs a man to "Find out where his [Gatsby's] money comes from. What clubs he belongs to. Who his parents are and where they lived. And his women, I want to know about his women." These aspects all point to the rumors of Gatsby's genealogy, class status, and sexual behavior. This film also emphasizes the theme of miscegenation; when it rains at Gatsby's party and after everyone comes inside, a yellow dog is the last to enter the house. Like Gatsby, the yellow dog suggests miscegenation. Further, when Tom is at Myrtle's apartment in New York, Tom steps on Myrtle's dog; this foreshadows how Gatsby will be indirectly crushed by Tom's wealth and power. Taken together, these visual representations suggest that Jack Clayton understands how Fitzgerald is "playing in the dark."

32. In *Tough Jews: Fathers, Sons, and Gangster Dreams* (New York: Simon & Schuster, 1998), Rich Cohen, echoing the life of Jay Gatsby, connects the fictional Meyer Wolfshiem to the real-life gangster Arnold Rothstein. Rich relates: "Of course, in the real world, Arnold Rothstein was just as smart and well put together as F. Scott Fitzgerald. . . . He was a businessman just like so many of those fathers who, returning each day from the city, disappear into neat suburban homes—whose wives, when all is said and done, have no idea what their husbands do. He had broken through the traditional confines of the underworld and come out in a place where the line between the criminal and the commendable is vague and unreal. He worked the underworld the way a great aristocrat works the upper world: moving gracefully through rooms and threshold" (52).

33. Ralph Ellison, *Shadow and Act* (1958; repr., New York: Vintage Books, 1972), 44.

34. Although the Barbary Coast can refer to a district in San Francisco, it is also an area of North Africa that runs from Egypt to the Atlantic.

35. Katrina Hazzard-Gordon, *Jookin': The Rise of Social Dance Formation in African-American Culture* (Philadelphia: Temple University Press, 1990), 76.

36. Jacqui Malone, *Steppin' on the Blues: The Visible Rhythms of African American Dance* (Chicago: University of Illinois Press, 1996), 143.

37. Ann Douglas, *Terrible Honesty: Mongrel Manhattan in the 1920s* (New York: Farrar, Straus and Giroux, 1995), 101.

38. Sherene H. Razack, in *Looking White People in the Eye: Gender, Race and Culture in Courtrooms and Classrooms* (Toronto: University of Toronto Press, 1998), draws on the analysis of Frantz Fanon, arguing, "Looking white people in the eye is an encounter for Fanon that is deeply psychically structured and sexualized, illuminating, as Homi Bhabha writes, 'the madness of racism, the pleasure of pain, the agnostic fantasy of

political power.' It is a moment when the 'white man's eyes break up the Black man's body and in that act of epistemic violence its own frame of reference is transgressed, its field of vision disturbed'" (4). Razack's analysis points out that Fitzgerald's sociolinguistic characterizations of these black "bucks," with their disturbing gazes, project the idea that these black men are sexually threatening to the "madness" of white supremacy.

39. The issue of breeding is a recurring theme in *The Great Gatsby*. Tom's elitist remarks about Gatsby suggest his inferior breeding; one of Myrtle Wilson's statements reinforces the issue of breeding relative to class. Myrtle, discussing her husband, declares, "I married him because he was a gentleman. . . . I thought he knew something about breeding but he wasn't fit to lick my shoe" (39).

40. Thomas Cripps, "The Making of *The Birth of a Nation*: The Emerging Politics of Identity in Silent Movies," in *The Birth of Whiteness: Race and the Emergence of U. S. Cinema*, ed. Daniel Bernardi (New Brunswick: Rutgers University Press, 1996), 135.

41. The Harlem Renaissance was marked by black veterans who had returned from France and Germany; as the novel reveals, Gatsby was a first lieutenant who had served in France and Germany. In *Negroes in American Society* (New York: Whittlesay House, 1949), Maurice R. Davie argues, "Thus, after the suicide of Lieutenant William J. French, in 1932 it was publicly revealed that he was one-eighth Negro, had passed for white for fourteen years in the Army, and had led white troops in France during the First World War" (405).

42. R. W. Stallman, "Conrad and *The Great Gatsby*," *Twentieth Century Literature* 1 (April 1955): 9.

43. Ralph Ellison, *Going into the Territory* (New York: Vintage Books, 1987), 104.

44. The word "sport" is used forty-seven times in the novel.

45. Tom Buchanan's apprehensions around miscegenation between blacks and whites must be put in the context of the unjustly calumniated black prizefighter—the first black heavyweight champion and "the white man's nightmare"—Jack Johnson. As Randy Roberts argues in *Papa Jack: Jack Johnson and the Era of White Hopes* (New York: Free Press, 1983), "Starting in 1909 the American public began to see the Bad Nigger in Jack Johnson. They saw his flashy clothes and his brightly colored, fast automobiles. They saw the way in which he challenged white authority in his numerous brushes with the law. They heard stories of his night life, the lurid tales of his week-long drunks and parties. Tales of his sexual bouts were also told, and his shaved head came to symbolize the sexual virility of the black male. But most shocking of all were the times he appeared in public with white women" (70). It is within this context that among other references to Jay Gatsby's blackness, like Jack Johnson with his "golden smile," Gatsby becomes the "bad nigger" or the bad "black buck."

46. If Tom considers Gatsby to be "white," then the shocking suggestion here is that Daisy is "black." This might explain why Tom hesitates about including Daisy in his world of Nordic superiority. As Gilbert Osofsky points out in *Harlem: The Making of a Ghetto, 1890–1930* (New York: Harper & Row, 1965), there was an unsuccessful attempt in 1910 to reestablish the state law banning intermarriage. The proposed "Act to Amend the Domestic Relations Law, in Relation to Miscegenation" sought to void all marriages "contracted between a person of white or Caucasian race and a person of the negro or black race" (42).

47. In *F. Scott Fitzgerald Manuscripts*, edited by Matthew Bruccoli (New York: Garland, 1990), Fitzgerald writes: "'Were all white here,' murmured Jordan, 'except possibly

Tom'" (133). This shocking statement, which was removed from the final manuscript, suggests Tom Buchanan's blackness or Otherness and reinforces the concept that Jay Gatsby successfully passes for white.

48. Chela Sandoval, "Theorizing White Consciousness for a Post-Empire World: Barthes, Fanon, and the Rhetoric of Love," in *Displacing Whiteness: Essays in Social and Cultural Criticism,* ed. Ruth Frankenburg (Durham: Duke University Press, 1997), 89.

49. Arthur Schlesinger Jr., *The Disuniting of America: Reflections on a Multicultural Society* (New York: W. W. Norton, 1993), 13.

50. Nathaniel Mackey, *Discrepant Engagement: Dissonance, Cross-Culturality and Experimental Writing* (New York: Cambridge University Press, 1993), 265.

51. Irving Lewis Allen, *The City in Slang: New York Life and Popular Speech* (New York: Oxford University Press, 1993), 165.

52. Leslie A. Fiedler, *Tyranny of the Normal: Essays On Bioethics, Theology and Myth* (Boston: David R. Godine, 1996), 150.

53. Quoted in Richard Lehan, *The Great Gatsby: The Limits of Wonder* (New York: Twayne, 1995), 23.

Chapter 5

1. Although my reading of the novel focuses on the tragic aspects, it should be noted that there are numerous comical moments in the text that provide a balance and reflect the tragic-comic duality of human existence. For example, Lena Grove's narrative, which frames *Light in August,* can be read as a comedy of rustic innocence.

2. C. Vann Woodward, *The Burden of Southern History* (Baton Rouge: Louisiana State University Press, 1983), 268.

3. Eric J. Sundquist, *To Wake the Nations:Race in the Making of American Literature* (Cambridge, MA: Harvard University Press, 1993), argues that in *Plessy v. Ferguson* the "central irony of Homer Plessy's deliberately staged challenge of a Louisiana segregated train car lay in the fact that he was seven-eights 'white'. . . he was thus 'black' only by the fictions of law and custom—and his case therefore tied together the radical decline in black civil rights that had occurred since Reconstruction and the fanatical adherence to 'one-drop' definitions of blackness that had begun to engulf not just the South but most of the nation by the mid-1890s" (228). Consequently, Christmas becomes trapped by the "fictions of law and custom" with regard to his racial identity.

4. As novel, in *Light in August* we have the geometric figure of a triangle in a circle. The three main characters, Gail Hightower, Joanna Burden, and Joe Christmas—connected by their tragic pasts—form a triangle trapped in the circular legacies of their grandfathers' actions. Additionally, Joe Christmas sums up his life by relating that he never got outside the circle of his past.

5. Eric J. Sundquist, *Faulkner: The House Divided* (Baltimore: Johns Hopkins University Press, 1983), 66. David M. Oshinsky, *"Worse Than Slavery": Parchman Farm and the Ordeal of Jim Crow Justice.* (New York: Free Press, 1996), describes the uniqueness of Mississippi. He argues, "Parchman is the quintessential penal farm, the closest thing to slavery that survived the Civil War. Its story covers the bleak panorama of race punishment in the darkest corner of the South. It begins in antebellum times, on the Mississippi frontier, though Parchman itself would not be constructed until 1904. And it con-

tinues to this day, a story filled with warnings and consequences, and perhaps lessons, for a nation deeply divided, black and white" (2).

6. Frederick L. Gwynn and Joseph L. Blotner, eds., *Faulkner in the University: Class Conferences at the University of Virginia* (Charlottesville: Virginia University Press, 1959), 74.

7. Despite Faulkner's assertion that Christmas's life is not based on the life of Jesus Christ, Christmas is betrayed; after cries for his death, he is subsequently crucified.

8. In *William Faulkner's "Light in August": A Description and Interpretation of the Revisions* (Charlottesville: University Press of Virginia, 1975), Regina K. Fadiman points out that in an earlier draft of the novel Faulkner presents Christmas's black blood as a matter of fact rather than speculation (64–65).

9. Eva Saks, "Representing Miscegenation Law," *Raritan—A Quarterly Review* 8.2 (1988): 40.

10. In Mark Twain, *Pudd'nhead Wilson* (1894; repr., New York: Penguin Books, 1986), Wilson unmasks the white Negro Tom by first declaring to the court "'that the person whose hand left the blood-stained finger-prints upon the handle of the Indian knife is the person who committed the murder'" (212). Here Twain conveys that a black man ("Tom") murders a white man with an Indian knife. Also, Roxy, Tom's mother, connects blood to behavior by stating that "It de nigger in you dat what it is. Thirty-one parts o' you is white en only one part nigger, en dat po little one part is yo soul" (157).

11. William Faulkner, *Light in August* (1931; repr., New York: Vintage Books, 1990), 449. All further references to this text will be given parenthetically.

12. Lee Jenkins, *Faulkner and Black-White Relations: A Psychoanalytic Approach* (New York: Columbia University Press, 1981), 101.

13. Saks, "Representing Miscegenation Law," 39.

14. F. James Davis, *Who Is Black?: One Nation's Definition* (University Park: Pennsylvania State University Press, 1991), 54.

15. Roland Barthes, "The Stucturalist Activity," trans. Richard Howard, *Partisan Review* 34 (1967): 86–87.

16. In Gwynn and Blotner, *Faulkner in the University*, Faulkner discussing the title change: "I used it [*Light in August*] because in my country in August there is a peculiar quality to light and that's what that title means" (74). Also, the initial title, *Dark House*, suggests Dickens's *Bleak House*, in which the narrative strands are woven together to convey the sense of a unified world understood and controlled by the author.

17. To a lesser extent, the theme of gender masquerading is represented in Faulkner's complex characterization of Joanna Burden.

18. Faulkner, *Faulkner in the University*, 210.

19. Faulkner's racist discourse has to be put in the miscegenation context of his being "mammy made." In "Funeral Sermon for Mammy Caroline Barr," in *Essay, Speeches and Public Letters by William Faulkner*, ed. James B. Meriwether (New York: Random House, 1965), Faulkner relates: "She still remained one of my earliest recollections, not only as a person, but as a fount of authority over my conduct and of security for my physical welfare, and of active and constant affection and love. . . . From her I learned to tell the truth, to refrain from waste, to be considerate of the weak and respectful to age" (117). In another speech, "A Letter to the Negro Leaders in the Negro Race," Faulkner extends the theme of miscegenation and introduces mimicry and masquerade. He states: "So if I were a Negro, I would say to my people: 'Let us be always unflaggingly and inflexibly flexible. But always decently, quietly, courteously with dignity

and without violence. And above all, with patience" (111). Of course, Faulkner's discourse is particularly ironic considering Mississippi's history of riotous and undignified behavior and its brutal violence—directed at black people.

20. Gwynn and Blotner, *Faulkner in the University,* 211. Black people were not the only ones to experience Faulkner's racist rancor. Discussing the Ikkemotubbe Indians, Faulkner states: "There are a few of them still in Mississippi, but they are a good deal like animals in a zoo: they have no place in the culture, in the economy, unless they become white men, and they have in some cases mixed with white people and their own conditions have vanished, or they have mixed with Negroes and they have descended into the Negroes' condition of semi-peonage" (43).

21. Fanon, *Black Skin, White Masks* (New York: Grove Press, 1967), 188.

22. Thomas Jefferson, *Notes on the State of Virginia* (New York: W. W. Norton, 1972), 143.

23. Both *Light in August* and *Notes on the State of Virginia* suggest America's anxiety around issues of race and mirror each other in terms of structural incongruity. As Robert A. Ferguson argues in *Law and Letters in American Culture* (Cambridge, MA: Harvard University Press, 1984), "Of the issues raised in the pessimistic remarks of *Notes*, only slavery resists rational management in Jefferson's hands, and it does so precisely because it defines legal terminology and solution within the intellectual framework of an eighteenth-century lawyer. Slavery exists but against natural law; it becomes, in consequence, a structural incongruity in *Notes*, spilling between and among sections" (51).

24. Patricia J. Williams, *The Alchemy of Race and Right: Diary of a Law Professor* (Cambridge, MA: Harvard University Press, 1991), 198.

25. Jacques Lacan, *Ecrits: A Selection,* trans. Alan Sheridan (New York: W. W. Norton, 1977), 148.

26. Gail Hightower's first name implies sexual ambivalence or sexual ambiguity that mirrors the racial ambiguity, whereas the last name implies an elite status removed from society. Further, the last name recalls Psalms 18:2: "The Lord is my rock , and my fortress, and my deliverer; my God, my strength, in whom I will trust; my buckler, and the horn of my salvation, and my *high tower*" (emphasis added).

27. John T. Irwin, *Doubling and Incest/Repetition and Revenge: A Speculative Reading of Faulkner* (Baltimore: Johns Hopkins University Press, 1973), 119.

28. When we consider the protagonist in *The Autobiography of an Ex-Coloured Man*, who is scrubbed into "whiteness" by his mother, the toothpaste that Joe Christmas uses becomes a transforming (whitening) agent. Toothpaste is an ingestion agent used to whiten by removing brown or yellow stain. Yet Christmas goes beyond the temporary ingestion to the digestion of the toothpaste. The "pinkcolored" toothpaste is in the room of Miss Atkins, the "fullbodied, smooth, pink-and-white" (120) dietician. Consequently, the parchment-colored Christmas's consumption of the toothpaste while "among the soft womansmelling garments" (121), which causes him to vomit, is symbolically a consumption of whiteness and the removal of blackness. Faulkner's suggestion of miscegenation is again quite explicit. This primal scene taints Christmas's appetite, establishing his aversion both to food prepared by women such as Mrs. McEachern and Joanna Burden and to sex with the "womanshenegro."

29. Faulkner's description of this sexualized and erotic triangle suggests the term "reckless eyeballing" used to refer to the fourteen-year-old Emmett Till, who, in 1955, was brutally mutilated and killed in Mississippi for looking at a white woman. Of course, with the young Christmas, the term would be "reckless hearing." Implicitly suggested here is the notion of a black man "raping" a white woman. Perhaps the only thing hindering

this charge is Christmas's young age. If he was a "Bigger" nigger, Christmas could have been charged with "rape" and subsequently lynched.

30. Anatole Broyard, quoted in Henry Louis Gates Jr., "White Like Me," *The New Yorker* June 1996, p. 68. As Gates relates, Broyard, a writer for the *New York Times*, was a black man who denied his family and passed for white. Summing up Broyard life's, Gates relates: "So here is a man who passed for white because he wanted to be a writer, and he did not want to be a Negro writer. It was a crass disjunction, but it is not his crassness or his disjunction. His perception was perfectly correct. He would have had to be a Negro writer, which was something he did not want to be. In his terms, he did not want to write about black love, black passion, black suffering, black joy; he wanted to write about love and passion and suffering and joy" (78).

31. Lacan, *Ecrits*, 4.

32. John Howard Griffin's *Black Like Me* and Grace Hasell's *Soul Sister*—passing-for-black narratives—are rare exceptions and describe temporary experiences that were undergone mainly to facilitate journalistic investigation. Although physically and psychologically challenged, both Griffin and Hasell returned to the privileged status of whiteness when their racial experiments were concluded.

33. As we have witnessed, Rena Walden's hair texture was a critical factor in John Warwick's desire to help his sister pass for white. Within both the white and the black communities, hair texture continues to play a critical role in one's subjectivity. In *Divided Sisters: Bridging the Gap Between Black Woman and White Woman* (New York: Doubleday, 1996), Midge Wilson and Kathy Russell argue: "Historically, within the African American community, hair texture was very much linked to the concerns about skin color. According to the standards of beauty set by the mulatto elite, who were in turn influenced by White society, a Black woman with straight or wavy hair was considered more attractive than a woman of the same color whose hair was tightly coiled, nappy, or kinky. Straight hair was declared 'good'; nappy hair was deemed 'bad'" (78). Despite this gendered focus, it should be noted that the same divisive classification of "good" hair and "bad" hair applied to black men, as well. Also, we recall the Ex-Coloured Man's narcissistic moment when he becomes fixated on the "size and liquid darkness" of his eyes. Since the vast majority of African American have eyes that are brown in color, lighter hues such as blues and gray are often associated with whiteness. Thus, since passing is largely based on ocular analysis, Christmas's eyes and hair, along with his skin color, are critical physical characteristics.

34. Frederick Douglass, *Narrative of the Life of Frederick Douglass, an American Slave* (New York: New American Library, 1968), 60.

35. Here Faulkner suggests a gender ambiguity to mirror Christmas's racial ambiguity.

36. Hugh M. Ruppersburg, with the editorial collaboration of James Hinkle and Robert McCoy, *Reading Faulkner:* Light in August (Jackson: University Press of Mississippi, 1994), xii, 111.

37. In Gwynn and Blotner, *Faulkner in the University*, Faulkner, discussing the Christ symbolism, states: "there are so few plots to use that sooner or later any writer is going to use something that has been used. And that Christ story is one of the best stories that man has invented, assuming that he did invent that story, and of course it will recur. Everyone that has had the story of Christ and the Passion as a part of his Christian background will in time draw from that. There was no deliberate intent to repeat it. That the people to me comes first. The symbolism comes second" (117).

38. Fanon, *Black Skin, White Masks*, 11.

39. Ibid., 72.

40. Faulkner's and Chesnutt's novels share three important aspects. First, both writers use the flashback as a narrative technique. Faulkner consistently describes Christmas as being catlike while Chesnutt describes John Warwick in a similar catlike manner. For example, when Christmas clandestinely goes down the rope to see Bobbie Allen, he is compared to a cat six times. Last, both authors use the Hametic legacy that black people are inferior to illustrate the historical context or shadow that Joe Christmas comes under. Joanna's father tells her that black people are a "race doomed and cursed to be forever and ever a part of the white race's doom and curse for its sins. Remember that. His doom and his curse. Forever and ever. . . . The curse of every white child that ever was born and that ever will be born" (252).

41. Christmas's food-throwing spectacle occurs the day after he "rapes" Joanna. Hissing, "I'll show you! I'll show the bitch!" Christmas "began to tear at her clothes. . . . But beneath the hands the body might have been the body of a dead woman not yet stiffened. But he did not desist; though his hands were hard and urgent it was with rage alone" (236).

42. C. J. S. Thompson, *Ladies or Gentleman?: Women Who Posed as Men and Men Who Impersonated Women* (New York: Dorset Press, 1993). Thompson makes a connection between seasonal celebrations and gender masquerades. Thompson points out: "The practice of one sex assuming the costume of the other formed part of the old English custom of 'mumming,' at one time common at the Christmas season. The men dressed themselves in women's clothes and the women donned the men's, and thus arrayed, they went from 'one neighbor's house to another making merry in their disguises.' This ancient custom is believed to have originated in the festival days added to the early Saturnalia" (15). In this regard, Faulkner describes the Du Boisian quality of Joanna Burden. Joanna is "two creatures that struggled in the one body like two moongleamed shapes struggling drowning in alternate throes upon the surface of a black thick pool beneath the last moon" (260).

43. Albert Murray, *South to a Very Old Place* (New York: Modern Library, 1995). Here Murray makes a poignant connection to Toni Morrison's *The Bluest Eye* (1970). Murray states: "This Joe Christmas is not ashamed of his black blood like Peola. He goes around telling people he thinks he got some and he doesn't even know it for sure. Miscegenation—some word, what? full of pubic hair—is something very special and very fundamental on the Faulknerian landscape, like incest in Greek tragedy" (133).

44. John B. Cullen and Flody C. Watkins, *Old Times in Faulkner County* (Chapel Hill: University of North Carolina Press, 1961), 89–98, remark that the killing of Joanna recalls Faulkner's childhood memory of the lynching of Nelse Patton, a black man from Oxford, Mississippi, who, in September 1908, murdered a white woman, Mattie McMillian, by cutting her throat so thoroughly with a razor that she was almost decapitated. In terms of literature, Joanna's decapitation anticipates the graphic beheading and burning of Mary Dalton in fellow Mississippian Richard Wright's *Native Son* (1940). Joseph Blotner, *Faulkner: A Biography* (New York: Random House, 1974), notes that, in a later murder that Faulkner heard about, a black man named Leonard Burt murdered his wife and set the house afire to conceal his crime. It can be argued that Faulkner appropriated these incidents in conveying the brutal murder of Joanna Burden.

45. Howard Eilberg-Schwartz, "Introduction: The Spectacle of the Female Head," in *The Denial of Women's Identity in Myth, Religion, and Culture*, ed. Howard Eilberg-Schwartz and Wendy Doniger (Berkeley: University of California Press, 1995), 1. Decapitation of

women is a recurring theme in literature. For example, when Bigger Thomas, in *Native Son*, feels threatened by Bessie, he repeatively bashes her in the head with a brick. Also, in *Alice in Wonderland*, we see this beheading theme. When Alice vociferously challenges the queen, the monarch shouts, "Off with her head."

46. Jefferson, *Notes on the State of Virginia*, 163.

47. Like Theodore Dreiser in *An American Tragedy* (1925) and F. Scott Fitzgerald in *The Great Gatsby* (1925), Richard Wright's oppressively tragic novel suggests passing in terms of an individual's attempt to transform himself by achieving a higher economic status.

48. Christmas's involvement in selling illegal whiskey suggests a connection between passing and criminality. Just as he disregards the strict boundaries of race, Christmas leaves his "nigger" job shoveling sawdust at the Jefferson mill and begins selling whiskey. This recalls John Warwick's prevaricating clandestine behavior and the Ex-Coloured Man's descent into gambling and the hustling of his musical skills for money. Further, as W. J. Cash makes clear in *The Mind of the South* (New York: Knopf, 1957), black people were employed by white bootleggers as deliverymen and salesmen. And the liquor business was a nexus of bootlegging where black men used and had sex with white prostitutes. Christmas's use of Joanna's cabin as a home and as a base of operations and his workng with Joe Brown as his partner in his bootlegging business further the criminality of miscegenation and masquerade. We recall that most of the women that Christmas becomes involved with, such as Bobbie Allen, are prostitutes. Thus, Faulkner's references to Joe Anna (Joanna and miscegenation) as a white prostitute are quite sophisticated.

49. With regard to Christmas's being the "bad nigger," Faulkner prefigures this pejorative prototype in his short story "That Evening Sun" in *Collected Stories of William Faulkner* (1931; repr., New York: Vantage Books, 1995). In this story, Jesus (no surname) is described as a "short black man, with a razor scar down his face" (290). He is Nancy Mannigoe's husband and murderer and Aunt Rachel's son. Jesus challenges the culture of white supremacy and is feared by both blacks and whites in the town of Jefferson, Mississippi.

50. This signifying phrase comes from Amiri Baraka's play *Dutchman* (1964). The suggestion is that a black man, through his dress and demeanor, is trying to pass for white. Here Baraka also addresses American racial and sexual stereotypes. Like Joanna Burden in *Light in August*, a white woman, Lula, wishes to seduce and control a black man, Clay. Antithetically, this ritual of seduction and murder ends with Lula stabbing Clay.

51. At the apex of their relationship, Joanna Burden informs Christmas that she is pregnant. Again Faulkner leaves the reader to speculate on the veracity of this revelation. Having had a oppressive and brutal childhood, Christmas would find the prospect of reproducing himself extremely disturbing. Christmas connects Joanna's change in behavior (they always meet in the bedroom to have sex) to marriage: "No more did he have to seek her through the house; the nights when he must seek her hidden and panting and naked about the dark house or among the shrubbery of the ruined park were as dead now as the hollow fencepost below the barn." Also, concerning marriage, stability, and security, Christmas thinks: "No. If I give in now, I will deny all the thirty years that I have lived to make me what I chose to be" (265). And, concerning Joanna's pregnancy, Christmas "believed that she was lying. He discovered now that he had been expecting her to tell him that for three months. But when he looked at her face, he knew that she was not." Thus, women and a permanent black identity are Christmas's worst

fears. All of the violence that Christmas engages in revolves around women and black people.

52. Mary Shelley, *Frankenstein* (New York: Penguin Books, 1983), 123.

53. Margo V. Perkins, "The Nature of Otherness: Class and Difference in Mary Shelley's *Frankenstein*," *Studies in the Humanities* 19.1 (1992): 27–42, makes a connection between the outsider and the privileged class. Perkins argues: "Depicting the relationship between a monstrous being and his creator, Mary Shelley's *Frankenstein* constitutes a provocative study in power relations, class, and the meaning of difference. Through the monster, Shelley creates an oppressed, dispossessed "Other" who is forced both to proclaim his humanity and to negotiate his survival against the values of an oppressive/ privileged ruling class, represented by the figure of Victor Frankenstein" (27). Like Hines's narcissistic and God-sanctioned racist discourse at the black churches, both Victor Frankenstein and Robert Walton engage in narcissistic discourse that proclaims their independent missions (one to create life and the other to go to Antarctica) to be sanctioned by Heavenly forces. I would argue that the hegemonic philosophy of white supremacy is implicit in the discourses of both Victor and Robert.

54. Eric J. Sundquist, *The House Divided* (Baltimore: Johns Hopkins University Press, 1983), 68.

55. Frantz Fanon, *The Wretched of the Earth* (New York: Grove Press, 1966), 27.

56. The names "Freeland" and "Freeman Town" became common after black people were emancipated after the Civil War. Faulkner conveys that, whether in the North or in the South, black people are segregated by racist social, political, and economic forces. It is these forces that motivate some black individuals to pass and masquerade as white. Also, the name "Freeland" figures quite importantly in Douglass's narratives. Passing for white equals "freedom" or escape from America's racist society.

57. Faulkner has repeatedly foreshadowed connections between the former Rev. Gail Hightower and Joe Christmas. Two critical connections are worth pointing out. First, when Christmas leaves Joanna, the lights of a car become fixed on him, and he "watched his body grow white out of the darkness like a kodak print emerging from the liquid" (108). The connection of this scene to Hightower is that Hightower develops photographs. The second concerns Hightower and his black cook. After Hightower's wife dies, rumors begin that suggest that their miscegenation relationship has led to his wife's insanity and death. Subsequently, Hightower is taken to the woods and beaten by masked (KKK) white men. Hightower accepts the beating and declines to reveal the identities of his persecutors. Like Percy Grimm, these men are doing the community's will. Both scenes suggest the miscegenation intersection of blackness and whiteness.

58. This horrific act reinforces the sexual ambiguity and latent homosexuality of Christmas, Hightower, and Grimm. We recall that Christmas's grandparents, along with Byron Burch, come to Hightower's house with a scheme to save Christmas's life. The scheme is for Hightower to claim that Christmas was with him the night that Joanna was killed. Byron states, "You could say he was here with you that night. . . . Folks would believe you. They would believe that anyway. They would rather believe that about you than to believe that he lived with her like a husband and then killed her" (390). Hysterically screaming, Hightower rejects this scheme.

59. Walter White, *Rope and Faggot* (New York: Arno Press and the *New York Times*, 1969), 56–57.

60. Fanon, *Black Skin, White Masks*, 165. Fanon relates that too often many white people

are "no longer aware of the Negro [*sic*] but only a penis; the Negro is eclipsed. He is turned into a penis. He is a penis" (170).

61. It should be noted that in the Scottsboro Case, in 1931, nine black boys were accused of raping two white women on a freight train, and many whites in Alabama called for the young boys to be lynched.

62. Richard B. Sewall, *The Vision of Tragedy* (New Haven: Yale University Press, 1980), argues that Faustus is "tragic because he recognizes the dilemma [the divided soul] as real. Even as he boasts that his soul is his own, to dispose of as he will, he hears the fearful echoes thundering in his ears" (59). Unlike the Ex-Coloured Man, Christmas is unable to make a permanent Faustian contract with whiteness. Yet, Christmas also represents the modern tragic theme of the divided soul. The past echoes violently in Christmas's present as he struggles with rumors of his dual racial heritage. Faulkner's explicit reference to Christopher Marlowe's *Dr. Faust* and Goethe's *Faust* occurs after Christmas attacks McEachern and escapes on his horse: "The youth upon its back rode lightly, balanced lightly, leaning well forward, exulting perhaps at that moment as Faustus had, of having put behind now at once and for all the Shall Not, of being free at last of honor and law" (207).

63. Michel Foucault, *Discipline and Punish: The Birth of the Prison*, trans. Alan Sheridan (New York: Vintage Books, 1979), 49–50.

64. Faulkner creates a synthesis of the past and the present and a synthesis of naming and unnaming when he positions Mrs. Hines in Christmas's former cabin, now occupied by Lena and her baby. Lena complains, "she [Mrs. Hines] keeps on calling him [her baby] Joey. When his name aint Joey. . . . She keeps on talking about— She is mixed up someway. And sometimes I get mixed up too, listening, having to. . . ." (409). We learn about Mrs. Hines that "she got not only the child but his parentage as well mixed up, since in that cabin those thirty years did not exist—the child and its father whom she had never seen, and her grandson whom she had not seen since he was a baby like the other, and whose father likewise to her had never existed, all confused" (447).

65. Faulkner, in "A Word to Virginians," in Gwynn and Blotner, *Faulkner in the University*, relating his theory of white superiority, gives advice to the "Negro." He states that the white man must take him in hand and "teach him that in order to be free and equal he must first be worthy of it, and then forever afterward work to hold and keep and defend it. . . . What he must learn are the hard things—self-restraint, honesty, dependability, purity; to act not even as well as just any white man, but to act as well as the best of white men" (211).

66. This poignant phrase comes from Frederick Douglass's *Narrative of 1845*, when he makes the connection between literacy and slavery. In response to his master Hugh Auld's opposition to teaching a slave to read, Douglass states: "These words sank deep into my heart, stirred up sentiments within that lay slumbering, and *called into existence* an entirely new train of thought. It was a new and special revelation, explaining dark mysterious things, with which my youthful understanding had struggled, but struggled in vain. I now understood what had been to me a most perplexing difficulty—to wit, the white man's power to enslave the black man" (emphasis added) (49). This description of the racial dynamics of power connects to Douglass's subsequent desire to end his life after realizing the absurdity of an educated slave. Douglass relates: "I often found myself regretting my own existence and wishing myself dead; and but for the hope of being free, I have no doubt but that I should have killed myself, or done something for which I should have been killed" (56). It is within this morbid desire that

Christmas, regretting his own existence, also seeks the freedom of death. We can trace this desire back to Doc Hines, whose racist discourse "called into existence" his grandson, Joe Christmas.

67. William Faulkner, "Address to the Southern Historical Association (1955) in *Essays, Speeches and Public Letters*, ed. James Meriwether (New York: Random House, 1965), 149.

Conclusion

1. Ann Douglas, *Terrible Honesty: Mongrel Manhattan in the 1920s* (New York: Farrar, Straus and Giroux, 1995), 449.
2. Nathan Irvin Huggins, *Revelations: American History, American Myths* (New York: Oxford University Press, 1995), 245–46.
3. Claude Anderson, *Black Labor: The Search for Power and Economic Justice* (Edgewood, MD: Duncan and Duncan, 1994), 10.
4. Susan Gubar, *Racechanges: White Skin, Black Face in American Culture.* (New York: Oxford University Press, 1997), 5.
5. See James H. Johnson Jr. and Walter C. Farrell Jr., "Race Still Matters," *Chronicle of Higher Education*, vol. 41, no. 43 (7 July 1995): A48. These writers relate that "light-skinned African Americans men were more likely that their dark-skinned counterparts to be working, although their unemployment rate (20 per cent) was still high compared with that of white males."
6. Jefferson, *Notes on the State of Virginia* (New York: W. W. Norton, 1972), 139.
7. Stanley Crouch, in "Race Is Over: Black, White, Red, Yellow—Same Difference," *New York Times Magazine*, 29 September 1996, makes the ludicrous argument that, because of increased cultural and racial miscegenation, the concept of race will slowly disappear. He states, "Even though error, chance and ambition are at the nub of the human future, I am fairly sure that race, as we currently obsess over it, will cease to mean as much 100 years from today. . . . One hundred years from today, Americans are likely to look back on the ethnic difficulties of our times as quizzically as we look at earlier periods of humans when misapprehension defined the reality" (170–71). Despite Crouch's view, America's wounded culture constantly reminds us that, like the end of racism, the end of race has been greatly exaggerated.

BIBLIOGRAPHY

Aaron, Daniel. "The 'Inky Curse': Miscegenation in the White American Literary Imagination." *Social Sciences Information* 22 (1983): 169–190.

Abrahams, Roger D. *Singing the Master: The Emergence of African-American Culture in the Plantation South*. New York: Penguin Books, 1992.

Adams, Michael Vannoy. *The Multicultural Imagination: Race, Color and the Unconscious*. New York: Routledge, 1996.

Akbar, Na'im. *Chains and Images of Psychological Slavery*. Jersey City: New Mind Production, 1984.

——. *Breaking the Chains of Psychological Slavery*. Tallahassee, Florida: Mind Productions and Associates Inc., 1996.

Aleinikoff, T. Alexander. "A Case for Race-Consciousness." *Columbia Law Review* 91. 5 (1991): 1060–1125.

Alexander, William T. *History of the Colored Race in America*. New York: Negro Universities Press, 1968.

Allen, Irving Lewis. *The City in Slang: New York Life and Popular Speech*. New York: Oxford University Press, 1993.

Allen, Theodore W. *The Invention of the White Race*, Vol. 1: *Racial Oppression and Social Control*. New York: Verso, 1994.

Anderson, Benedict. *Imagined Communities: Reflections on the Origins and Spread of Nationalism*. New York: Verso, 1991.

Anderson, Claude. *Black Labor, White Wealth*. Edgewood, MD.: Duncan and Duncan, 1994.

Anderson, Richard. "Gatsby's Long Shadow: Indurance and Endurance." *New Essays on the Great Gatsby*. Ed. Matthew J. Bruccoli. New York: Cambridge University Press, 1985. 15–40.

Anderson, Jervis. *This Was Harlem*. New York: Farrar, Straus and Giroux, 1982.

Andrews, Karen M. "White Women's Complicity and the Taboo: Faulkner's Layered Critique of the 'Miscegenation Complex.'" *Women's Studies* 22.4 (1993): 497–506.

Andrews, William L. "Miscegenation in the Late-Nineteenth-Century Novel." *Southern Humanities Review* 17 (1974): 13–24.

———. "William Dean Howells and Charles W. Chesnutt: Criticism and Race Fiction in the Age of Booker T. Washington." *American Literature* 48 (1976): 327–329.

———. *The Literary Career of Charles W. Chesnutt*. Baton Rouge: Louisiana State University Press, 1980.

———. "The Black Male in American Literature." *The American Black Male: His Present Status and His Future*. Ed. Richard G. Majors and Jacob U. Gordon. Chicago: Nelson-Hall, 1994. 60–68.

———. "Junctions on the Color Line." *Confessions of the Critics* Ed. H. Aram Veeser. New York: Routledge, 1996. 241–255.

———, ed. "The Representation of Slavery and the Rise of Afro-American Literary Realism, 1865–1920." *African American Autobiography: A Collection of Critical Essays*. Englewood Cliffs: Prentice Hall, 1993. 77–89.

Ani, Marima. *Yurugu: An African-Centered Critique of European Cultural Thought and Behavior*. Trenton, NJ: Africa World Press, 1994.

Appiah, Anthony Kwame. "The Uncompleted Argument: Du Bois and the Illusion of Race. *"Race," Writing, and Difference*. Ed. Henry Louis Gates Jr. Chicago: University of Chicago Press, 1986. 21–37.

———. "The Conversation of Race. *Black American Literature Forum* 23 (1989): 37–60.

———. "Race." *Key Words in Contemporary Literary Studies*. Ed. Frank Lentricchia and Tom McLaughlin. Chicago: University of Chicago Press, 1989. 247–287.

———. "Racisms." *Anatomy of Racism*. Ed. David Theo Goldberg. Minneapolis: University of Minnesota Press, 1990. 3–17.

———, and Amy Gutman. *Color Conscious: The Political Morality of Race*. Princeton: Princeton University Press, 1996.

Applebaum, Harvey M. "Miscegenation Statues: A Constitutional and Social Problem." *Georgetown Law Journal* 53 (1964): 49–91.

Archer, Leonard C. *Black Images in the American Theater: NAACP Protest Campaigns—Stage, Screen, Radio and Television*. New York: Pageant-Poseidon, Ltd., 1973.

Arendt, Hannah. "Race Thinking Before Racism." *Review of Politics* 6 (January 1944): 36–73.

Avins, Alfred. "Anti-Miscegenation Laws and the Fourteenth Amendment: The Original Intent." *Virginia Law Review* 52 (1966): 1224–1255.

Awkward, Michael. *Negotiating Difference: Race, Gender, and the Politics Positionality*. Chicago: University of Chicago Press, 1995.

Ayers, Edward L. *Vengeance and Justice*. New York: Oxford University Press, 1984.

———. *The Promise of the New South: Life After Reconstruction*. New York: Oxford University Press, 1992.

Baker, Houston A., Jr. "A Forgotten Prototype: *The Autobiography of an Ex-Coloured Man* and *Invisible Man*." *Virginia Quarterly Review* 49 (1973): 413–429.

———. *Blues, Ideology, and Afro-American Literature: A Vernacular Theory*. Chicago: University of Chicago Press, 1984.

———. *Modernism and the Harlem Renaissance*. Chicago: University of Chicago Press, 1987.

Bakhtin, M. M. *The Dialogic Imagination: Four Essays*. Trans. Caryl Emerson and Michael Holquist. Austin: University of Texas Press, 1981.

Baldwin, James. "On Being 'White' and Other Lies." *Essence* April (1984): 90–92.

———. "Color." *The Price of the Ticket: Collected Nonfiction, 1948–1985*. New York: St. Martin/Marek, 1985. 319–324.

———. "Faulkner and Desegregation." *The Price of the Ticket: Collected Nonfiction, 1948–1985*. New York: St. Martin/Marek, 1985. 147–152.

———. "Stranger in the Village." *Price of the Ticket: Collected Nonfiction, 1948–1985*. New York: St. Martin/Marek, 1985. 79–90.

Baldwin, Joseph. "Psychological Aspects of European Cosmology in American Society." *Western Journal of Black Studies* 9.4 (1985): 216–223.

Baldwin, Louis Fremont. *How the Ethiopian Is Changing His Skin*. San Francisco: Pilot, 1929.

Balibar, Etienne, and Immanuel Wallerstein. *Race, Nation, Class: Ambiguous Identities*. Trans. of Etienne Balibar by Chris Turner. London: Verso, 1991.

Banton, Michael. "Analytical and Folk Concepts of Race and Ethnicity." *Ethnic and Racial Studies* 2.2 (1979): 127–138.

———. *Racial Theories*. New York: Cambridge University Press, 1987.

Barksdale, Richard K. *Praisesong of Survival: Lectures and Essays 1957–89*. Urbana: University of Illinois Press, 1992.

Barth, Fredrik, ed. *Ethnic Groups and Boundaries: The Social Organization of Culture Difference*. Boston: Little, Brown, 1969.

Barthes, Roland. *Mythologies*. Trans. Amnette Lavers. New York: Hill and Wang, 1974.

———. *S/Z*. New York: Hill, 1974.

Bastide, Roger. "Color, Racism, and Christianity." *Color and Race*. Ed. John Hope Franklin. Boston: Houghton Mifflin, 1968. 34–74.

Baughman, Judith S. *American Decades 1920–1929*. Detroit: Gale Research International, 1996.

Beale, Frances. "Double Jeopardy: To Be Black and Female." *The Black Woman: An Anthology*. Ed. Toni Cade. New York: New American Library, 1970. 90–100.

Beck, Warren. *Faulkner: Essays*. Madison: University of Wisconsin Press, 1976.

Behr, Edward. *Prohibition: Thirteen Years that Changed America*. New York: Arcade, 1996.

Bell, Bernard W. *The Afro-American Novel and Its Tradition*. Amherst: University of Massachusetts Press, 1987.

Bell, Derrick A. "Interracial Sex and Marriage." *Race, Racism, and American Law*. Boston: Little, Brown, 1973. 53–81.

———. *Faces at the Bottom of the Well: The Permanence of Racism*. New York: Basic Books, 1992.

———. "Property Rights in Whiteness." *Critical Race Theory: The Cutting Edge*. Ed. Richard Delagado. Philadelphia: Temple University Press, 1995. 75–83.

Bennett, Juda. *The Passing Figure: Racial Confusion in Modern American Literature*. New York: Peter Lang, 1996.

Bennett, Lerone, Jr. *The Shaping of Black America: The Struggles and Triumphs of African-Americans, 1619 to the 1990s*. 1975. Reprint. New York: Penguin Books, 1993.

———. *Before the Mayflower: A History of the Negro in America 1619–1964*. New York: Penguin Books, 1968.

———. "Thomas Jefferson's Negro Grandchildren." *Ebony* 10 (1954): 78–80.

Benston, Kimberly W. "I Yam What I Am: The Topos of Un(naming) in Afro-American Literature." *Black Literature and Literary Theory*. Ed. Henry Louis Gates Jr. New York: Methuen, 1984. 151–172.

Bentley, Nancy. "White Slaves: The Mulatto Hero in Antebellum Fiction." *American Literature* 65.3 (1993): 501–522.

Bercovitch, Sacvan. *The American Jeremiad*. Madison: University of Wisconsin Press, 1978.

Berger, John. *Ways of Seeing*. London: British Broadcasting Company and Penguin Books, 1972.

Bergner, Gwen. "Who Is That Masked Woman? or, The Role of Gender in Fanon's *Black Skin, White Masks.*" *PMLA* 110.1 (fall 1995): 75–88.

Berland, Alwyn. Light in August: *A Study in Black and White*. New York: Twayne, 1992.

Berlant, Lauren. "National Brands/National Body: *Imitation of Life.*" *Comparative American Identities: Race, Sex, and Nationality in the Modern Text*. Ed. and with an introduction by Hortense J. Spillers. New York: Routledge, 1991. 110–140.

Berlin, Edward. *Ragtime: A Musical and Cultural History*. Berkeley: University of California Press, 1980.

Berman, Ronald. *The Great Gatsby and Modern Times*. Champaign: University of Illinois Press, 1994.

——. The Great Gatsby *and Fitzgerald's World of Ideas*. Tuscaloosa: University of Alabama Press, 1997.

Berry, Brewton. *Almost White*. New York: Macmillan, 1963.

Berzon, Judith R. *Neither Black nor White: The Mulatto Character in American Fiction*. New York: New York University Press, 1978.

Bewley, Marius. "Scott Fitzgerald and the Collapse of the American Dream." *Modern Critical Views: F. Scott Fitzgerald*. Ed. Harold Bloom. New York: Chelsea House, 1985. 23–47.

Bhabha, Homi K. *The Location of Culture*. New York: Routledge, 1994.

——. "Interrogating Identity: The Postcolonial Prerogative." *Anatomy of Racism*. Ed. David Theo Goldberg. Minneapolis: University of Minnesota Press, 1990. 183–209.

Birmingham, Stephen. *Certain People: America's Black Elite*. Boston: Little, Brown, 1977.

Blackburn, Julia. *The Book of Colour*. London: Jonathan Cape, 1995.

Blackett, R. J. M. "Fugitive Slaves in Britain: The Odyssey of William and Ellen Craft." *Journal of American Studies* 12 (1978): 41–62.

——. "The Odyssey of William and Ellen Craft." *Beating Against the Barriers: Biographical Essays in Nineteenth-Century Afro-American History*. Baton Rouge: Louisiana State University Press, 1986. 87–137.

Blassingame, John W. *The Slave Community: Plantation Life in the Antebellum South*. New York: Oxford University Press, 1972.

Bleikasten, Andre. *The Ink of Melancholy*. Bloomington, Indiana University Press, 1980.

——. "Fathers in Faulkner." *The Fictional Father: Lacanian Readings of the Text*. Ed. Robert Con Davis. Amherst: University of Massachusetts Press, 1981. 115–146.

——. "*Light in August*: The Closed Society and Its Subjects." *New Essays on* Light in August. Ed. Michael Millgate. New York: Cambridge University Press, 1987. 81–102.

Blesh, Rudi, and Harriet Janis. *They All Played Ragtime: The True Story of an American Music*. London: Sidgwick and Jackson, 1958.

Bloom, Harold, ed. *Black American Prose Writers of the Harlem Renaissance*. New York: Chelsa House, 1994.

Blotner, Joseph. *Faulkner: A Biography*. New York: Vintage Books, 1991.

Bluestein, Gene. "Faulkner and Miscegenation." *Arizona Quarterly* 43.2 (1987): 151–164.

Bogle, Donald. *Toms, Coons, Mulattoes, Mammies, and Bucks: An Interpretative History of Blacks in Films*. New York: Continuum, 1989.

Boker, Pamela A. *The Grief Taboo in American Literature: Loss and Prolonged Adolescence in Twain, Melville, and Hemingway.* New York: New York University Press, 1996.

Bondoc, Anna. "Close, But No Banana." *To Be Real: Telling the Truth and Changing the Face of Feminism.* Ed. and with an introduction by Rebecca Walker. New York: Anchor Books, 1995. 167–184.

Bone, Robert A. *The Negro Novel in America.* New Haven: Yale University Press, 1969.

——. *Down Home.* New York: G. P. Putnam's Sons, 1975.

Boskin, Joseph. *Sambo: The Rise and Demise of an American Jester.* New York: Oxford University Press, 1986.

Brandt, Joseph. *Dismantling Racism: The Continuing Challenge to White America.* Minneapolis: Augsberg Fortress, 1991.

Brandt, Nat. *Harlem at War: The Black Experience in WWII.* Syracuse, NY: Syracuse University Press, 1996.

Brodhead, Richard, ed. *The Journals of Charles W. Chesnutt.* Durham: Duke University Press, 1993.

Brodie, Fawn M. "The Great Jefferson Taboo." *American Heritage* 22 (1972): 49–57, 97–100.

——. *Thomas Jefferson: An Intimate History.* New York: Bantam Books, 1974.

Brodsky, Louis Daniel. "Faulkner and the Racial Crisis, 1956." *Southern Review* 20.4 (1988): 791–807.

——. "Faulkner's Life Masks." *Southern Review* 22 (1986): 738–765.

Bronz, Stephen. *Roots of Negro Social Consciousness: The 1920: Three Harlem Renaissance Writers.* New York: Libra, 1964.

Brooks, Cleanth. *William Faulkner: The Yoknapatawpha Country.* New Haven: Yale University Press, 1963.

Brooks, Gwendolyn. "To Those of My Sisters Who Kept Their Naturals." *Blacks.* Chicago: David Company, 1987. 459–60.

Brooks, Neil. "On Becoming an Ex-Man: Postmodern Irony and the Extinguishing of Certainties in *The Autobiography of an Ex-Coloured Man.*" *College Literature* 22 (1995): 17–29.

Brooks, Peter. *Reading for the Plot: Design and Intention in Narrative.* New York: Vintage Books, 1985.

——. *Body Work: Objects of Desire in Modern Narrative.* Cambridge, MA: Harvard University Press, 1993.

Brown, Richard Maxwell. *Strain of Violence: Historical Studies of American Violence and Vigilantism.* New York: Oxford University Press, 1975.

Brown, Sterling. "Negro Character as Seen by White Authors." *Dark Symphony: Negro Literature in America Fiction.* Ed. James A. Emanuel and Theodore Gross. New York: Free Press, 1968. 139–171.

——. *The Negro in American Fiction.* 1937. Reprint. Port Washington, NY: Kennikat Press, 1968.

——. "A Century of Negro Portraiture in American Literature." *Massachusetts Review* 7 (1966): 73–96.

Brown, William Wells. *Clotel; Or the President's Daughter.* 1853. Reprint. New York: Collier Books, 1972.

Bruce, Dickson D., Jr. *Black American Writing from the Nadir: The Evolution of a Literary Tradition 1877–1915.* Baton Rouge: Louisiana State University Press, 1989.

——. "W. E. B. Du Bois and the Idea of Double Consciousness." *American Literature* 64.2 (June 1992): 299–309.

Bruccoli, Matthew J. *Some Sort of Epic Grandeur: The Life of F. Scott Fitzgerald*. New York: Harcourt Brace Jovanovich, 1981.

——. "Introduction." *New Essays on* The Great Gatsby. Ed. Matthew Bruccoli. New York: Cambridge University Press, 1985. 1–14.

——. *"The Last of the Novelists": F. Scott Fitzgerald and* The Last Tycoon. Carbondale: Southern Illinois University Press, 1997.

——, ed. *As Ever, Scott Fitz-: Letters Between F. Scott Fitzgerald and His Literary Agent Harold Ober 1919–1940*. New York: J. B. Lippincott, 1972.

——. *The Notebooks of F. Scott Fitzgerald*. New York: Harcourt Brace Jovanovich/Bruccoli Clark, 1978.

——. *F. Scott Fitzgerald Manuscripts*. New York: Garland, 1990.

Bruccoli, Matthew J., ed., with Judith S. Baughman. *F. Scott Fitzgerald: A Life in Letters*. New York: Charles Scribner's Sons, 1994.

Bruccoli, Matthew J., and Margaret M. Duggan, eds. *Correspondence of F. Scott Fitzgerald*. New York: Random House, 1980.

Bruccoli, Matthew J., and Jackson R. Bryer, eds. *F. Scott Fitzgerald in His Own Times: A Miscellany*. Kent: Kent State University Press, 1971.

Brundage, Karla. "Passing." *Multi-America: Essays on Cultural Wars and Cultural Peace*. Ed. Ishmael Reed. New York: Penguin Books, 1997. 116–122.

Bullock, Penelope. "The Mulatto in American Fiction." *Phylon* 6 (1945): 78–82.

Bullough, Vern L., and Bonnie Bullough. *Cross Dressing, Sex, and Gender*. Philadelphia: University of Pennsylvania Press, 1993.

Burg, B. R. "The Rhetoric of Miscegenation: Thomas Jefferson, Sally Hemmings, and Their Historians." *Phylon* 47 (1986): 128–138.

Burges, Austin Earle. *What Price Integration?* Dallas: American Guild Press, 1956.

Burma, John H. "The Measurement of Negro 'Passing.'" *American Journal of Sociology* 52 (1946): 18–22.

Butterfield, Stephen. *Black Autobiography in America*. Amherst: University of Massachusetts Press, 1974.

Callahan, John F. *The Illusions of a Nation: Myth and History in the Novels of F. Scott Fitzgerald*. Urbana: University of Illinois Press, 1971.

——. *In the African-American Grain: Call-and Response in Twentieth-Century Black Fiction*. Middletown, CT: Wesleyan University Press, 1989.

Camporesi, Piero. *Juice of Life: The Symbolic and Magic Significance of Blood*. Foreword by Umberto Eco. New York: Continuum, 1995.

Carroll, Richard A. "Black Radical Spirit: An Analysis of James Weldon Johnson's Critical Perspective." *Phylon* 32 (1971): 344–364.

Cartey, Wilfred. *Black Images*. New York: Teachers College Press, 1970.

Carton, Evan. "Pudd'nhead Wilson and the Fiction of Law Custom." In *American Realism: New Essays*. Ed. Eric J. Sundquist. Baltimore: Johns Hopkins University Press, 1982. 82–94.

Cash, W. J. *The Mind of the South*. New York: Knopf, 1957.

Casper, Leonard. "Miscegenation as Symbol: *Band of Angels*." *Robert Penn Warren: A Collection of Critical Essays*. Ed. John Lewis Longley Jr. New York: New York University Press, 1965. 140–48.

Castle, Terry. *Masquerade and Civilization: The Carnivalesque in Eighteenth-Century English Culture and Fiction*. Stanford: Stanford University Press, 1986.

Caughie, Pamela L. "'Not Entirely Strange . . . Not Entirely Friendly': Passing and Pedagogy." *College English* 54.7 (1992): 775–793.

———. "Let It Pass: Changing the Subject, Once Again." *PMLA* 112 (1997): 26–39.

Cell, John W. *The Highest Stage of White Supremacy: The Origins of Segregation in South Africa and the American South*. New York: Cambridge University Press, 1982.

Chabrier, Gwendolyn. *Faulkner Families: A Southern Saga*. New York: Gordian Press, 1993.

Chapkis, Wendy. *Beauty Secrets*. Boston: South End Press, 1986.

Cheng, Vincent J. *Joyce, Race, and Empire*. New York: Cambridge University Press, 1995.

Chesnutt, Charles Waddell. "The Future American: What the Race Is Likely to Become in the Process of Time." *Boston Evening Transcript* 18 August 1899: 20.

———. *The House Behind the Cedars*. 1900. Reprint. Introduction by Donald B. Gibson. New York: Penguin Books, 1993.

———. "The Future American: A Stream of Dark Blood in the Veins of the Southern Whites." *Boston Evening Transcript* 25 August 1900: 15.

———. "The Future American: A Complete Race Amalgamation Likely to Occur." *Boston Evening Transcript* 1 September 1900: 24.

———. "The Free Colored People of North Carolina." *Southern Workman* 31 (1902): 136–141.

———. "Race Prejudice: Its Causes and Its Cures: An Address Delivered Before the Boston Historical and Literary Association." *Alexander Magazine* 1 (1905): 21–26.

———. "What Is a White Man?" *The Minority Presence in American Literature 1600–1900*, Vol. 2. Ed. Philip Butcher. Washington, DC: Howard University Press, 1977. 276–282.

Chodorow, Nancy. *The Reproduction of Motherhood: Psychoanalysis and the Sociology of Gender*. Berkeley: University of California Press, 1978.

Choen, Rich. *Tough Jews: Fathers, Sons, and Gangster Dreams*. New York: Simon and Schuster, 1998.

Churchill, Ward. *Fantasies of the Master Race*. Monroe, ME: Common Courage Press, 1992.

Clarke, Deborah. "Gender, Race, and Language in *Light in August*." *American Literature: A Journal of Literary History, Criticism and Bibliography* 61.3 (1989): 398–413.

Clayton, Bruce. "The Proto-Dorian Convention: W. J. Cash and the Race Question." *Race, Class and Politics in Southern History*. Ed. Jeffrey J. Crow, Paul D. Escott, and L. Flynn Jr. Baton Rouge: Louisiana State University Press, 1989. 260–288.

Cleage, Pearl. "Hairpiece." *African American Review* 27 (1993): 37–41.

Cliff, Michelle. *Claiming an Identity They Taught Me to Despise*. Watertown, MA: Persephone Press, 1980.

———. *Bodies of Water*. New York: Dutton, 1990.

Clifford, James. *The Predicament of Culture*. Cambridge, MA: Harvard University Press, 1988.

Collier, Eugenia. "The Endless Journey of an Ex-Coloured Man." *Phylon* 32 (1971): 365–373.

Collier, James Lincoln. *The Reception of Jazz in America: A New View*. Brooklyn: Institute for Studies in American Music, 1988.

Collins, Patricia Hill. *Black Feminist Thought: Knowledge, Consciousness, and the Politics of Empowerment*. New York: Routledge, 1990.

Cook, Bruce A. "What Is It Like to Be a Negro?" *Commonwealth* 27 (October 1961): 129.

Cooke, Michael C. *Afro-American Literature in the Twentieth Century: The Achievement of Intimacy*. New Haven: Yale University Press, 1984.

———. "Naming, Being and Black Experience." *Yale Review* 68 (1978): 167–186.

Cooper, Wendy. *Hair: Sex, Society, Symbolism*. New York: Stein and Day, 1971.

Copher, B. "Three Thousand Years of Biblical Interpretation with Reference to Black Peoples." *Journal of the Interdenominational Theological Center* 13 (spring 1986): 225–246.

Cornell, Drucilla. "The Violence of the Masquerade: Law Dressed Up as Justice." *Working Through Derrida*. Ed. Gary Madison. Evanston, IL: Northwestern University Press, 1993. 77–93.

Cose, Ellis. *The Rage of a Privileged Class*. New York: HarperCollins, 1993.

Craft, William, and Ellen Craft. *Running a Thousand Miles for Freedom or, The Escape of William and Ellen Craft from Slavery*. 1860. *Great Slave Narratives*. Reprint. Ed. Arna Bontemps. Boston: Beacon Press, 1969. 269–331.

Crawford, M. "Identity, Passing and Subversion." *Feminism and Psychology* 2.3 (1992): 429–431.

Crenshaw, Kimberle Williams. "Race, Reform, and Retrenchment: Transformation and Legitimation in Antidiscrimination Law." *Harvard Law Review* 101 (1988): 1331–1387.

——. "Demarginalizing the Intersection of Race and Sex: A Black Feminist Critique of Antidiscrimination Doctrine, Feminist Theory, and Antiracist Politics." *Feminist Legal Theory: Readings in Law and Gender*. Ed. Katharine J. Bartlett and Rosanne Kennedy. Boulder: Westview Press, 1991. 57–80.

——. "Color Blindness, History, and the Law." *The House That Race Built: Black Americans, U.S. Terrain*. Ed. and with an introduction by Wabneema Lubiano. New York: Pantheon Books, 1997. 280–288.

Cripps, Thomas. *Slow Fade to Black: The Negro in American Film 1900–1942*. New York: Oxford University Press, 1977.

——. "Film." *Split Image: African American in the Mass Media*. Ed. Jannette L. Dates and William Barlow. Washington, DC: Howard University Press, 1990. 125–172.

——. "The Making of the *Birth of a Nation*: The Emerging Politics of Identity in Silent Movies." *The Birth of Whiteness: Race and the Emergence of U.S. Cinema*. Ed. Daniel Bernardi. New Brunswick: Rutgers University Press, 1996. 38–55.

——. "'Race Movies' as Voices of the Black Bourgeoisie: *The Scar of Shame*." *Representing Blackness: Issues in Film and Video*. Ed. and with an introduction by Valerie Smith. New Brunswick: Rutgers University Press, 1997. 47–59.

Croly, David G. *Miscegenation: The Theory of the Blending of the Races, Applied to the American White Man and Negro*. New York: H. Dexter Hamilton, 1864.

Crosland, Andrew T. *A Concordance to F. Scott Fitzgerald's* The Great Gatsby. Detroit: Gale Research Company, 1975.

Crouch, Stanley. *The All-American Skin Game, or The Decoy of Race: The Long and the Short of It 1990–1994*. New York: Pantheon Books, 1995.

——. "Race Is Over." *New York Times* Magazine, 29 September 1996: 170–171.

Cruse, Harold. *Plural but Equal: A Critical Study of Blacks and Minorities in America Plural Society*. New York: William Morrow, 1987.

Cullen, Countee. *Colour*. New York: Harper and Brothers, 1925.

Cunningham, George P. "'Called into Existence': Desire, Gender, and Voice in Frederick Douglass's *Narrative of 1845*." *differences: A Journal of Feminist Cultural Studies* 1.3 (1989): 108–135.

Curtis, Susan. *Dancing to a Black Man's Tune: A Life of Scott Joplin*. Columbia: University of Missouri Press, 1994.

Cutler, James E. *Lynch-Law, An American Investigation into the History in the United States*. 1905. Reprint. New York: Negro Universities Press, 1969.

Cutter, Martha J. "Sliding Significations: Passing as a Narrative and Textual Strategy in Fiction." *Passing and the Fictions of Identity*. Ed. Elaine K. Ginsberg. Durham: Duke University Press, 1996. 75–100.

Daggett, Harriet Spiller. "The Legal Aspect of Amalgamation in Louisiana." *Texas Law Review* 11 (1993): 162–184.

Daniel, Bradford. "Why They Can't Wait: An Interview with a White Negro." *The Progressive* (July 1964): 15–19.

Datcher, Michael. "Violence Is American." *Soulfires: Young Black Men on Love and Violence.* Ed. by Daniel J. Wideman and Rohan B. Preston. New York: Penguin Books, 1996. 83–85.

Davie, Maurice R, *Negroes in American Society.* New York: McGraw-Hill, 1949.

Davis, Angela. *Women, Race, and Class.* New York: Vintage Books, 1983.

———. *Women, Culture, and Politics.* New York: Random House, 1984.

Davis, Arthur P. "The Tragic Mulatto Theme in Six Works of Langston Hughes." *Phylon* 16 (1955): 195–204.

———. *From the Dark Tower: Afro-American Writers 1900 to 1960.* Washington, DC: Howard University Press, 1974.

Davis, F. James. *Who Is Black?: One Nation's Definition.* University Park: Pennsylvania State University Press, 1991.

Davis, T., and Henry Louis Gates Jr., eds. *The Slave Narrative.* New York: Oxford University Press, 1985.

Davis, Thadious M. *Faulkner's "Negro": Art and the Southern Context.* Baton Rouge: Louisiana State University Press, 1983.

Day, Beth. *Sexual Life Between Blacks and Whites: The Roots of Racism.* New York: World, 1972.

Dearborn, Mary V. "Miscegenation and the Mulatto, Inheritance and Incest: The Pocahontas Marriage, Part II." *Pocahontas's Daughter: Gender and Ethnicity in American Culture.* New York: Oxford University Press, 1986. 131–158.

Decker, Jeffrey Louis. *Made in America: Self-Styled Success from Horatio Alger to Oprah Winfrey.* Minnesota: University of Minnesota Press, 1997.

Deffaa, Chip, ed. *F. Scott Fitzgerald: The Princeton Years. Selected Writings, 1914–1920.* Fort Bragg, CA: Cypress House Press, 1996.

Degler, Carl N. *Neither Black nor White: Slavery and Race Relations in Brazil and the United States.* Madison: University of Wisconsin Press, 1971.

De Jongh, James. *Vicious Modernism: Black Harlem and the Literary Imagination.* Cambridge: Cambridge University Press, 1990.

Delgado, Richard. "Words That Wound: A Tort Action for Racial Insults, Epithets, and Name Calling." *Words That Wound: Critical Race Theory, Assaultive Speech, and the First Amendment.* Ed. Mari J. Matsuda, R. Lawrence III, Richard Delgado, and Kimberle William Crenshaw. Boulder: Westview Press, 1993. 89–110.

Delmar, P. Jay. "Coincidence in Charles W. Chesnutt's *The House Behind the Cedars.*" *American Literary Realism* 15 (1982): 97–103.

de Man, Paul. "Autobiography as De-facement." *MLN* 94 (1979): 919–930.

Dennis, Rutledge M. "Social Darwinism, Scientific Racism, and the Metaphysics of Race." *Journal of Negro Education* 64.3 (1995): 243–251.

Dickens, Homer. *What a Drag: Men as Women and Women as Men in the Movies.* New York: Quill, 1984.

Dijkestra, Bram. *Evil Sisters: The Threat of Female Sexuality and the Cult of Manhood.* New York: Knopf, 1996.

Dixon, Thomas. *The Leopard Spots: A Romance of the White Man Burden.* New York: Doubleday, 1903.

——. *The Clansman: An Historical Romance of the Ku Klux Klan*. 1905. Reprint. Ridgewood, NJ: Gregg Press, 1967.

Doane, Mary Ann. *Femmes Fatales: Feminism, Film Theory, and Psychoanalysis*. New York: Routledge, 1991.

Dominquez, Virginia. *White by Definition: Social Classification in Creole Louisiana*. New Brunswick: Rutgers University Press, 1986.

D'Orso, Michael. *Like Judgment Day: The Ruin and Redemption of a Town Called Rosewood*. New York: Boulevard Books, 1996.

Douglas, Ann. *Terrible Honesty: Mongrel Manhattan in the 1920s*. New York: Farrar, Straus and Giroux, 1995.

Douglass, Frederick. *Narrative of the Life of Frederick Douglass, an American Slave*: 1845. Ed. Philip S. Foner. Reprint. New York: International, 1950.

——. *The Life and Writings of Frederick Douglass: Early Years*. 1817–1849. Ed. Philip S. Foner. New York: International, 1960.

Doyle, Laura. *Bordering on the Body: The Racial Matrix of Modern Fiction and Culture*. New York: Oxford University Press, 1994.

Drake, St. Clair, and Horace R. Cayton. *Black Metropolis: A Study Of Negro Life in a Northern City*, Vol. 1. Revised and enlarged edition with introductions by Richard Wright and E. C. Hughes. New York: Harcourt, Brace and World, 1962.

Du Bois, William E. B. "The Souls of White Folk." *The Independent* 69 (August 18, 1910): 339–342.

——. "Intermarriage." *The Crisis* (February 1913): 181–182.

——. "On Being Ashamed of Oneself: An Essay on Race Pride." *Crisis* 40 (1933): 199–200.

——. *The Souls of Black Folk: Essays and Sketches*. 1903. Reprint. Introductions by Nathan Hare and Alvin Poussaint. New York: New American Library, 1969.

——. *Dust of Dawn: An Essay Toward an Autobiography of a Race Concept*. 1940. Introduction by Irene Diggs. New Brunswick: Transaction, 1984.

——. "The Conservation of Races." *Writings*. Ed. Nathan Huggins. New York: Library of America, 1986. 815–827.

duCille, Ann. *The Coupling Convention: Sex, Text, and Tradition in Black Women's Fiction*. New York: Oxford University Press, 1993.

——. *Skin Trade*. Cambridge, MA: Harvard University Press, 1996.

Dunbar, Paul Laurence. "We Wear the Mask." *American Negro Poetry*. Revised edtion. Ed. Arna Bontemps. New York: Hill and Wang, 1974. 14.

Dworkin, Andrea. *Intercourse*. New York: Free Press, 1987.

Dyer, Richard. "White." *Screen* 29.3 (1988): 44–64.

Eagleton, Terry. *Ideology*. London: Verso, 1991.

Early, Gerald. *The Culture of Bruising: Essays on Prizefighting, Literature and Modern Culture*. Honeywell, NJ: Ecco Press, 1994.

Early, Gerald, ed. "Introduction." *My Soul's High Song: The Collected Writings of Countee Cullen, Voice of the Harlem Renaissance*. New York: Doubleday, 1991. 3–73.

Eble, Kenneth E. *F. Scott Fitzgerald*. Boston: Twayne, 1963.

——. "*The Great Gatsby* and the Great American Novel." *New Essays on* The Great Gatsby. Ed. Matthew J. Bruccoli. New York: Cambridge University Press, 1985, 79–100.

Eilberg-Schwartz, Howard, and Wendy Doniger, eds. *Off with Her Head!: The Denial of Women's Identity in Myth, Religion, and Culture*. Berkeley: University of California Press, 1995.

Elder, Arlene. *The "Hindered Hand": The Cultural Implications of Early African-American Fiction*. Westport, CT: Greenwood Press, 1978.

Ellis, Joseph J. *American Sphinx: The Character of Thomas Jefferson*. New York: Knopf, 1997.

Ellison, Curtis W., and E. W. Metcalf. *Charles W. Chesnutt: A Reference Guide*. Boston: G. K. Hall, 1977.

Ellison, Ralph. *Shadow and Act*. 1953. Reprint. New York: Vintage Books, 1972.

———. *Going to the Territory*. New York: Vintage Books, 1987.

———. *Invisible Man*. 1952. Reprint. New York: Vintage Books, 1989.

———. *The Collected Essays of Ralph Ellison*. Ed. and with an introduction by John F. Callahan. New York: Modern Library, 1995.

———. *Flying Home and Other Stories*. Ed. and with an introduction by John F. Callahan. New York: Random House, 1996.

Ellsworth, Scott. *Death in a Promised Land: The Tulsa Race Riot of 1921*. Baton Rouge: Louisiana State University Press, 1982.

Esonwanne, Uzo. "'Race' and Hermeneutics: Paradigm Shift—From Scientific to Hermeneutic Understanding of Race. *African American Review* 26.4 (1992): 565–582.

Evans, Veichal J. "Chester Himes on Miscegenation." *Western Journal of Black Studies* 7.2 (1983): 74–77.

Fadiman, Regina K. *William Faulkner's* Light in August*: A Description and Interpretation of the Revisions*. Charlottesville: University Press of Virginia, 1975.

Fahey, William A. *F. Scott Fitzgerald and the American Dream*. New York: Thomas Y. Crowell, 1973.

Fanon, Frantz. *The Wretched of the Earth*. New York: Grove Press, 1963.

———. *Towards the African Revolution: Political Essays*. Trans. Haakon Chevalier. New York: Grove Press, 1967.

———. *Black Skin, White Masks*. New York: Grove Press, 1967.

———. *A Dying Colonialism*. Harmondsworth: Pelican Books, 1970.

Faulkner, Howard J. "Homespun Justice: The Lynching in American Fiction." *South Dakota Review* 22.4 (1984): 104–119.

———. "James Weldon Johnson: Portrait of the Artist as Invisible Man." *Black American Literature Forum* 19 (1985): 147–151.

———. "A Vanishing Race." *CLA Journal* 37.3 (1994): 274–292.

Faulkner, William. "If I Were a Negro." *Ebony* (September 1956): 70–72.

———. *Essays, Speeches and Public Letters*. Ed. James B. Meriwether. New York: Random House, 1965.

———. *Absalom, Absalom!* 1936. Reprint. New York: Vintage Books, 1990.

———. *Light in August*. 1932. Reprint. New York: Vintage Books, 1990.

———. *Go Down Moses*. 1942. Reprint. New York: Vintage Books, 1990.

———. "That Evening Sun." *Collected Stories of William Faulkner*. 1931. New York: Vintage Books, 1995.

Fauset, Jessie Redmon. *Plum Bun: A Novel Without A Moral*. 1928. Reprint. Introduction by Deborah E. McDowell. Boston Beacon Press, 1990.

———. Review of *The Autobiography of an Ex-Coloured Man*. *Crisis* 5 (1912): 38.

Feagin, Joe R., and Hernan Vera. *White Racism: The Basics*. New York: Routledge, 1995.

Fehrenbacher, Don E. *The Dred Scott Case: Its Significance in American Law and Politics*. New York: Oxford University Press, 1978.

Feldstein, Stanley, ed. *The Poisoned Tongue: A Documentary History of American Racism and Prejudice*. New York: William Morrow, 1972.

Ferguson, Ann. *Blood at the Root: Motherhood, Sexuality and Male Dominance*. London: Pandora Press, 1989.

Ferguson, SallyAnn H. "Rena Walden: Failed 'Future American.'" *Southern Literary Journal* 25 (1982): 74–82.

——. "'Frank Fowler': A Racial Pun." *Southern Atlantic Review* 50 (1985): 47–53.

——. "Genuine Blacks and Future Americans." *MELUS* 15 (1988): 109–119.

Ferguson, Robert A. "The Judicial Opinion as Literary Genre." *Yale Journal of Law and the Humanities* 2.1 (winter 1990): 201–219.

——. *Law and Letters in American Culture*. Cambridge, MA: Harvard University Press, 1984.

Fernandes, Florestan. *The Negro in Brazilian Society*. Ed. Phyllis B. Eveleth. Trans. Jacqueline D. Skiles, A. Brunel, and Arthur Rothwell. New York: Atheneum, 1971.

Fetterley, Judith. "*The Great Gatsby*: Fitzgerald's Droit du Seigneur." *New Essays on* The Great Gatsby. Comp. Harold Bloom. New York: Chelsea House, 1991.

Fieldler, Leslie A. *Love and Death in the American Novel*. Rev. ed. New York: Scarborough Books, 1982.

——. *Tyranny of the Normal: Essays On Bioethics, Theology and Myth*. Boston: David R. Godine, 1996.

Fields, Barbara J. "Ideology and Race in American History." *Region, Race, and Reconstruction*. Ed. J. Morgan Kousser and James M. McPherson. New York: Oxford University Press, 1982. 143–177.

Fish, Jefferson M. "Mixed Blood." *Psychology Today* (November–December 1995): 55–61, 76, 80.

Fishkin, Shelley Fisher. "Interrogating 'Whiteness,' Complicating 'Blackness': Remapping American Culture." *Criticism and the Color Line: Desegregating American Literary Studies*. Ed. Henry B. Wonham. New Brunswick: Rutgers University Press, 1996. 251–290.

Fitzgerald, F. Scott. *The Great Gatsby*. 1925. New York: Simon and Schuster, 1995.

——. *The Jazz Age*. 1931. Introduction by E. L. Doctorow. New York: New Directions, 1996.

Fleming, Robert E. "Irony as a Key to Johnson's *The Autobiography of an Ex-Coloured Man*." *American Literature* 43 (1971): 83–96.

——. "Contemporary Themes in Johnson's *Autobiography of an Ex-Coloured Man*." *Negro American Literature Forum* 4.4 (1970): 120–124, 141.

Flusche, Michael. "On the Color Line." *North Carolina Historical Review* 53 (1976): 1–24.

Foucault, Michel. *Discipline and Punish: The Birth of the Prison*. Trans. Alan Sheridan. New York: Vantage Books, 1979.

——. *The Foucault Reader*. Ed. Paul Rabinow. New York: Pantheon Books, 1984.

Fowler, David. *Northern Attitudes Towards Interracial Marriages: Legislation and Public Opinion in the Middle Atlantic and the States of the Old Northwest, 1780–1930*. New York: Garland, 1987.

Fowler, Doreen, and Ann J. Abadie, eds. *Faulkner and Race: Faulkner and Yoknapatawpha, Conference*. Jackson: University Press of Mississippi, 1987.

Fowler, Doreen, and Campbell McCool. "On Suffering: A Letter from William Faulkner." *American Literature* 57 (December 1985): 650–652.

Fradella, Sal. *Jack Johnson*. Boston: Branden, 1990.

Francis, Allison. "Why Am I Still Onstage at the Cotton Club?" *MultiAmerica: Essays on*

Cultural Wars and Cultural Peace. Ed. Ishmael Reed. New York: Penguin Books, 1997. 123–126.

Frankenberg, Ruth. *White Women, Race Matters: The Social Construction of Whiteness*. Minneapolis: University of Minnesota Press, 1993.

Franklin, John Hope. "*Birth of a Nation*—Propaganda as History." *Massachusetts Review* 20.3 (1979): 417–433.

———. "Color and Race in the Modern World." Introduction to *Color and Race*. Ed. John Hope Franklin. Boston: Houghton Mifflin, 1968. vii–xvi.

Franklin, John Hope, and Alfred E. Moss. *From Slavery to Freedom: A History of Negro Americans*. 1967. Reprint. New York: Knopf, 1988.

Frazier, E. Franklin. "Children in Black and Mulatto Families." *American Journal of Sociology* 39 (1933): 12–29.

———. *The Negro Family in the United States*. New York: Holt, Rhinehart and Winston, 1948.

———. *The Black Bourgeoisie*. New York: Free Press, 1957.

Fredrickson, George M. *The Black Image in the White Mind: The Debate on Afro-American Character and Destiny 1817–1914*. New York: Harper and Row, 1972.

———. *White Supremacy: A Comparative Study in American and South African History*. New York: Oxford University Press, 1982.

———. *The Arrogance of Race: Historical Perspectives on Slavery, Racism, and Social Inequality*. Middletown, CT: Wesleyan University Press, 1988.

Freud, Sigmund. *Totem and Taboo: Some Points of Agreement Between the Mental Lives of Savages and Neurotics*. 1913. Trans. James Strachey. New York: W. W. Norton, 1950.

———. *Jokes and Their Relationship to the Unconscious*. 1905. Biographical introduction by Peter Gay. Reprint. New York: W. W. Norton, 1989.

Friedman, Lawrence J. *The White Savage: Racial Fantasies and the Postbellum South*. Englewood Cliffs, NJ: Prentice Hall, 1970.

Fry, Northrope. *Anatomy of Criticism: Four Essays*. Princeton: Princeton University Press, 1957.

Frye, Marilyn. "On Being White: Toward a Feminist Understanding of Race and Race Supremacy." *The Politics of Reality: Essays in Feminist Theory*. Trumansburg, NY: Crossing Press, 1983. 110–127.

Funderburg, Lise. *Black, White, Other: Biracial Americans Talk about Race and Identity*. New York: William Morrow, 1994.

Gaines, Jane. "White Privilege and Looking Relations—Race and Gender in Feminist Film Theory." *Screen* 29.4 (1988): 12–27.

———. "Introduction: Fabricating the Female Body." *Fabrications: Costume and the Female Body*. Ed. Jane Gaines and Charlotte Herzog. New York: Routledge, 1990. 1–27.

———. "The Scar of Shame: Skin Color and Caste in Black Silent Melodrama." *Representing Blackness: Issues in Film and Video*. Ed. and with an introduction by Valerie Smith. New Brunswick: Rutgers University Press, 1997. 61–81.

Gains, Kevin. "Assimilationist Minstrelsy as Racial Uplift Ideology." *American Quarterly* 45 (1993): 22–35.

Gallo, Rose Adrienne. *F. Scott Fitzgerald*. New York: Frederick Ungar, 1978.

Gallop, Jane. *Reading Lacan*. Ithaca: Cornell University Press, 1985.

Garber, Marjorie. *Vested Interests: Cross-Dressing and Cultural Anxiety*. New York: Harper Perennial, 1993.

Garrett, George. "Fire and Freshness: A Matter of Style in *The Great Gatsby*." *New Essays on*

The Great Gatsby. Ed. Matthew J. Bruccoli. Cambridge: Cambridge University Press, 1985. 101–116.

Garrett, Marvin P. "Early Recollections and Structural Irony in *The Autobiography of an Ex-Coloured Man.*" *Critique* 13 (1971): 5–14.

Gates, Henry Louis, Jr. *Figures in Black: Words, Signs, and the "Racial" Self*. New York: Oxford University Press, 1987.

——. *Signifying Monkey: A Theory of African-American Literary Criticism*. New York: Oxford University Press, 1988.

——. "The Black Man's Burden." *Black Popular Culture, a Project by Michelle Wallace*. Ed. Gina Dent. Seattle: Bay Press, 1992. 75–83.

——. "In the Kitchen." *Colored People*. New York: Knopf, 1994. 40–49.

——. "White Like Me." *The New Yorker*, 17 June 1996: 66–81.

——. "The Passing of Anatole Broyard." *Thirteen Ways of Looking at a Black Man*. New York: Random House, 1997. 180–214.

Gates, Henry Louis, Jr., and Nellie Y. McKay, eds. *The Norton Anthology: African American Literature*. New York: W. W. Norton, 1996.

Gatewood, Willard B. *Aristocrats of Color: The Black Elite, 1880–1920*. Bloomington: Indiana University Press, 1990.

Gayle, Addison, Jr. *The Black Aesthetic*. Garden City, NY: Doubleday, 1972.

——. *The Way of the New World: The Black Novel in America*. Garden City, NY: Anchor/Doubleday, 1976.

George, Louis W. "Beauty Culture and Colored People." *Messenger* (July 1918): 18.

Gergen, Kenneth J. "The Significance of Skin Color in Human Relation." *Color and Race*. Ed. John Hope Franklin. Boston: Houghton Mifflin, 1968. 112–128.

Gibson, Aliona I. *Nappy: Growing Up Black and Female in America*. New York: Harlem River Press, 1995.

Gibson, Donald B. *The Politics of Literary Expression: A Study of Major Black Writers*. Westport, CT: Greenwood Press, 1981.

Giddings, Paula. *When and Where I Enter: The Impact of Black Women on Race and Sex in American Culture*. New York: William Morrow, 1984.

Gilbert, Sandra M., and Susan Gubar. *No Man's Land: The Place of the Woman Writer in the Twentieth Century*, Vol. 2: *Sexchanges*. New Haven: Yale University Press, 1989.

Gillman, Susan. *Dark Twins: Imposter and Identity in Mark Twain's America*. Chicago: University of Chicago Press, 1989.

Gilman, Sander L. *On Blackness Without Blacks: Essays on the Image of the Black in Germany*. Boston: G. K. Hall, 1982.

——. *Difference and Pathology: Stereotypes of Sexuality, Race, and Madness*. Ithaca: Cornell University Press, 1985.

——. *Jewish Self-Hatred: Anti-Semitism and the Hidden Language of the Jews*. Baltimore: Johns Hopkins University Press, 1986.

——. *The Jew's Body*. New York: Routledge, 1991.

——. *Freud, Race, and Gender*. Princeton: Princeton University Press, 1993.

Gilman, Sander L., and Edward Chamberlin, eds. *Degeneration: The Dark Side of Progress*. New York: Columbia University Press, 1985.

Gilmore, Al-Tony. "Jack Johnson and White Women: The National Impact." *Journal of Negro History* 58 (1973): 18–38.

——. *Bad Nigger!: The National Impact of Jack Johnson*. Port Washington, NY: Kennikat Press, 1975.

Gilroy, Paul. *The Black Atlantic: Modernity and Double Consciousness.* Cambridge, MA: Harvard University Press, 1993.

Ginsberg, Elaine K., ed. "Introduction: The Politics of Passing." *Passing and the Fictions of Identity.* Durham: Duke University Press, 1996. 1–18.

Gloster, Hugh M. *Negro Voices in America Fiction.* 1948. New York: Russell and Russell, 1965.

Goddard, Henry H. *Human Efficiency and Levels of Intelligence.* Princeton: Princeton University Press, 1920.

Goffman, Kimbal (Stroud). "Black Pride." *Speech and Power: The African-American Essay and Its Cultural Content from Polemics to Pulpit,* Vol. 1. Ed. Gerald Early. Hopewell: Ecco Press, 1992. 12–19.

Goldberg, David Theo. "Introduction." *Anatomy of Racism.* Ed. David Theo Goldberg. Minneapolis: Minnesota University Press, 1990. xi–xxiii.

——. *Racist Culture: Philosophy and the Politics of Meaning.* Cambridge: Blackwell, 1993.

Golden, Marita. "whitegirls." *Skin Deep: Black Women and White Women Talk About Race.* Ed. Marita Golden and Susan Richards Shreve. New York: Doubleday, 1995. 24–36.

Goldfield, Michael. "The Color Politics in the United States: White Supremacy as the Main Explanation for the Peculiarities of American Politics from Colonial Times to the Present." *The Bounds of Race: Perspectives on Hegemony and Resistance.* Ed. and with an introduction by Dominick Lacapra. Ithaca: Cornell University Press, 1991. 104–133.

Gordon-Reed, Annette. *Thomas Jefferson and Sally Hemmings: An American Controversy.* Charlottesville: University Press of Virginia, 1997.

Gossett, Thomas F. *Race: The History of an Idea in America.* New York: Schocken, 1963.

Gould, Stephen Jay. *The Mismeasure of Man.* New York: Norton, 1981.

Graham, Lawrence Otis. *Member of the Club: Reflections on Life in a Racially Polarized World.* New York: HarperCollins, 1995.

——. *Our Kind of People: Inside America's Black Upper Class.* HarperCollins Publishers, 2000.

Grant, Madison. *The Passing of the Great Race or the Racial Basis of European History.* New York: Scribner, 1916.

Grant, Percy Stickney. "American Ideas and Race Mixture." *North American Review* 195 (1912): 513–525.

Grayson, Deborah R. "Is It Fake?: Black Women's Hair as Spectacle and Spectacular." *Camera Obscura: Feminism, Culture, and Media Studies* 36 (1995): 13–31.

Greenberg, Jack. *Race Relations and American Law.* New York: Columbia University Press, 1959.

Greenfeld, Howard. *F. Scott Fitzgerald.* New York: Crown, 1974.

Grier, William H., and Price M. Cobbs. *Black Rage.* New York: Basic Books, 1968.

Griffin, John Howard. *Black Like Me.* 1960. Reprint. New York: New American Library, 1964.

——. *A Time to Be Human.* New York: Macmillan, 1977.

Grimshaw, Allen D., ed. *Racial Violence in the United States.* Chicago: Aldine, 1969.

Gubar, Susan. *Racechanges: White Skin, Black Face in American Culture.* New York: Oxford University Press, 1997.

Guillanumin, Colette. "The Idea of Race and Its Elevation to Autonomous, Scientific, and Legal Status." *Sociological Theories: Race and Colonialism.* New York: UNESCO, 1980. 37–67.

Gunning, Sandra. *Race, Rape, and Lynching: The Red Record of American Literature 1890–1912.* New York: Oxford University Press, 1996.

Gurganus, Allan. *White People.* New York: Knopf, 1991.

Gwaltney, John L. *Drylongso: A Self Portrait of Black America.* New York: Random House, 1980.

Gwynn, Frederick L., and Joseph L. Blotner, eds. *Faulkner in the University: Class Conferences at the University of Virginia, 1957–1958.* Charlottesville: University Press of Virginia, 1959.

Gysin, Fritz. "Predicaments of Skin Boundaries in Recent African American Fiction." *The Black Columbiad: Defining Moments in African American Literature and Culture.* Ed. Werner Sollors and Maria Diedrich. Cambridge, MA: Harvard University Press, 1994. 286–297.

Hacker, Andrew. *Two Nations: Black and White, Separate, Hostile, Unequal.* New York: Scribners, 1992.

Haizlip, Shirlee Taylor. *The Sweeter the Juice: A Family Memoir in Black and White.* New York: Simon and Schuster, 1994.

———. "Passing." *American Heritage* 46.1 (1995): 46–54.

Halberstam, Judith. *Skin Shows: Gothic Horror and the Technology of Monsters.* Durham: Duke University Press, 1995.

Hall, David. "Race and Constitution: Epilogue." *New York Law School Journal of Human Rights* 5:2 (1988): 425–431.

Hall, Gwendolyn Midlo. *Africans in Colonial Louisiana: The Development of Afro-Creole Culture in the Eighteenth Century.* Baton Rouge: Louisiana State University Press, 1992.

Hall, Jacquelyn Dowd. *Revolt Against Chivalry: Jessie Daniel Ames and the Women's Campaign Against Lynching.* New York: Columbia University Press, 1979.

Hall, Kermit L., William M. Wiecek, and Paul Finkleman. *American Legal History: Cases and Materials.* New York: Oxford University Press, 1991.

Hall, Stuart. "Cultural Studies: Two Paradigms." *Media, Culture and Society* 2 (1980): 57–72.

———. "Culture, the Media and the 'Ideological' Effect." *People's History and Socialist Theory.* Ed. Ralph Samuel. London: Routledge and Kegan Paul, 1981. 227–240.

———. "What Is This 'Black' in Black Popular Culture." *Black Popular Culture, a Project by Michelle Wallace.* Ed. Gina Dent. Seattle: Bay Press, 1992. 21–33.

Halttunen, Karen. *Confidence Men and Painted Women: A Study of Middle-Class Culture in America, 1830–70.* New Haven: Yale University Press, 1982.

Hamilton, V. *Adam Clayton Powell, Jr.: The Political Biography of an American Dilemma.* New York: Collier, 1991.

Haraway, Donna. *Private Visions: Gender, Race, and Nature in the World of Modern Science.* New York: Routledge, 1990.

Hardaway, Roger D. "Unlawful Love: A History of Arizona Miscegenation Law." *Journal of Arizona History* 27 (1986): 377–390.

Hare, Nathan. *The Black Anglo-Saxons.* 1965. Reprint. Chicago: Third World Press, 1991.

Harper, Frances E. W. *Iola Leroy or Shadows Uplifted.* 1893. Introduction by Hazel V. Carby. Boston: Beacon Press, 1987.

Harper, Philip Brian. "Fiction and Reform ll." *The Columbia History of the American Novel.* Ed. Emory Elliot et al. New York: Columbia University Press, 1991. 216–239.

Harris, Cheryl I. "Whiteness as Property." *Harvard Law Review* 106.8 (1993): 1706–1791.

Harris, Trudier. *Exorcising Blackness: Historical and Literary Lynching and Burning Rituals.* Bloomington: Indiana University Press, 1984.

Hartman, S. V., and Farah Jasmine Griffin. "Are You Colored as That Negro?: The Politics of Being Seen in Julie Dash's *Illusions.*" *Black American Literature Forum* 25.2 (1991): 361–373.

Hasell, Grace. *Soul Sister*. Greenwich, CT: Fawcett, 1969.

——. *Black/White Sex*. Introduction by Wintrop D. Jordan. New York: William Morrow, 1972.

Haskins, James. *The Creoles of Color of New Orleans*. New York: Thomas Y. Crowell, 1975.

Hathaway, Heather. "'Maybe Freedom Lies in Hating': Miscegenation and the Oedipal Conflict." *Refiguring the Father: New Readings of Patriarchy*. Ed. Patricia Yaeger and Beth Kowaleski-Wallace. Carbondale: University of Illinois Press, 1989. 153–167.

Hazard-Gordon, Katrina. *Jookin': The Rise of Social Dance Formations in African-American Culture*. Philadelphia: Temple University Press, 1990.

Hegel, G. W. G. *The Phenomenology of Mind*. Trans. and with an introduction by J. B. Baillie. New York: Humanities Press, 1977.

Hermance, Joel N. *Charles W .Chesnutt, 1877–1920*. New York: Hill and Wang, 1967.

——. *Charles W. Chesnutt: America's First Great Black Novelist*. Hamden: Archon Books, 1974.

Herrmann, Anne. "'Passing' Women Performing Men." *The Female Body: Figures, Styles, Speculations*. Ed. Laurence Goldstein. Ann Arbor: University of Michigan Press, 1991. 178–189.

Herton, Calvin. *Sex and Racism in America*. New York: Grove Press, 1965.

Higginbotham, A. Leon, Jr. *In the Matter of Color-Race and the American Legal Process: The Colonial Period*. New York: Oxford University Press, 1978.

——. *Shades of Freedom: Racial Politics and Presumptions of the American Legal Process*. New York: Oxford University Press, 1996.

Higham, John. *Strangers in the Land: Patterns of American Nativism, 1860–1925*. New York: Atheneum, 1975.

Hirsch, Arnold D., and Joseph Logsdon, eds. *Creole New Orleans: Race and Americanization*. Baton Rouge: Louisiana State University Press, 1992.

Hoch, Paul. *White Hero, Black Beast: Racism, Sexism and the Mask of Masculinity*. London: Pluto Press, 1979.

Hodges, Graham Russell, and Alan Edward Brown. *"Pretends to Be Free": Runaway Slave Advertisements from Colonial and Revolutionary New York and New Jersey*. Ed. and with an introduction by Graham Russell Hodges and Alan Edward Brown. New York: Garland, 1994.

Holloway, Karla F. C. *Codes of Conduct: Race, Ethics, and the Color of Our Character*. New Brunswick: Rutgers University Press, 1972.

Honnighausen, Lothar. "Black as White Metaphor: A European View of Faulkner Fiction." *Faulkner and Race: Faulkner and Yoknapatawpha, Conference 1986*. Ed. Doreen Fowler and Ann J. Abadie. Jackson: University Press of Mississippi, 1987. 192–221.

hooks, bell. *Feminist Theory from Margin to Center*. Boston: South End Press, 1984.

——. "From Black Is a Woman Color." *Callaloo* 12.2 (1989): 382–388.

——. "Straightening Our Hair." *Z Magazine* (summer 1988): 14–18.

——. *Black Looks: Race and Representation*. Boston: South End Press, 1992.

Horowitz, Helen Lefkowitz, and Kathy Peiss, eds. *Love Across the Color Line: The Letters of Alice Hanley to Channing Lewis*. Amherst: University of Massachusetts Press, 1996.

Horsman, Regniald. *Race and Manifest Destiny: The Origins of Racial Anglo-Saxonism*. Boston: Harvard University Press, 1986.

Horton, James Oliver. *Free People of Color: Inside the African American Community*. Washington, DC: Smithsonian Institution Press, 1993.

Hovey, Jaime. "'Kissing a Negress in the Dark': Englishness as a Masquerade in Woolf's *Orlando*." *PMLA* 112.3 (1997): 393–404.

Howe, Irving. *William Faulkner*. New York: Vintage Books, 1952.

Huggins, Nathan Irvin. *Harlem Renaissance*. New York: Oxford University Press, 1971.

——. *Revelations: American History, American Myths*. Ed. Brenda Smith Huggins. New York: Oxford University Press, 1995.

Hughes, Langston. *The Ways of White Folks*. 1933. Reprint. New York: Vintage Books, 1962.

——. *Mulatto: A Tragedy of the Deep South*. *Five Plays by Langston Hughes*. Ed. Webster Smalley. Bloomington: Indiana University Press, 1968. 1–36.

——. "Limitations of Life." *Black Theater U.S.A.: Forty-Five Plays by Black Americans*. Ed. James V. Hatch. New York: Free Press, 1974. 655–657.

——. "Who Is Passing for Who?" *Laughing to Keep from Crying*. Mattituck, NY: Aeonian Press, 1976.

Hull, Gloria. *Color, Sex and Poetry: Three Women Writers of the Harlem Renaissance*. Bloomington: Indiana University Press, 1987.

Hull, Gloria, Patricia Bell Scott, and Barbara Scott, eds. *All the Women Are White, All the Blacks Are Men, but Some of Us Are Brave*. Old Westbury, NY: Feminist Press, 1982.

Hungerford, Harold. "Past and Present in *Light in August*." *American Literature* 55 (1983): 183–198.

Hutcheon, Linda. *A Theory of Parody: The Teachings of Twentieth-Century Art Forms*. New York: Methuen, 1985.

Hutchinson, George. *The Harlem Renaissance in Black and White*. Cambridge, MA: Harvard University Press, 1995.

Hyde, Alan. *Bodies of Law*. Princeton: Princeton University Press, 1997.

Ignatiev, Noel. *How the Irish Became White*. New York: Routledge, 1995.

Irwin, John T. *Doubling and Incest/Repetition and Revenge: A Speculative Reading of Faulkner*. Baltimore: Johns Hopkins University Press, 1975.

——. *American Hieroglyphics: The Symbol of the Egyptian Hieroglyphics in the American Renaissance*. Baltimore: Johns Hopkins University Press, 1980.

Isaacs, Harold R. "Group Identity and Political Change: The Role of Color and Physical Characteristics." *Color and Race*. Ed. John Hope Franklin. Boston: Houghton Mifflin, 1968. 75–97.

Jackson, Jack. *The Autobiography of Jack Johnson: In the Ring and Out*. New York: Carol, 1992.

Jackson, Miles M. "Letters to a Friend: Correspondence from James Weldon Johnson to George A. Towns." *Phylon* 29 (1968): 182–198.

Jackson, R. Byer, ed. *F. Scott Fitzgerald: The Critical Reception*. New York: Burt Franklin, 1978.

James, C. L. R. *Beyond a Boundary*. Introduction by Robert Lipsyte. Durham: Duke University Press, 1993.

——. "The West Indian Middle Classes." In *I Am Because We Are: Readings in Black Philosophy*. Ed. and with an introduction by Fred Hord (Mzee Lasana Okpara) and Jonathan Scott Lee. Amherst: University of Massachusetts Press, 1995. 152–161.

Jameson, Frederick. *The Prison-House of Language: A Critical Account of Structuralism and Russian Formalism*. Princeton: Princeton University Press, 1972.

Jason, Wendell. Charles W. Chesnutt's "Outrageous Fortune." *CLAJ* 20 (1976): 195–204.

Jefferson, Thomas. *Notes on the State of Virginia*. 1782. Reprint. New York: W. W. Norton, 1972.

——. *Thomas Jefferson: Writings*. New York: Library of America, 1984.

——. *The Writings of Thomas Jefferson.* 20 vols. Ed. Andrew A. Lipscomb and Albert E. Bergh. Washington, DC, 1903.

Jenkins, Lee. *Faulkner and Black-White Relations: A Psychoanalytic Approach.* New York: Columbia University Press, 1981.

Jenkins, Ron. *Subversive Laughter: The Liberating Power of Comedy.* New York: Free Press, 1994.

Johnson, Charles. *Being and Race: Black Writing Since 1970.* Bloomington: Indiana University Press, 1988.

Johnson, James Hugo. *Race Relations in Virginia and Miscegenation in the South, 1776–1860.* Foreword by Winthrop Jordan. Amherst: University of Massachusetts Press, 1970.

Johnson, James Weldon. *The Book of American Negro Poetry.* 1922. Reprint. New York: Harcourt Brace and World, 1969.

——. *Negro Americans What Now?* New York: Da Capo Press, 1973.

——. *Along This Way.* 1933. Reprint. Introduction by Sondra Kathryn Wilson. New York: Penguin Books, 1990.

——. *The Autobiography of an Ex-Coloured Man.* 1912. Reprint. New York: Penguin Books, 1990.

——. *Black Manhattan.* 1930. Reprint. Introduction by Sondra Kathryn Wilson. New York: Da Capo Press, 1991.

Jones, Gail. *Corregidora.* Boston: Beacon Press, 1986.

Jones, Lisa. *Bulletproof Diva: Tales of Race, Sex, and Hair.* New York: Doubleday, 1994.

Jones, Nettie. *Mischief Makers.* New York: Weidenfeld and Nicolson, 1989.

Jordan, June. "What Would I Do White." *No More Masks.* Ed. Florence Howe. New York: Harper Perennial, 1993. 264–266.

Jordan, Winthrop D. *White over Black: American Attitudes Toward the Negro, 1550–1812.* New York: W. W. Norton, 1968.

——. *The White Man's Burden: Historical Origins of Racism in the United States.* New York: Oxford University Press, 1974.

Joyce, Joyce Ann. *Warriors, Conjurers and Priests: Defining African-centered Literary Criticism.* Chicago: Third World Press, 1994.

Julien, Isaac. "Black Is, Black Ain't: Notes on De-Essentialing Black Identities." *Black Popular Culture, a Project by Michelle Wallace.* Ed. Gina Dent. Seattle: Bay Press, 1992. 255–263.

Kahane, Claire. "The Artificial Niggers." *Massachusetts Review* (spring 1978): 183–198.

Karon, Bertram P. *Black Scars.* New York: Springer, 1975.

Kartiganer, Donald M. *The Fragile Thread: The Meaning of Form in Faulkner's Novels.* Amherst: University of Massachusetts Press, 1979.

Katz, William Loren. *The Invisible Empire: The Ku Klux Klan's Impact on History.* Seattle: Open Hand, 1986.

Kawash, Samira. "*The Autobiography of an Ex-Coloured Man*: (Passing for) Black Passing for White." *Passing and the Fictions of Identity.* Ed. Elaine K. Ginsberg. Durham: Duke University Press, 1996. 59–74.

Kent, George E. "Faulkner and the Heritage of White Racial Consciousness: Notes on White Nationalism in Literature." *Blackness and the Adventure of Western Culture.* Chicago: Third World Press, 1972. 164–182.

——. "Patterns of the Harlem Renaissance." *The Harlem Renaissance Remembered.* Ed. Arna Bontemps. New York: Dodd, Mead, 1972. 27–51.

Kernberg, Otto. *Borderline Conditions and Pathological Narcissism*. Northvale, NJ: Jason Aronson, 1985.

Kinnamon, Keneth, and Michel Fabre, eds. *Conversations with Richard Wright*. Jackson: University Press of Mississippi, 1993.

Kinney, James. *Amalgamation: Race, Sex and Rhetoric in the Nineteenth-Century American Novel*. Westport, CT: Greenwood Press, 1985.

Kisseloff, Jeff. *You Must Remember This: An Oral History of Manhattan from the 1890s to War World II*. New York: Schocken, 1989.

Klotman, Phyllis Rauch. *Another Man Gone: The Black Runner in Contemporary Afro-American Literature*. Port Washington, NY: Kennikat Press, 1977.

———. "'Tearing a Hole in History': Lynching as Theme and Motif." *Black American Literature Forum* 19.2 (1985): 55–63.

Kostelanetz, Richard. "The Politics of Passing: The Fiction of James Weldon Johnson." *Negro American Literature Forum* 3 (1969): 22–24, 29.

Kouwenhoven, John A. *Beer Can by the Highway: Essays on What's American about America*. 1961. Foreword by Ralph Ellison. Baltimore: Johns Hopkins University Press, 1988.

Kovel, Joel. *White Racism: A Psychohistory*. 1970. Reprint. New York: Columbia University Press, 1984.

Kreiswirth, Martin. "Plots and Counterplots: The Structure of *Light in August*." *New Essays on Light in August*. Ed. Michael Millgate. Cambridge: Cambridge University Press, 1987. 55–79.

Kreuger, David. "Money, Meanings and Madness: A Psychoanalytic Perspective." *Psychoanalytic Review* 78 (1991): 209–224.

Lacan, Jacques. *Ecrits: A Selection*. 1966. Trans. Alan Sheridan. Reprint. New York: W. W. Norton, 1977.

———. *The Four Fundamental Concepts of Psycho-Analysis*. Trans. Alan Sheridan. New York: W. W. Norton, 1978.

Lacan, Jacques, and Ecole Frudienne. *Feminine Sexuality*. Ed. Juliet Mitchell and Jacqueline Rose. Trans. Jacqueline Rose. New York: W. W. Norton, 1982.

Ladd, Barbara. *Nationalism and the Color Line in George W. Cable, Mark Twain and William Faulkner*. Baton Rouge: Louisiana State University Press, 1996.

Landry, Bart. *The New Black Middle Class*. Berkeley and Los Angeles: University of California Press, 1987.

Lang, Robert, ed. *The Birth of a Nation*. New Brunswick: Rutgers University Press, 1994.

Larson, R. *An Intimation of Things Distant: The Collected Fiction of Nella Larsen*. New York: Doubleday, 1992.

Lasch, Christopher. *The Culture of Narcissism: American Life in an Age of Diminishing Expectations*. New York: Warner, 1979.

Lawrence, D. H. *Studies in Classic American Literature*. 1923. Reprint. New York: Penguin Books, 1977.

Lazarre, Jane. *Beyond the Whiteness of Whiteness: Memoir of a White Mother of Black Sons*. Durham: Duke University Press, 1996.

Leckie, Barbara. "'I Should Have Had My Own': Language, Madness, and Women." *Praxis* (1987): 58–75.

Lee, Reba. *I Passed for White, by Reba Lee as Told to Mary Hastings Bradley*. New York: Longmans, Green, 1955.

Lehan, Richard. "Inventing Gatsby." *Major Literary Characters in Gatsby*. Ed. with an introduction by Harold Bloom. New York: Chelsea House, 1991. 189–195.

——. *The Great Gatsby: The Limits of Wonder*. New York: Twayne, 1995.

Leighton, Isabel, ed. *The Aspirin Age, 1919–1941*. New York: Simon and Schuster, 1949.

Leonard, William Torbert. *Masquerade in Black*. Metuchen, NJ: Scarecrow Press, 1986.

Lerner, Gerda. *The Creation of Patriarchy*. New York: Oxford University Press, 1986.

Lessing, Doris. *Prisons We Choose to Live Inside*. New York: Harper, 1987.

Levin, Harry. *The Power of Blackness*. New York: Vintage Books, 1958.

Levine, Lawrence W. *Black Culture and Black Consciousness: Afro-American Folk Thought from Slavery to Freedom*. New York: Oxford University Press, 1977.

Levy, Eugene. "Ragtime and Race Pride: The Career of James Weldon Johnson." *Journal of Popular Culture* 1 (1968): 357–370.

——. *James Weldon Johnson: Black Leader, Black Voice*. Chicago: University of Chicago Press, 1973.

Lewis, David Levering. *When Harlem Was in Vogue*. New York: Knopf, 1981.

Lewis, J. M. "Caucasian Body Hair Management: A Key to Gender and Species Identification in U.S. Culture." *Journal of American Culture* 10 (1987): 7–14.

Lewis, Roger. "Money, Love, and Aspiration in *The Great Gatsby*." *New Essays on The Great Gatsby*. Ed. Matthew J. Bruccoli. New York: Cambridge University Press, 1985. 41–57.

Lincoln, C. Eric. "Color and Group Identity in the United States." *Color and Race*. Ed. John Hope Franklin. Boston: Houghton Mifflin, 1968. 249–263.

——. *Coming Through the Fire: Surviving Race and Place in America*. Durham: Duke University Press, 1996.

Locke, Alain, ed. *The New Negro*. 1925. Reprint. Preface by Robert Hayden. New York: Atheneum, 1968.

Lofgren, A. *The Plessy Case: A Legal-Historical Interpretation*. New York: Oxford University Press, 1987.

Lombardo, Paul A. "Miscegenation, Eugenics, and Racism: Historical Footnotes to *Loving v. Virginia*." *University of California Davis Law Review* 21.2 (1988): 421–452.

Long, Robert Emmet. *The Achieving of* The Great Gatsby: *F. Scott Fitzgerald, 1920–1925*. East Brunswick, NJ: Associated University Presses, 1979.

Longley, John L., Jr. "Joe Christmas: The Hero in the Modern World." *Tragic Mask*. Chapel Hill: University of North Carolina Press, 1963. 192–205.

Lopez, Ian F. Haney. *White by Law: The Legal Construction of Race*. New York: New York University Press, 1996.

Lott, Eric. "'The Seeming Counterfeit': Racial Politics and Early Blackface Minstrelsy." *American Quarterly* 43.1 (1991): 223–254.

——. *Love and Theft: Blackness, Minstrelsy and the American Working Class*. New York: Oxford University Press, 1993.

——. "White Like Me: Racial Cross-Dressing and the Construction of American Whiteness." *Cultures of United States Imperialism*. Ed. Amy Kaplan and Donald Pease. Durham: Duke University Press, 1993. 474–495.

Loury, Glenn C. "Free at Last? A Personal Perspective on Race and Identity in America." *Lure and Loathing: Essays on Race, Identity, and the Ambivalence of Assimilation*. Ed. Gerald Early. New York: Penguin Books, 1993. 1–12.

Low, Gail Ching-Liang. "White Skins/Black Masks: The Pleasure and Politics of Imperialism." *New Formations* 9 (winter 1989): 83–104.

Lowen, Alexander. *Narcissism: Denial of the True Self*. New York: Macmillan/Collier, 1985.

Ludwig, Arnold M. *How Do We Know Who We Are?: A Biography of the Self*. New York: Oxford University Press, 1997.

Macdonald, Ross. *Black Money.* New York: Vintage Books, 1996.

MacKethon, Lucinda H. "*Black Boy* and *Ex-Coloured Man*: Version and Inversion of the Slave Narrator Quest for Voice." *CLAJ* 32.2 (1988): 123–147.

Madison, Grant. *The Passing of the Great Race, or The Racial Basis of European History.* New York: Scribner, 1918.

Mailer, Norman. "The White Negro." *The Penguin Book of the Beats.* Ed. Ann Charters. New York: Penguin Books, 1993. 581–605.

Malcolm X. *The Autobiography of Malcolm X*, with the assistance of Alex Haley. Introduction by M. S. Handler. Epilogue by Alex Haley. New York: Grove Press, 1965.

Malone, Jacqui. *Steppin' on the Blues: The Visible Rhythms of African American Dance.* Chicago: University of Illinois Press, 1996.

Margolies, Edward. *Native Sons: A Critical Study of Twentieth-Century Black American Authors.* Philadelphia: Lippincott, 1968.

Matthews, John T. *The Play of Faulkner's Language.* Ithaca: Cornell University Press, 1982.

Mayer, Milton. "The Issue Is Miscegenation." *White Racism: Its History, Pathology, and Practice.* Ed. Barry Schwartz and Robert Disch. New York: Dell, 1970. 207–217.

McBride, James. *The Color of Water: A Black Man's Tribute to His White Mother.* New York: Riverhead Books, 1996.

McCarthy, Timothy P. "Legalizing Anxiety: Plessy, Passing and the Conundrum of Race in American Culture." *Race and Reason.* New York: Institute for Research in African-American Studies, 1996. 20–25.

McCaskill, Barbara. "'Yours Very Truly': Ellen Craft—The Fugitive as Text and Artifact." *African American Review* 28.4 (1994): 509–529.

McClintock, Anne. *Imperial Leather: Race, Gender and Sexuality in the Colonial Contest.* New York: Routledge, 1995.

McIntyre, Charshee C. L. *Criminalizing a Race: Free Blacks During Slavery.* New York: Kayode, 1992.

McKay, Claude. "Near-White." *Gingertown.* 1932. Reprint. Freeport, NY: Books for Libraries Press, 1972. 72–104.

McMillen, Neil R., and Noel Polk. "Faulkner on Lynching." *The Faulkner Journal* 8.1 (1992): 3–14.

Meeter, Glenn. "Male and Female in *Light in August* and *The Hamlet*: Faulkner Mythical Method." *Studies in the Novel* 20 (1988): 404–416.

Mellow, James R. *Invented Lives: F. Scott and Zelda Fitzgerald.* Boston: Houghton Miffin, 1984.

Mencke, John G. *Mulattoes and Race Mixture: American Attitudes and Images, 1865–1918.* Ann Arbor: UMI Research Press, 1979.

Mercantante, Anthony S. *Good and Evil in Myth and Legend.* 1978. Reprint. New York: Barnes and Noble, 1996.

Mercer, Kobena. "Black Hair/Style Politics." *New Formations* 3 (1987): 33–54.

Meriwether, James B., ed. *Essays, Speeches and Public Letters by William Faulkner.* New York: Random House, 1966.

Meriwether, James B., and Michael Millgate, eds. *Lion in the Garden: Interviews with William Faulkner, 1926–1962.* New York: Random House, 1968.

Meyers, Jeffrey. *Scott Fitzgerald: A Biography.* New York: HarperCollins, 1994.

Michaels, Walter Benn. "The Souls of White Folk." *Literature and the Body: Essays on Population and Persons.* Ed. Elaine Scarry. Baltimore: Johns Hopkins University Press, 1988. 185–209.

——. "Race into Culture: A Critical Genealogy of Cultural Identity." *Critical Inquiry* 18.4 (1992): 655–685.

——. "The No-Drop Rule." *Identities*. Ed. Kwame Anthony Appiah and Henry Louis Gates Jr. Chicago: University of Chicago Press, 1995. 401–412.

——. *Our America: Nativism, Modernism, and Pluralism*. Durham: Duke University Press, 1995.

Micheaux, Oscar. *The Masquerade: An Historical Novel*. New York: Book Supply Company, 1947.

Miller, John Chester. *The Wolf by the Ears: Thomas Jefferson and Slavery*. Charlottesville: University Press of Virginia, 1991.

Miller, Henry. *On the Fringe: The Dispossessed in America*. Lexington, MA: D. C. Heath, 1991.

Millgate, Michael. "Introduction." *New Essays on* Light in August. Ed. Michael Millgate. Cambridge: Cambridge University Press, 1987. 1–29.

——. "A Novel: Not an Anecdote: Faulkner's *Light in August*." *New Essays on* Light in August. Ed. Michael Millgate. Cambridge: Cambridge University Press, 1987. 31–53.

——. *The Achievement of William Faulkner*. 1963. Reprint. Athens: University of Georgia Press, 1989.

Minh-ha, Trinh T. *Woman, Native, Other: Writing Postcoloniality and Feminism*. Bloomington: Indiana University Press, 1989.

Minter, David. *William Faulkner: His Life and Work*. Baltimore: Johns Hopkins University Press, 1980.

Mirzoeff, Nicholas. *Bodyscape: Art, Modernity and the Ideal Figure*. New York: Routledge, 1995.

Mizener, Arthur. *The Far Side of Paradise: A Biography of F. Scott Fitzgerald*. Boston: Houghton Mifflin, 1951.

Moddelmog, Debra A. "Faulkner's Theban Saga: *Light in August*." *Southern Literary Journal* 18 (1985): 13–29.

Moreland, Richard C. "Faulkner and Modernism." *The Cambridge Companion to William Faulkner*. Ed. Philip M. Weinstein. Cambridge: Cambridge University Press, 1995. 17–30.

Morganthu, Tom. "What Color Is Black?" *Newsweek*, 13 February 1995: 64.

Morris, Wesley, with Barbara Alverson Morris. *Reading Faulkner*. Madison: University of Wisconsin Press, 1989.

Morrison, Toni. *Playing in the Dark: Whiteness and the Literary Imagination*. Cambridge, MA: Harvard University Press, 1992.

——. "On the Backs of Blacks." *Time* Special Issue, "The New Face of America" (fall 1993): 57.

——. "The Pain of Being Black: An Interview with Toni Morrison." With Bonnie Angelo. *Conversations with Toni Morrison*, ed. Danille Taylor-Guthrie. Jackson University Press of Mississippi, 1994. 255–61.

——. "Unspeakable Things Unspoken: The Afro-American Presence in American Literature." *Criticism and the Color Line: Desegregating American Literary Studies*. Ed. Henry B. Wonham. New Brunswick: Rutgers University Press, 1996. 16–29.

Moses, Wilson J. "The Lost World of the Negro, 1895–1919: Black Literary and Intellectual Life Before the 'Renaissance.'" *Black American Literature Forum* 21.1–2 (1987): 61–84.

Mullen, Harryette. "Optic White: Blackness and the Production of Whiteness." *Diacritics* 24 (1994): 71–89.

Mulvey, Laura. "Visual Pleasure and Narrative Cinema." *Feminism and Film Theory.* Ed. Constance Penley. New York: Routledge, 1988. 57–68.

Mumford, Kevin J. "Homosex Changes: Race, Culture Geography, and the Emergence of the Gay." *American Quarterly* 48.3 (1996): 395–414.

Murray, Albert. *The Omni-Americans: New Perspectives on Black Experience and American Culture—Some Alternatives to the Folklore of White Supremacy.* New York: Outerbridge and Dienstfrey, 1970.

———. *South to a Very Old Place.* 1971. Reprint. New York: Modern Library, 1995.

Myrdal, Gunnar, with Richard Sterner and Arnold Rose. *An American Dilemma: The Negro Problem and Modern Democracy.* 1944. Reprint. New York: Harper and Row, 1962.

———. "Passing." *The Negro in Twentieth Century America.* Ed. John Hope Franklin and Isidore Starr. New York: Vintage Books, 1967. 12–13.

Neal, Angela M., and Midge L. Wilson. "The Role of Skin Color and Features in the Black Community: Implications for Black Women and Therapy." *Clinical Psychology Review* 9 (1989): 323–333.

Nelson, Dana D. *The Word in Black and White: Reading Race in American Literature, 1638–1867.* New York: Oxford University Press, 1993.

Nelson, William Javier. "Racial Definition: Background for Divergence." *Phylon* 47.4 (1986): 318–326.

Newby, I. A. *Jim Crow Defense: Anti-Negro Thought in America, 1900–1930.* Baton Rouge: Louisiana State University Press, 1965.

Newton, Esther. *Mother Camp: Female Impersonation in America.* Englewood Cliffs, NJ: Prentice Hall, 1972.

Nielsen, Alan Lynn. *Reading Race: White American Poets and the Racial Discourse in the Twentieth Century.* Athens: University of Georgia Press, 1988.

Nilon, H. *Faulkner and the Negro.* New York: Citadel Press, 1965.

Njeri, Itabari. *The Last Plantation: Color, Conflict and Identity: Reflections of a New World Black.* Boston: Houghton Mifflin, 1997.

Nowatzki, Robert. "Race, Rape, Lynching and Manhood Suffrage: Construction of White and Black Masculinities in Turn-of-the-Century White Supremacist Literature." *Journal of Men's Studies: A Scholarly Journal about Men and Masculinities* 3.2 (1994): 161–170.

Olney, James. "'I Was Born': Slave Narratives, Their Status as Autobiography and as Literature." *The Slave Narrative.* Ed. T. Davis and Henry Louis Gates Jr. New York: Oxford University Press, 1985. 148–175.

Olsen, Otto H. *The Thin Disguise:* Plessy v. Ferguson, *A Documentary Presentation.* New York: Humanities Press, 1967.

Oshinsky, David O. *"Worse Than Slavery": Parchman Farm and the Ordeal of Jim Crow Justice.* New York: Free Press, 1996.

Oullivan, Maurice J., Jr. "Of Souls and Pottage: James Weldon Johnson's *The Autobiography of an Ex-Coloured Man. CLAJ* 23 (1979): 60–70.

Ottley, Roi. *New World A-Coming.* New York: Arno Press and The New York Times, 1968.

———. "Five Million White Negroes." *Ebony* (March 1948): 22–28.

Outlaw, Lucius. "Toward a Critical Theory of Race." *Anatomy of Racism.* Ed. David Theo Goldberg. Minneapolis: University of Minnesota Press, 1990. 58–84.

Page, Lisa. "High Yellow White Trash." *Skin Deep: Black Women and White Women Write About Race.* Ed. Marita Golden and Susan Richards Shreve. New York: Doubleday, 1995. 13–23.

Parker, David. *"The Great Gatsby:* Two Versions of the Hero." *Modern Critical Views: F. Scott Fitzgerald.* Ed. Harold Bloom. New York: Chelsea House, 1985. 141–156.

Parker, Freddie L., Ed. *Stealing a Little Freedom: Advertisements for Slave Runaways in North Carolina, 1791–1840*. New York: Garland, 1994.

Parr, Susan Resneck. "The Idea of Order at West Egg." *New Essays on* The Great Gatsby. Ed. Matthew J. Bruccoli. New York: Cambridge University Press, 1985. 59–78.

Pascoe, Peggy. "Race, Gender, and Intercultural Relation: The Case of Interracial Marriage." *Frontiers* 12.1 (1991): 5–18.

Paterson, Orlando. *Slavery and Social Death*. Cambridge, MA: Harvard University Press, 1982.

Paul, Ru. *Lettin' It All Hang Out: An Autobiography*. New York: Hyperion, 1995.

Payne, Ladell. "Themes and Cadences: James Weldon Johnson's Novel." *Southern Literary Journal* 11.2 (1979): 43–55.

Peavy, D. *Go Slow Now: Faulkner and the Race Question*. Eugene: University of Oregon Press, 1971.

Peterson, Carla L. "The Remaking of America: Gertrude Stein's 'Melanctha' and African-American Musical Traditions." *Criticism and the Color Line: Desegregating American Literary Studies*. Ed. Henry B. Wonham. New Brunswick: Rutgers University Press, 1996. 140–157.

Petesch, Donald A. "Faulkner on Negroes: The Conflict Between the Public Man and the Private Art." *Southern Humanities Review* 10 (1976): 55–64.

——. *A Spy in the Enemy Country: The Emergence of Modern Black Literature*. Iowa City: Iowa University Press, 1989.

Pfeiffer, Kathleen. "Individualism, Success, and American Identity in *The Autobiography of an Ex-Coloured Man*." *African American Review* 30.3 (1996): 403–419.

Pickens, Ernestine Williams. *Charles W. Chesnutt and the Progressive Movement*. New York: Pace University Press, 1994.

Pieterse, Jan Nederveen. *White on Black: Images of Africa and Blacks in Western Popular Culture*. New Haven: Yale University Press, 1992.

Pinckney, Alphonso. *The American Way of Violence*. New York: Vintage Books, 1972.

Pinkard, Terry. *Hegel's Dialectic: The Explanation of Possibility*. Philadelphia: Temple University Press, 1988.

Piper, Adrian. "Passing for White, Passing for Black." *Transition* 58 (1992): 4–32.

Pisiak, Roxanna. "Irony and Subversion in James Weldon Johnson *The Autobiography of an Ex-Coloured Man*." *Studies in American Fiction* 21.1 (1993): 83–96.

Quarles, Benjamin. *The Negro in the Making of America*. New York: Collier, 1964.

Radford, Jill, and Diana E. H. Russell. "Introduction." *Femicide: The Politics of Woman Killing*. New York: Twayne, 1992.

Ramsey, Priscilla. "A Study of Black Identity in 'Passing' Novels of the Nineteenth and Early Twentieth Centuries." *Studies in Black Literature* 7.2 (1976): 1–7.

Raveau, F. H. M. "An Outline of the Role of Color in Adaptation Phenomena." *Color and Race*. Ed. John Hope Franklin. Boston: Houghton Mifflin, 1968. 98–111.

——. "Role of Color in Identification Processes." *Ethnic Identity: Cultural Continuities and Change*. Ed. George De Vos and Lola Romanucci-Ross. Chicago: University of Chicago Press, 1982. 353–359.

Reed, Joseph W. *Three American Originals: John Ford, William Faulkner, and Charles Ives*. Middletown, CT: Wesleyan University Press, 1984.

Reed, Tennessee. "Being Mixed in America." *MultiAmerica: Essays on Cultural Wars and Cultural Peace*. Ed. Ishmael Reed. New York: Viking, 1997. 113–115.

Render, Sylvia Lyons. *Charles W. Chesnutt*. Boston: Twayne, 1980.

Render, Sylvia Lyons, ed. *The Short Fiction of Charles W. Chesnutt*. Washington, DC: Howard University Press, 1981.

Reuter, Edward Byron. *The Mulatto in the United States: Including a Study of the Role of Mixed Blood Races Throughout the World*. Boston: Richard Badger. Reprint. New York: Negro University Press, 1969.

Rhines, Jesse Algeron. *Black Film/White Money*. New Brunswick: Rutgers University Press, 1996.

Rhys, Jean. *The Wild Sargasso Sea*. London: Deutsch, 1966.

Rich, Adrienne. "Disloyal to Civilization: Feminism, Racism Gynephobia." *On Lies, Secrets, and Silence*. New York: W. W. Norton, 1979. 275–310.

Richter, Gregory C. *The Incest Theme in Literature and Legend: Fundamentals of a Psychology of Literary Creation*. Trans. and with an introduction by Peter Rudnytsky. Baltimore: Johns Hopkins University Press, 1992.

Riviere, Joan. "Womanliness as Masquerade." *International Journal of Psychoanalysis* 10 (1920): 303–313. Reprinted in *Formations of Fantasy*. Ed. Victor Burgin, James Donald, and Cora Kaplan. London: Methuen, 1986. 35–44.

Roberts, Diane. *Faulkner and Southern Womanhood*. Athens: University of Georgia Press, 1994.

Roberts, Randy. *Papa Jack: Jack Johnson and the Era of White Hope*. New York: Free Press, 1983.

Robinson, Amy. "It Takes One to Know One: Passing and Communities of Common Interest." *Critical Inquiry* 20 (1994): 715–736.

Rodgers, David Lawrence. "The Irony of Idealism: William Faulkner and the South's Construction of the Mulatto." *The Discourse of Slavery: Aphra Behn to Toni Morrison*. Ed. Carl Plasa and Betty J. Ring. Foreword by Isobel Armstrong. New York: Routledge, 1994. 166–190.

Roediger, David R. *The Wages of Whiteness*. New York: Verso, 1991.

——. *Towards the Abolition of Whiteness: Essays on Race, Politics, and Working Class History*. London and New York: Verso, 1994.

Rogin, Michael. *Blackface, White Noise: Jewish Immigrants in the Hollywood Melting Pot*. Berkeley: University of California Press, 1996.

Rooks, Noliwe M. *Hair Raising: Beauty, Culture, and African American Women*. New Brunswick: Rutgers University Press, 1996.

Root, Maria P. P., ed. *Racially Mixed People in America*. Newbury Park, CA: Sage, 1992.

Rothenberg, Paula, ed. *Racism and Sexism: An Integrated Study*. New York: St. Martin Press, 1988.

Rourke, Constance. *American Humor: A Study of National Character*. 1931. Reprint. Tallahassee: Florida University Press, 1959.

Rowe, John Carlos. "To Live Outside the Law, You Must Be Honest: The Authority of the Margin in Contemporary Theory." *Cultural Critique* I (2): 67–77.

Rue, Loyal. *By the Grace of Guile: The Role of Deception in Natural History and Human Affairs*. New York: Oxford University Press, 1994.

Ruppersburg, Hugh M. *Reading Faulkner: Light in August*. With the editorial collaboration of James Hinkle and Robert McCoy. Jackson: University Press of Mississippi, 1994.

Rushing, Andrea Benton. "Hair-Raising." *Feminist Studies* 14 (1988): 325–335.

Russell, Kathy, and Midge Wilson. *Divided Sisters: Bridging the Gap Between Black Women and White Women*. New York: Doubleday, 1996.

Russell, Kathy, Midge Wilson, and Ronald Hall. *Color Complex: The Politics of Skin Color Among African Americans*. New York: Harcourt Brace Jovanovich, 1992.

Rutherford, Jonathan, ed. *Identity, Community, Culture, Difference*. London: Lawrence, 1990.

Said, Edward. *Culture and Imperialism*. New York: Knopf, 1993.

Saks, Eva. "Representing Miscegenation Law." *Raritan* 8.2 (1988): 39–69.

Sammons, Jeffrey. *Beyond the Ring*. Urbana: University of Illinois Press, 1988.

Sandstrom, Glen. "Identity Diffusion: Joe Christmas and Quentin Compson." *American Quarterly* 19 (1967): 207–223.

Sartre, Jean-Paul. *Being and Nothingness*. Trans. Hazel E. Barnes. New York: Washington Square, 1966.

Scales-Trent, Judy. *Notes of a White Black Woman: Race, Color, Community*. University Park: Pennsylvania State University Press, 1995.

Shapiro, Meyer. "Recent Abstract Painting." *Modern Art*. New York: Braziller, 1982.

Schlesinger, Arthur M., Jr. *The Disuniting of America: Reflections on a Multicultural Society*. New York: W. W. Norton, 1993.

Schuyler, George. "Who Is 'Negro'? Who Is 'White'?" *Common Ground* 1 (1940): 53–56.

——. *Black No More*. 1931. Reprint. Foreword by James A. Miller. Boston: Northeastern University Press, 1989.

Schwenk, Katrin. "Lynching and Rape: Border Cases in African American History and Fiction." *The Black Columbian: Defining Moments in African American Literature and Culture*. Ed. Werner Sollors and Maria Diedrich. Cambridge, MA: Harvard University Press, 1994. 312–324.

Scott, Daryl Michael. *Contempt and Pity: Social Policy and the Image of the Damaged Black Psyche 1880–1996*. Chapel Hill: University of North Carolina Press, 1997.

Sedlack, Robert P. "The Evolution of *The House Behind the Cedars*." *CLA Journal* 19 (1976): 123–135.

Senna, Danzy. "To Be Real." *To Be Real: Telling the Truth and Changing the Face of Feminism*. Ed. and with an introduction by Rebecca Walker. New York: Anchor Books, 1995. 5–20.

Settle, Glen. "Fitzgerald's Daisy: The Siren Voice." *American Literature: A Journal of Literary History, Criticism and Bibliography*. 57.1 (1985): 115–124.

Sewall, Richard. *The Vision of Tragedy*. New Haven: Yale University Press, 1980.

Sharpe, Ernest J., Jr. "The Man Who Changed His Skin." *American Heritage* 40.1 (1989): 44–55.

Shelley, Mary. *Frankenstein*. 1818. Reprint. New York: Penguin Books, 1983.

Shipman, Pat. *The Evolution of Racism: Human Differences and the Use and Abuse of Science*. New York: Simon and Schuster, 1994.

Showalter, Elaine. "Critical Cross-Dressing: Male Feminist and the Woman of the Year." *Men in Feminism*. Ed. Alice Jardine and Paul Smith. New York: Methuen, 1987. 116–132.

Shuffleton, Frank. "Thomas Jefferson: Race, Culture, and the Failure of Anthropological Method." *A Mixed Race: Ethnicity in Early America*. Ed. Frank Shuffleton. New York: Oxford University Press, 1993.

Sickels, Robert J. *Race, Marriage, and the Law*. Albuquerque: University of New Mexico Press, 1972.

Silk, Catherine, and John Silk. *Racism and Anti-Racism in American Popular Culture: Portrayals of African-Americans in Fiction and Film*. Manchester: Manchester University Press, 1990.

Singh, Amritjit. *The Novels of the Harlem Renaissance*. University Park: Pennsylvania State University Press, 1976.

Skerrett. Joseph T., Jr. "Irony and Symbolic Action in James Weldon Johnson's *The Autobiography of an Ex-Coloured Man*." *American Quarterly* 32 (1980): 540–558.

Skidmore, Thomas E. *Black into White: Race and Nationality in Brazilian Thought*. 1972. Reprint. Durham: Duke University Press, 1993.

Slater, Peter Greg. "Ethnicity in *The Great Gatsby*." *Twentieth Century Literature* 19 (1973): 53–62.

Slatoff, Walter J. *Quest for Failure: A Study of William Faulkner*. Ithaca: Cornell University Press, 1960.

Smith, Billy G., and Richard Wojtowicz. *Blacks Who Stole Themselves: Advertisements for Runaways in the Pennsylvania Gazette, 1728–1790*. Philadelphia: University of Pennsylvania Press, 1989.

Smith, Helena M. "No-Nation Bastards." *Studies in the Humanities* 1.1 (1969): 18–28.

Smith, Sidonie. *Where I'm Bound: Patterns of Slavery and Freedom in Black American Autobiography*. Westport, CT: Greenwood Press, 1974.

Smith, Valerie. *Self-Discovery and Authority in Afro-American Narrative*. Cambridge, MA: Harvard University Press, 1987.

——. "Reading the Intersection of Race and Gender in Narratives of Passing." *Diacritics* 24.2–3 (1994): 43–57.

Snead, James A. *Figures of Division: William Faulkner's Major Novels*. New York: Methuen, 1986.

——. "*Light in August* and the Rhetorics of Racial Divisions." *Faulkner and Race: Faulkner and Yoknapatawpha, Conference, 1986*. Ed. Doreen Fowler and Ann J. Abadie. Jackson: University Press of Mississippi, 1987. 152–169.

——. *White Screens/Black Images: Hollywood from the Dark Side*. Ed. Colin MacCabe and Cornel West. New York: Routledge, 1994.

Snowden, Frank M. *Before Color Prejudice: The Ancient View of Blacks*. Cambridge, MA: Harvard University Press, 1983.

Sollors, Werner. *Beyond Ethnicity: Consent and Descent in American Culture*. New York: Oxford University Press, 1986.

——. "'Never Was Born': The Mulatto, an American Tragedy?" *Massachusetts Review* 27 (1986): 293–316.

——. "Introduction: The Invention of Ethnicity." *The Invention of Ethnicity*. Ed. Werner Sollors. New York: Oxford University Press, 1989. ix–xx.

——. "National Identity and Ethnic Diversity: 'Of Plymouth Rock and Jamestown and Ellis Island'; or Ethnic Literature and Some Redefinitions of America." *History and Memory in African-American Culture*. Ed. Genevieve Fabre and Robert G. O'Meally. New York: Oxford University Press, 1994. 92–121.

——. "How Americans Became White: Three Examples." *MultiAmerica: Essays on Cultural Wars and Cultural Peace*. Ed. Ishmael Reed. New York: Penguin Books, 1997. 3–5.

——. *Neither Black nor White Yet Both: Thematic Explorations of Interracial Literature*. New York: Oxford University Press, 1997.

Spickard, Paul R. *Mixed Blood: Intermarriage and Ethnic Identity in Twentieth-Century America*. Madison: University of Wisconsin Press, 1989.

Spillers, Hortense J. "Notes on an Alternative Model—Neither/Nor." *The Year Left* 2: *An American Socialist Yearbook*. Ed. Mike Davis, Manning Marable, Fred Pfeil, and Michael Sprinker. London: Verso, 1987. 176–194.

——. "Mama Baby, Papa Maybe: An American Grammar Book." *Diacritics* 17 (1987): 65–81.
——. " 'The Permanent Obliquity of an In(pha)llibly Straight': In the Time of the Daughters and the Fathers." *Changing Our Own Words: Essays on Criticism, Theory, and Writing by Black Women*. Ed. Cheryl A. Wall. New Brunswick: Rutgers University Press, 1989. 127–149.
——. "Introduction: Who Cuts the Border? Some Readings on America." *Comparative American Identities: Race, Sex, and Nationality in the Modern Text*. Ed. Hortense J. Spillers. New York: Routledge, 1991. 1–25.
——. "Cross-Currents, Discontinuities: Black Women's Fiction." *Conjuring: Black Women, Fiction, and Literary Tradition*. Ed. Marjorie Pryse and Hortense J. Spillers. Bloomington: Indiana University Press, 1995. 249–261.
Stafford, Barbara. *Body Criticism*. Cambridge, MA: MIT Press, 1991.
Stammp, Kenneth. *The Peculiar Institution: Slavery in the Ante-Bellum South*. New York: Vintage Books, 1956.
Stanton, William. *The Leopard Spots: Scientific Attitudes Toward Race in America, 1815–1859*. Chicago: University of Chicago Press, 1960.
Staples, Brent. *Parallel Time: Growing Up in Black and White*. New York: Pantheon Books, 1994.
Starling, Marion Wilson. *The Slave Narrative: Its Place in American History*. Boston: Hall, 1981.
Stavola, Thomas J. *Scott Fitzgerald: Crisis in an American Identity*. New York: Barnes and Noble, 1979.
Stein, Judith. "Defining the Race 1890–1930." *The Invention of Ethnicity*. Ed. Werner Sollors. New York: Oxford University Press, 1989. 77–104.
Steinberg, Stephen. *The Ethnic Myth: Race, Ethnicity, and Class in America*. Boston: Beacon Press, 1981.
Stember, Herbert. *Sexual Racism: The Emotional Barrier to an Integrated Society*. New York: Harper Colophon Books, 1978.
Stepan, Nancy Leys, and Sander L. Gilman. "Appropriating the Idioms of Science: The Rejection of Scientific Racism." *The Bounds of Race: Perspectives on Hegemony and Resistance*. Ed. and with an introduction by Dominick Lacapra. Ithaca: Cornell University Press, 1991. 72–103.
Stepto, Robert B. *From Behind the Veil: A Study of Afro-American Narrative*. Chicago: University of Illinois Press, 1979.
Sterling, Dorothy. "Ellen Craft: The Valiant Journey." *Black Foremothers: Three Lives*. Old Westbury: Feminist Press, 1979. 2–59.
Still, William. *The Underground Rail Road*. 1872. Reprint. New York: Arno Press, 1968.
Stoddard, Lothrop. *The Rising Tide of Color Against White World Supremacy*. New York: Charles Scribner's Sons, 1920.
——. *Clashing Tides of Colour*. New York: Charles Scribner's Sons, 1935.
Stoler, Ann Laura. *Race and the Education of Desire: Foucault's History of Sexuality and the Colonial Order of Things*. Durham: Duke University Press, 1995.
Stone, Merlin. *Three Thousand Years of Racism*. New York: New Sibyline Books, 1981.
Sundquist, Eric J. *Faulkner: The House Divided*. Baltimore: Johns Hopkins University Press, 1983.
——. "Faulkner, Race, and the Forms of American Fiction." *Faulkner and Race: Faulkner and Yoknapatawpha, Conference, 1986*. Ed. Doreen Fowler and Ann J. Abadie. Jackson: University Press of Mississippi, 1987. 1–34.

———. "Mark Twain and Homer Plessy." *Mark Twain's Pudd'nhead Wilson: Race, Conflict and Culture*. Ed. Susan Gilman and Forest G. Robinson. Durham: Duke University Press, 1990. 46–72.

———. *The Hammers of Creation: Folk Culture in Modern African American Fiction*. Athens: University of Georgia Press, 1992.

———. *To Wake the Nations: Race in the Making of American Literature*. Cambridge, MA: Harvard University Press, 1993.

———. "Red, White, Black and Blue." *Transition* 6.2 (1996): 94–115.

Takaki, Ronald T. *Iron Cages: Race and Culture in Nineteenth-Century America*. Seattle: University of Washington Press, 1979.

Talalay, Kathryn. *Composition in Black and White: The Life of Philippa Schuyler*. New York: Oxford University Press, 1995.

Tate, Greg. "Nobody Loves a Genius Child: Jean-Michel Basquiat, Flyboy in the 80s Art Boom Buttermilk." *Jean-Michel Basquiat: The Notebooks*. *The Village Voice*, 14 November 1989: 31–35.

Tate, Mary Jo. *F. Scott Fitzgerald A to Z: The Essential Reference to His Life and Work*. Foreword by Matthew J. Bruccoli. New York: Facts on File, 1997.

Taylor, Walter. *Faulkner's Search for a South*. Chicago: University of Illinois Press, 1983.

Terkel, Studs. *Race: How Blacks and Whites Think and Feel About the American Obsession*. New York: New Press, 1992.

Terry, Eugene. "Charles W. Chesnutt: A Victim of the Color Line." *Contributions to Black Studies* 1 (1977): 13–44.

Terry, Jennifer, and Jacqueline Urla. *Deviant Bodies: Critical Perspectives on Difference in Science and Popular Culture*. Bloomington: Indiana University Press, 1995.

Thomas, Alexander, and Samuel Sillen. *Racism and Psychiatry*. Secaucus, NJ: Citadel Press, 1974.

Thompson, C. J. S. *Ladies or Gentleman?: Women Who Posed as Men and Men Who Impersonated Women*. New York: Dorset Press, 1993.

Thompson, Robert Farris. *Flash of the Spirit: African and Afro-American Art and Philosophy*. New York: Random House, 1983.

Tischker, Nancy M. *Black Masks: Negro Character in Modern Southern Fiction*. University Park: Pennsylvania State University Press, 1967.

Tocqueville, Alex de. *Democracy in America*. 1835. Trans. Henry Reeve. Ed. Phillips Bradley. New York: Knopf, 1951.

Toll, Robert C. *Blacking Up: The Minstrel Show in Nineteenth-Century America*. New York: Oxford University Press, 1974.

Toomer, Jean. *Cane*. 1923. Reprint. Introduction by Darwin T. Turner. New York: W. W. Norton, 1988.

Trelease, Allen W. *White Terror: The Ku Klux Klan Conspiracy and Southern Reconstruction*. Baton Rouge: Louisiana State University Press, 1971.

Tucker, John. "William Faulkner's *Light in August*: Toward a Structuralist Reading." *Modern Language Quarterly* 43 (1983): 138–155.

Turnbull, Andrew, ed. *The Letters of F. Scott Fitzgerald*. New York: Scribner's, 1963.

Twain, Mark. *Pudd'nhead Wilson and Those Extraordinary Twins*. 1894. Reprint. Introduction by Malcolm Bradbury. New York: Penguin Books, 1969.

Tyler, Carole Anne. "Passing: Narcissism, Identity, and Difference." *Differences: A Journal of Feminist Cultural Studies* 6.2–3 (1994): 212–248.

Uro, Joseph R. "Menstrual Blood and 'Nigger' Blood: Joe Christmas and the Ideology of Sex and Race." *Mississippi Quarterly* 41 (1988): 391–401.

Vance, Carole S., ed. *Pleasure and Danger: Exploring Female Sexuality*. Boston: Routledge and Kegan Paul, 1985.

Vauthier, Simone. "Texualité et Stereotypes: Of African Queens and Afro-American Princes and Princesses: Miscegenation in *Old Hepsy.*" *Publications du Conseil Scientifique de la Sorbonne Nouvelle* 3 (1980): 87–106.

Wade-Gayles, Gloria. *No Crystal Stair: Visions of Race and Sexuality in Black Women Fiction*. New York: Pilgrim Press, 1984.

———. "The Making of a Permanent Afro." *Catalyst: A Magazine of Heart and Mind* (summer 1988): 20–26.

Wald, Gayle. "'A Most Disagreeable Mirror': Reflections on White Identity in *Black Like Me.*" *Passing and the Fictions of Identity*. Ed. Elaine K. Ginsberg. Durham: Duke University Press, 1996. 151–77.

Waldo, Terry. *This Is Ragtime*. New York: Hawthorn Books, 1976.

Walker, Alice. "Oppressed Hair Puts a Ceiling on the Brain." *Living by the Word*. New York: Harcourt Brace Jovanovich, 1988. 60–74.

Ward, Samuel Ringgold. *Autobiography of a Fugitive Negro*. New York: Arno Press, 1965.

Warhol, Andy. *The Andy Warhol Diaries*. Ed. Pat Hackett. New York: Warner, 1989.

Warmbold, Joachim. "If Only She Didn't Have Negro Blood in Her Veins: The Concept of Metissage in German Colonial Literature." *Journal of Black Studies* 23.2 (1992): 200–210.

Warren, Kenneth W. *Black and White Strangers: Race and American Literary Realism*. Chicago: University of Chicago Press, 1993.

———. "Troubled Black Humanity in *The Souls of Black Folk* and *The Autobiography of an Ex-Coloured Man.*" *The Cambridge Companion to American Realism and Naturalism*. Ed. Donald Pizer. Cambridge: Cambridge University Press, 1995. 263–277.

Warren, Robert Penn. "Faulkner: The South, the Negro, and Time." *Faulkner: A Collection of Critical Essays*. Ed. Robert Penn Warren. Englewood Cliffs, NJ: Prentice Hall, 1966. 251–271.

Washington, Booker T. *Up from Slavery*. 1901. Reprint. New York: Doubleday, 1963.

Washington, Joseph R. *Marriage in Black and White*. Boston: Beacon, 1970.

Watson, Graham. *Passing for White: A Study of Racial Assimilation in a South African School*. New York: Tavistock, 1970.

Watson, James G. *William Faulkner, Letters and Fictions*. Austin: University of Texas Press, 1987.

Watson, Steven. *The Harlem Renaissance: Hub of African-American Culture, 1920–1930*. New York: Pantheon Books, 1995.

Welsh, Alexander. "On the Difference Between Prevailing and Enduring." *New Essays on Light in August*. Ed. Michael Millgate. New York: Cambridge University Press, 1987. 123–151.

Weinauer, Ellen M. "'A Most Respectable Looking Gentleman': Passing, Possession, and Transgression in *Running a Thousand Miles for Freedom.*" *Passing and the Fictions of Identity*. Ed. Elaine K. Ginsberg. Durham: Duke University Press, 1996. 37–56.

Weinstein, Arnold. "Fusion and Confusion in *Light in August.*" *Faulkner Journal* 1.2 (1986): 2–16.

Weinstein, Philip M. "Marginalia: Faulkner's Black Lives." *Faulkner and Race: Faulkner and*

Yoknapatawpha, Conference, 1986. Ed. Doreen Fowler and Ann J. Abadie. Jackson: University Press of Mississippi, 1987. 170–191.

Well-Barnett, Ida B. *On Lynching*. 1892. Reprint. New York: Arno Press, 1969.

Welsing, Frances Cress. *The Isis Papers: The Keys to the Colors*. Chicago: Third World Press, 1991.

Werner, Craig. "Minstrel Nightmares: Black Dreams of Faulkner's Dreams of Blacks." *Faulkner and Race: Faulkner and Yoknapatawpha, Conference, 1986.* Ed. Doreen Fowler and Ann J. Abadie. Jackson: University Press of Mississippi, 1987. 35–57.

——. "The Politics of Passing: Identity and Community in Charles W. Chesnutt's *The Marrow of Tradition* and James Weldon Johnson'a *The Autobiography of an Ex-Coloured Man*." *Kentucky Philological Review* 6 (1991): 27–31.

West, Cornel. *Race Matters*. Boston: Beacon Press, 1993.

Westbrook, Robert. *Intimate Lives: F. Scott Fitzgerald and Sheliah Graham, Her Son's Story*. New York: HarperCollins, 1995.

White, Mimi. "*The Birth of a Nation*: History as Pretext." *The Birth of a Nation*. Ed. Robert Lang. New Brunswick: Rutgers University Press, 1994. 214–224.

White, Walter. *Flight*. New York: Knopf, 1926.

——. "Why I Remain a Negro." *Saturday Review of Literature* 11 (1947): 13–14, 49–52.

——. *Rope and Faggot*. 1929. Preface by Roy Wilkens. Arno Press and The New York Times, 1969.

——. *A Man Called White: The Autobiography of Walter White*. 1948. Reprint. Foreword by Andrew Young. Athens: University of Georgia Press, 1995.

White, William Lindsay. *Lost Boundaries*. New York: Harcourt Brace, 1948.

Wicker, Tom. *Tragic Failure: Racial Integration in America*. New York: William Morrow, 1996.

Wiegman, Robyn. "Anatomy of Lynching." *Journal of the History of Sexuality* 3.3 (1993): 445–467.

——. *American Anatomies: Theorizing Race and Gender*. Durham: Duke University Press, 1995.

William, Bettye J. "Early Twentieth-Century Novelists of Afrocentric Feminist Thought." *CLAJ* 39.2 (1995): 165–178.

Williams, Gregory Howard. *Life on the Color Line: The True Story of a White Boy Who Discovered He Was Black*. New York: Penguin Books, 1995.

Williams, Michael. "Cross-dressing in Yoknapatawpha County." *Mississippi Quarterly* 47 (1994): 369–390.

Williams, Patricia J. *The Alchemy of Race and Rights: Diary of a Law Professor*. Cambridge, MA: Harvard University Press, 1991.

——. *The Rooster Egg: On the Persistence of Prejudice*. Cambridge, MA: Harvard University Press, 1995.

——. *Seeing A Color-Blind Future: The Paradox of Race*. New York: Farrar, Straus and Giroux, 1997.

Williams, Rhonda M. "Living at the Crossroads: Explorations in Race, Nationality, Sexuality, and Gender." *The House That Race Built: Black Americans, U.S. Terrain*. Ed. and with an introduction by Wabneema Lubiano. New York: Pantheon Books, 1997. 136–156.

Williamson, Joel. *New People: Miscegenation and Mulattoes in the United States*. New York: Free Press, 1980.

———. *The Crucible of Race: Black-White Relations in the American South Since Emancipation.* New York: Oxford University Press, 1984.

———. *A Rage for Order.* New York: Oxford University Press, 1986.

———. *William Faulkner and Southern History.* New York: Oxford University Press, 1993.

Wilson, Amos N. *Black-on-Black Violence: The Psychodynamics of Black Self-Annihilation in Service of White Domination.* New York: Afrikan World Infosystems, 1990.

Wilson, Edmund. "F. Scott Fitzgerald." *F. Scott Fitzgerald: A Collection of Critical Essays.* Ed. Arthur Mizener. Englewood Cliff, NJ: Prentice Hall, 1963. 80–85.

Wilson, Reagan. *Baptized in Blood: The Religion of the Lost Cause, 1865–1920.* Athens: University of Georgia Press, 1980.

Wilson, Douglas. "Thomas Jefferson and the Character Issue." *Atlantic Monthly* 270 (1992): 57–74.

Wilson, James D. "Incest and American Romantic Fiction." *Studies in the Literary Imagination* 7.1 (1974): 31–50.

Wilson, Sondra Kathryn, ed. *The Selected Writings of James Weldon Johnson,* Vols. 1 and 2: *Social, Political, and Literary Essays.* New York: Oxford University Press, 1995.

Winokur, Mark. "Black Is White/White Is Black: 'Passing' as a Strategy of Racial Compatibility in Contemporary Hollywood Comedy." *Unspeakable Images: Ethnicity and the American Cinema.* Ed. Lester D. Friedman. Chicago: University of Illinois Press, 1991. 190–211.

Wittenberg, Judith Bryant. "Race in *Light in August*: Wordsymbols and Observed Reflections." *The Cambridge Companion to William Faulkner.* Ed. Philip M. Weinstein. New York: Cambridge University Press, 1995. 146–167.

Wittke, Carl. *Tambo and Bones: A History of the American Minstrel Stage.* Westport, CT: Greenwood Press, 1968.

Woodward, C. Vann. *Origins of the New South, 1877–1913.* Baton Rouge: Louisiana State University Press, 1951.

———. *The Burden of Southern History.* Baton Rouge: Louisiana State University Press, 1960.

———. *The Strange Career of Jim Crow.* New York: Oxford University Press, 1966.

———. "The National Decision Against Equality." *American Counterpoint: Slavery and Racism in the North-South Dialogue.* Boston: Little, Brown, 1971. 212–233.

Wright, Bobby. *The Psychopathic Racial Personality and Other Essays.* Chicago: Third World Press, 1984.

Wright, Lawrence. "One Drop of Blood." *The New Yorker* 25 July 1994: 46–55.

Wright, Luther, Jr. "Who Black, Who White, and Who Cares: Reconceptualizing the United States Definition of Race and Racial Classifications." *Vanderbilt Law Review* 48 (1995): 513–569.

Wright, Richard. "Between the World and Me." *Partisan Review* 2 (1935): 18–19.

———. "Man of All Work." *Eight Men.* 1940. Reprint. Foreword by David Bradley. New York: Thunder Mouth Press, 1987. 117–162.

———. *White Man Listen.* 1957. Reprint. New York: Harper Perennial, 1995.

Wynter, Sylvia. "Sambos and Minstrels." *Social Text* 1 (1979): 149–156.

X, Malcolm. *The End of White Supremacy: Four Speeches.* Ed. and with an introduction by Benjamin Karim. New York: Arcade, 1989.

Young, Robert J. C. *White Mythologies: Writing History and the West.* London: Routledge, 1990.

———. *Colonial Desire: Hybridity in Theory, Culture and Race*. New York: Routledge, 1995.

Zack, Naomi. *Race and Mixed Race*. Philadelphia: Temple University Press, 1993.

Zender, Karl F. *The Crossing of the Ways: William Faulkner, the South, and the Modern World*. New Brunswick: Rutgers University Press, 1989.

AFRICAN AMERICAN LITERATURE AND CULTURE

EXPANDING AND EXPLODING THE BOUNDARIES

General Editor
Carlyle V. Thompson

The purpose of this series is to present innovative, in-depth, and provocatively critical literary and cultural investigations of critical issues in African American literature and life. We welcome critiques of fiction, poetry, drama, film, sports, and popular culture. Of particular interest are literary and cultural analyses that involve contemporary psychoanalytical criticism, new historicism, deconstructionism, critical race theory, critical legal theory, and critical gender theory.

For additional information about this series or for the submission of manuscripts, please contact:

Peter Lang Publishing, Inc.
Acquisitions Department
275 Seventh Avenue, 28th floor
New York, New York 10001

To order other books in this series, please contact our Customer Service Department:

(800) 770-LANG (within the U.S.)
(212) 647-7706 (outside the U.S.)
(212) 647-7707 FAX

Or browse online by series:

www.peterlangusa.com